100 Years
of Test Match Cricket
At Edgbaston
by Brian Halford

A Britespot Publication

Foreword

By Dennis Amiss MBE

Edgbaston has always had a proud tradition as the home of Warwickshire County Cricket Club, but the famous Birmingham stadium has also played another major role in the history of world cricket.

Way back in May 1902 the first ever Test Match took place at this ground when an England team boasting some of the most famous players of the day took on the touring Australian side in a most amazing game of cricket. The details of this game and the other matches played over the past 100 years brought to life in this book written by the noted and well respected journalist, Brian Halford.

The story of International cricket at Edgbaston has been painstakingly researched, and each of the 38 Test Matches played here are featured in detail, including scorecards of the game, match by match reports and wonderful photographs which illuminate the mighty feats of individual skill and determination which have been played out in front of thousands upon thousands of spectators who have passed through the Edgbaston gates.

The book chronicles the greats of world cricket who have left an indelible imprint in the history books as well as those players' who graced the Edgbaston pitch on briefly and have almost been lost in the mists of time. It is much more than a reference book, as it features more than just details of scores on the field of play – it is a true record of the story behind the game.

As a Warwickshire man through and through I was fortunate enough to represent my country 50 times both home and abroad, and played for England at Edgbaston on a number of occasions, so I feel proud to have chance to write this foreword to such an important work. This book is a fitting tribute to the history of Test cricket in Birmingham, and one which will be a source of entertainment and valuable reference for many years.

100 YEARS OF TEST MATCH CRICKET AT EDGBASTON
A Britespot Publication

First Published in Great Britain by
Britespot Publishing Solutions Limited
Chester Road, Cradley Heath, West Midlands B64 6AB

July 2002

ISBN 1 904103 11 1

Cover design and layout
© Britespot Publishing Solutions Limited

Printed and bound in Great Britain by
Cradley Print Limited, Chester Road, Cradley Heath, West Midlands B64 6AB

Acknowledgments
Thanks to Mary Bonner, Paul Lazenby, Rob Brooke, Phil Britt, David Wildgoose and the staff of
the Birmingham Post & Mail library for their much appreciated assistance.
I would also like to thank Roger Wootton, Graham Morris, Patrick Eagar, Popperfoto, Allsport and Empics for
supplying the rest of the photos and Keith Cook of Warwickshire County Cricket Club.
May I also thank Roger Marshall, Linda Perkins and Paul Burns of Britespot Publishing for producing this publication.

Pictures supplied in association with

The Birmingham Post

Contents

Chapter 1

1902

England v Australia May 29 1902

Thursday May 29, 1902. In South Africa, Boer leaders are in conclave to decide whether to accept Britain's terms for an end to the savage conflict which has been raging for almost three years. In England, Prince Edward, ready to be crowned king in the summer, appendicitis permitting, is thrilled by the munificence of Bilston District Council which votes to set aside £25 for celebratory street bunting. In Birmingham, the Klein Family (the World's Greatest Cyclists) are busy in rehearsal for their performance later that day at the Empire and, across the city at Edgbaston cricket ground, at just after 11am, a chap called Archibald Campbell MacLaren flips a coin into the air and another by the name of Joseph Darling enunciates his choice of heads or tails. Test match cricket had arrived in the Second City.

It was an immensely proud day for Warwickshire County Cricket Club and the city of Birmingham. Only 11 years after hosting first-class cricket for the first time (a North v South fixture in 1891), Edgbaston became the twelfth arena to stage the sport in its highest form. When Darling's Australian team parked their socks in the Edgbaston dressing-rooms it was a defining moment not only in the history of English cricket but also the city's heritage. Set in motion was a century - and counting - of top class sportsmen arriving in Birmingham to parade their skills, in turn attracting droves of spectators to inject revenue into the region. The sense of adventure shown by the county club's founding fathers in pushing for Test status as quickly as possible was to have considerable short-term cost - that first match culminated in a financial

The old enemy. Australia's squad for the inaugural Edgbaston Test

loss of over £2,000 - but has benefited the city ever since.

Bringing the England team to Birmingham was not a goal lightly achieved. The MCC had to be convinced that this fledgling first-class county could handle such a prestigious event. To secretary Rowland Ryder fell the burden of organisation - and what a burden. Thirty-six times in 12 months Warwickshire's general committee gathered. Considering the nature of many committees, whether that glut of gatherings made the task 36 times easier or 36 times more complicated is open to debate but Ryder picked his way through the forest of complexities. Almost single-handedly, without the assistance of a telephone, a typewriter or a precedent, he organised a Test match. It was an astounding feat.

Temporary stands were horse-drawn, piece by piece, across the city from Villa Park football ground. Two hundred catering staff, 60 gatemen and 60 policemen were hired. Railway companies were contacted to arrange cheap fares from towns within a 60-mile radius of Birmingham. Every

trouble was taken to ensure the contentment of the touring party during their stay at the Grand Hotel. All of this, remember, without the aid of a telephone. For weeks preceding the match, a frenzy of messengers and telegrams criss-crossed the city. Finally the historic day arrived and what followed during those first three days transpired to be a microcosm of the subsequent century of Test cricket at Edgbaston. On the field, brilliant cricket. Off the field, delicate decisions. And heading towards the field in a downward direction at high velocity - precipitation. Ah yes, rain. Plenty of rain. Several times during the century to follow it was to save England's bacon. It started off firmly on Australia's side.

Edgbaston joined the Test elite at the heart of the Golden Age and it is arguable whether a better XI has ever taken the field for England than that which MacLaren led into that Ashes opener in 1902. The team was a smorgasbord of natural talent from the flair and flamboyance of amateurs Charles Fry, Gilbert Jessop and Kumar Ranjitsinhji to the steely professional skills of Johnny Tyldesley, Wilfred Rhodes and George Hirst. The Australians, too, were

hugely strong, not least in batting. Hugh Trumble was kept out by a dislocated thumb but there was the mighty Victor Trumper, Darling, Clem Hill, Monty Noble and Warwick Armstrong. A power-packed batting unit which was, incredibly, to be shot out for what remains Australia's lowest score in a Test match.

After MacLaren won the toss, England hit early trouble. Fry, who only three weeks earlier had played for Southampton against Sheffield United in the FA Cup final, nicked a drive at Ernest Jones then MacLaren was left stranded when Ranjitsinhji inexplicably turned down a straightforward run to third man and Hill's throw was right over the bails. Clearly unnerved by his error, Ranji was soon bowled when he missed an attempt to leg-glance Armstrong.

Tyldesley, invariably a prolific scorer at Edgbaston, turned the innings around. Dropped on 43, the Lancashire legend took full advantage of his escape with savage cuts and crisp leg-side hits over the infield. With resolute support from Stanley Jackson and Hirst, Tyldesley delighted the exuberant crowd

whose pleasure stretched into the evening as some merry last-wicket swings from Bill Lockwood and Rhodes propelled England to 351 for nine at the close of an enthralling first day. Disappointment for the home members arrived only from the failure of Warwickshire wicket-keeper Dick Lilley.

Ten thousand people were in on the second day only for the clouds that had swirled ominously throughout the first to this time unload themselves. The start of play was delayed until 2.55pm when that tenth-wicket alliance grew to 81 before MacLaren's declaration at half-past three. Rhodes, England's number 11, remained unbeaten on 38 - then got busy with the ball to sweep away the entire Australian innings for 36.

He started bowling from the City End and was summarily dispatched for four through mid-off by Trumper. With Australia 8 for 0, MacLaren had an idea. He called up Somerset's Len Braund for an over to allow Rhodes and Hirst to change ends. Good idea. Exploiting the damp wicket with consummate skill, Rhodes wrecked the formidable Australian batting to lodge figures of 11-3-17-7.

Simple scoreboard, simple message. England in control.

A little more cricket followed as Australia resumed at 5.15pm and meandered along to 46 for two but the rain had long sentenced the match to a draw. The excellence of Tyldesley and Rhodes was not to be rewarded with victory and all that the decision to squeeze in that last session of play achieved for the club was to trigger a clutch of requests from disgruntled spectators for compensation for clothes ruined in the scrimmage at the City End. Still, Edgbaston had joined Melbourne, The Oval, Sydney, Old Trafford, Lord's, The Adelaide Oval, St George's Park in Port Elizabeth, Newlands in Cape Town, The Old Wanderers ground in Johannesburg, Trent Bridge and Headingley in the esteemed circle of Test venues. The club's sense of adventure was warmly embraced and supported by their sporting brethren in the region - many clubs chipped in to help cover the financial loss recorded on the Test.

His long-time Yorkshire cohort Hirst contributed 11-4-15-3. Only the redoubtable Trumper progressed beyond five. He resisted for 70 minutes and mustered half his team's total before his off-stump was uprooted by Hirst. In front of a scintillated and disbelieving crowd, Australia's entire first innings occupied only 23 overs and 80 minutes.

That rain, however, was brewing. Following on, on a gloomy second evening, Australia reached eight without loss but the players had scarcely reached the pavilion at the close before the deluge set in. England's hopes of christening Edgbaston with a victory were well and truly washed away as rain swept down all night and well into the next day. The downpour shifted problems from Darling and his batsmen to Ryder and his staff. Next morning much of the field was underwater when play was scheduled to start yet large crowds gathered outside the ground. With only the remotest chance of cricket being played, Ryder faced a difficult decision. Should he let the hordes in?
At 3.45pm, with the sun at last out and the umpires having decided that play could commence, albeit pointlessly in view of the match situation, the gates were opened. The subsequent rush for the best vantage-points caused pandemonium at the City End where there was, in fact, only one gate. Hoardings were pushed over and numerous spectators ended up horizontal in the mud and on the freshly-laid tarmac.

Yorkshire genius Wilfred Rhodes

Chapter 2

1909

England v Australia May 27 1909

Seven years elapsed between the first two Tests to be played at Edgbaston but half the 22 players who participated in the inaugural match were still around and playing well enough to earn selection for the second - the opener in the five-match Ashes series of 1909.

Archie MacLaren, now 37, had been reappointed to the England captaincy and still among his team were Charles Fry, Johnny Tyldesley, Wilfred Rhodes, George Hirst, Gilbert Jessop and Dick Lilley. Four Australians - Monty Noble (now captain), Victor Trumper, Warwick Armstrong and Sydney Gregory - had bridged the intervening years. Seven years on, just like the first time, the English bowlers were to dominate the three days but this time the weather was kinder and allowed them to finish the job.

England's first win at Edgbaston was safely banked although Rhodes, the destroyer of 1902, was required to deliver just a single over during the entire match as left-armers Hirst and Colin Blythe shared all 20 Australian wickets.

Hirst and Blythe, as characters, could barely have contrasted more. Hirst was a blunt, exuberant Yorkshireman forged, like Rhodes, from the tough learning grounds of west Yorkshire league cricket. At 37, he retained an awesome physique which he used to deliver the ball, from an unusually long, bounding run, at a seaming, swinging fast-medium. Hirst regarded no cause as lost. His presence, alone, lifted his team-mates and intimidated opponents.

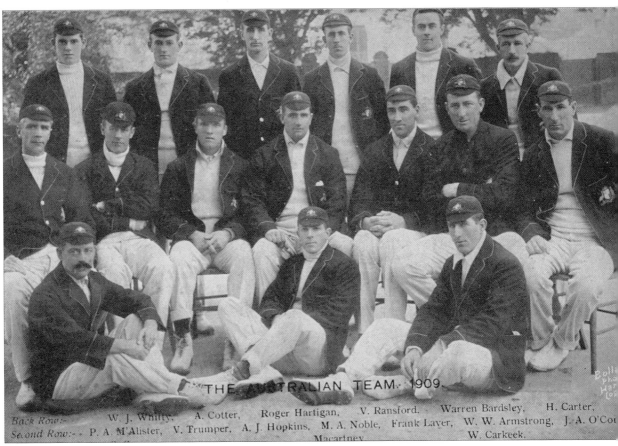

Australia's squad for the 1909 Edgbaston Test

A. C. MacLaren, Lancashire

While the Yorkshireman towered over a dressing-room Blythe, from Tonbridge in Kent, was much more introverted. An epilepsy sufferer, the 29-year-old was moody; intense sometimes to the point of tortured. His high intelligence manifested itself in his slow bowling. A master of flight and variation, never was Blythe more at ease than when being attacked by batsmen. To Hirst's leonine clout, Blythe added the guile of a fox.

The two left-armers were primed and ready for action but on the opening day all they could do was, along with 2,000 spectators, wait for a series of heavy showers to sweep over Edgbaston. At 4pm, even the hardly sprinkling was on the brink of losing hope when there was a sudden brightening up. Play began at 5pm amid an atmosphere of noisy relief.

Surprisingly, Noble chose to bat on the wet wicket. Hirst and Blythe licked their lips, rolled up their sleeves and got to work. In half an hour's play before bad light closed back in, each collected a wicket. Blythe ousted Albert Cotter with the assistance of Hirst at mid-off then Warren Bardsley

fell to a brilliant left-handed slip catch by MacLaren. Australia closed at 22 for two.

On a much brighter second morning Armstrong dug in deep. Support for him was thin, though, as the two left-armers scarcely delivered a bad ball. Armstrong's vigil was ended when Hirst rattled his leg-stump and from 46 for three the tourists declined to 74 all out. Hirst 23-8-28-4. Blythe 23-6-44-6. Australian batsmen didn't seem to fancy Edgbaston at all.

England, at first, fared little better as they were hit by a treble burst from Charlie Macartney. The 'Governor General''s future lay chiefly in lacerating opposing bowlers but here his slow left-arm accounted for Jack Hobbs, MacLaren and Fry (the latter out first ball to maintain his Edgbaston Test average of 0.00) to reduce England to 13 for three. Tyldesley and Nottinghamshire's Arthur Jones rebuilt the total to within 13 of Australia's. Although they perished in successive overs and Armstrong worked his way through the lower order (including Lilley in his 31st Test for a duck), Hirst, Jessop and Rhodes nurdled enough runs to supply a useful lead of 47.

Second time around, Australia drastically reshuffled their batting order in an attempt to deal with Hirst and Blythe. Only numbers 10 and 11 John O'Connor and Bill Whitty retained the same places in the order. This time Noble took Macartney in to open the batting with him but neither lasted long. Blythe spun one inside Macartney's defence before Noble perished to a magnificent catch. The captain clipped Hirst firmly off his pads, timing the ball sweetly, only for Jones at short-leg to thrust out his left hand and somehow cling on to the ball. An instant's silence to digest the brilliance of the moment was followed by a thunderclap of cheering from the stands.

Third-wicket pair Gregory and Vernon Ransford, elevated from six and seven in the first innings, halted the slide and at last forced MacLaren into that most drastic course of action - a bowling change. Northamptonshire seamer George Thompson, making his debut, was given four overs but, despite trying a spell at each end, received short shrift as Australia recovered to 67 for two - 20 runs ahead - by the close of the second day.

England's supporters fill the Edgbaston field after their team's victory

Refreshed overnight, Hirst and Blythe resumed their domination on the final morning. Blythe outthought the third-wicket pair, first tempting Gregory to sky to mid-wicket where Thompson, running round from mid-on, completed a splendid catch, then deceiving Ransford in flight to bowl him off his pads. From 103 for four - 56 runs ahead - Australia collapsed to 125 for nine and although last pair O'Connor and Whitty added 26 in 20 minutes, when Lilley clamped his mitts round an edge from O'Connor, England's target was just 105 and Hirst and Blythe had completed a full house of 20 wickets.

Now it was time for John Berry Hobbs, trapped lbw first ball in the first innings, to unveil his class. At 12.55pm he strode out with Fry. At 3.10pm they returned to the pavilion with the job done. Hobbs was masterful. Having seen his partner's early vulnerability - Fry reached only three when dropped by O'Connor at mid-on - the Surrey maestro took responsibility and engineered the strike with consummate skill. By the time the target was reached by a Fry smite to the square-leg boundary,

MR. G. L. JESSOP.

Constables on duty (bottom left corner) to control the happy crowd

Hobbs had struck nine fours. The two batsmen, warmly applauded by the opposition, strode up the pavilion steps through the appreciative Warwickshire members to join their beaming colleagues in the dressing-room.

Hobbs had performed the coup de grace with some glorious strokes on the final afternoon but England's first victory at Edgbaston owed everything to the skills of Hirst and Blythe. Richly did they enjoy the moment. Hearty was the post-match supper. By the time Birmingham next hosted a Test match, 15 years into the future, Hirst's great playing career would be in its final throes. Come the summer of 1924 the Yorkshireman would be coaching at Eton School and donning his whites for his beloved Yorkshire only on an occasional basis. Blythe had been dead almost seven years, killed in action in France.

A collection of autographed balls from all the participating players to celebrate England's victory.

Chapter 3

1924

England v South Africa June 14 1924

The Australian batsmen had endured a wretched time of it - 36 all out in only 23 overs - in their first Test innings at Edgbaston in 1902. Twenty-two years later South Africa paid their first Test match visit to the ground and registered an innings which made the Aussies' earlier effort appear a paragon of longevity and fortitude.

Assailed by Sussex pair Arthur Gilligan and Maurice Tate, Herbie Taylor's South Africans were swept away in the space of only 75 deliveries in their first

innings. Of their paltry total of 30 runs, more than a third were extras. Edgbaston's early proclivity for setting long-standing records had surfaced again. Eighty years on, South Africa have still never been dismissed for a smaller total in Test cricket.

The seeds of their downfall in Birmingham on those three June days in 1924 had been sown two summers earlier - at a practice session in Hove. The 1922 season was proving an unsuccessful one for Sussex so captain Gilligan gathered his players

South Africa pay their first visit to Edgbaston

The South African line up of 1924

together for a full day of practice. During it, he happened to face Tate who was busily purveying his usual brand of slow off-breaks. Suddenly, Tate slipped in a surprise.

"Down came a quick one which spreadeagled my stumps," Gilligan later recalled. "He did this three times. I said 'Maurice you must change your style of bowling immediately.'" Change it he did and by 1924 opposing batsmen were suffering. When, just before the opening Test, Gilligan was appointed captain of England he wasted no time in convincing the selectors that his Sussex team-mate was, at 29, ready for Test cricket.

Gilligan (himself a bowler of menace and pace) and Tate rapidly became the most feared opening bowling pair in county cricket. They approached the Test at Edgbaston in top form having just bowled out Surrey and Middlesex (two of the strongest batting sides in the country) for 53 and 41 respectively in successive matches at The Oval and Lord's. Now they turned their attention to South Africa.

This time the England team showed just one survivor from the previous Edgbaston Test 15 years earlier; Jack Hobbs, now 41 and firmly established as the hero of every young boy who followed cricket. Hobbs' experience and class would be precious to an XI which included, as well as a new captain, five debutants - Tate, Percy Chapman, Roy Kilner, Herbert Sutcliffe and George Wood. On a balmy morning, Hobbs took up exactly where he had left off 15 years and two weeks earlier.

Only 48 hours before the Test was due to start, Warwickshire's championship match with Yorkshire had been abandoned because the ground was drenched. So, when South Africa captain Taylor won the toss, he was quick to insert England in the hope that his bowlers would harness moisture still evident in the pitch. In fact, the wicket played well and Hobbs and Sutcliffe were soon accumulating elegantly. In two hours 10 minutes they added 136, the first of 15 three-figure opening stands they were to construct for their country, and when they fell in quick succession there was no respite for the toiling South Africans. As the afternoon grew hot, the bowlers became jaded and dispirited as Frank Woolley and Patsy Hendren inherited command with a third-wicket alliance of 83. Percy Fender added a chippy 36 and Kilner drove with power to reach 40 out of 398 for seven at the close. The South Africans had leaned too heavily on George Parker, an expatriate fast-bowler plucked from Bradford League side Eccleshill to make his Test debut. Parker was rewarded with five wickets from his first bowl in Test cricket but, with a cumbersome approach and a follow-through which took him almost the length of the wicket, he failed to last the day after bowling 33 overs and had to retire, exhausted, a few minutes before the close.

Next morning England advanced to 438, a position of some comfort. Comfort was then upgraded to outright hedonism as the Sussex maestros got to work. The first ball of the innings was a no-ball, from which Taylor took a single. The second dislodged Bob Catterall's off-stump. Moments later Tate marked out his run and delivered his first missile in Test cricket. It was a trifle short but Manfred Susskind helped it obligingly to Kilner at short-leg. When a Gilligan break-back eluded Dave Nourse's defence, South Africa were six for three.

Mick Commaille, returning to Test cricket at the age of 41 after a 14-year absence, scampered a single off Gilligan which transpired to be his only scoring stroke while watching six partners perish. In a magnificent display of straight bowling the Sussex

pair routed the rest without the assistance of a fielder. Gilligan took out Tom Ward and Parker with successive balls to close the innings after only 75 balls and 48 minutes.

For those patriots in the crowd who simply wanted to watch England win, this was manna from heaven. Those spectators who relish more of a contest were next to be rewarded, however, as South Africa showed their mettle and salvaged their reputation. Taylor and Commaille ground out 54 for the first wicket to launch a resolute rearguard action. All the top order batted solidly, most of all Catterall and James Blanckenberg who dug in with enormous determination to lift South Africa to 274 for four (Catterall 52, Blanckenberg 56) at the close of the second day.

The fightback promoted a tinge of concern at the lack of depth to England's bowling attack. Although six bowlers had been used, only Gilligan and Tate had enjoyed success so predictably the captain entrusted himself and his county colleague with the ball on the final morning. Gilligan immediately struck a major blow with the wicket of Blanckenberg before he had added to his overnight score. Catterall then cast a shadow over his good work by crazily calling Hugh Deane for a fourth run which he had no chance of making - a wanton waste of a wicket in a rearguard action. Catterall resisted on but South Africa's first-innings capitulation had left them with too steep a mountain to climb - a term which, incidentally, in 2002 is the hoariest old sporting cliche of them all but, in 1924, was fresh and original so can be used in that context at this point. Hobbs' catch at cover point, to dismiss Sidney Pegler, concluded England's comprehensive victory by an innings and 18 runs.

For Warwickshire, eager to encourage the MCC to allocate them more Test matches, the only disappointment during the three days was from poor attendances but these were attributed to the minimum admission charge having been pitched too high at half a crown. Enough people of the moneyed variety attended, at least, to pose the constabulary with a new challenge. Six hundred of those new-fangled "motor-cars" had to be accommodated outside the ground and were excellently parked up by the police.

Part of Warwickshire County Cricket Club plans for " Going Gay " this season - preparing the site of the new tea gardens at Edgbaston

Chapter 4

1929

England v South Africa June 15 1929

The opening Test match of England's 1929 series against South Africa commenced at Edgbaston exactly 93 days after England's players trudged off the Melbourne Cricket Ground at the conclusion of a long and arduous Ashes series in Australia. Ninety-three days was just about enough time for Harold Larwood, JC White, Wally Hammond, Patsy Hendren and Maurice Tate - the five men who played in both games - to have recovered from the exertions of the earlier match.

That Melbourne Test was a monumental occasion. It lasted the little matter of eight days at the end of which, after 33 hours and 17 minutes of cricket, Australia won by five wickets. It was a hard-earned victory, yet somewhat hollow as it simply prevented a whitewash in the series. England's players, already 4-0 up approaching the end of one of most gruelling of all tours (there was no hopping around by jet in those days of course) were, to use the technical term, cream-crackered.

Wally Hammond, Gloucestershire and England

The emphatic Ashes triumph underlined England's domination of world cricket and sent the nation's cricket lovers into the summer of 1929 expecting South Africa to be beaten with ease. Australia had been unable to contain the brilliant Wally Hammond, who amassed a staggering 905 runs at 113.12 in the Ashes series, or deal with White and Larwood, who shared 43 wickets. These were great cricketers, close to or in their prime and Warwickshire were overjoyed that Hammond, White and Larwood would be unpacking their jockstraps in the Edgbaston dressing-room for the opening Test against of 1929.

The county needed a fillip. Crowds, and therefore gate receipts, had taken a dive as Birmingham's sporting populace, with limited cash in their pocket as the depression bit, elected to direct it increasingly towards the burgeoning sports of greyhound racing and speedway. Warwickshire's team, languishing low in the championship, were doing little to attract punters. Edgbaston needed a rattling good Test match to tempt them back for county matches and with England luxuriating in the warm afterglow of the Ashes, all seemed set fair for such an occasion. It was not to be. "If all Test matches were comparable with the dreary affair that is dragging along at Edgbaston," the Birmingham Post lamented after the second day, "public opinion would soon compel their exclusion from English cricket programmes as unwarrantable weariness to the flesh and spirit of honest citizens." South Africa were regarded as cannon fodder. Their form so far on tour had been moderate and they arrived in Birmingham directly from Stoke-on-Trent where 56-year-old Sydney Barnes had rattled through them to the tune of 32-11-41-8. Despite the absence of Jack Hobbs with a shoulder injury, England expected to win comfortably.

There were 11,000 in the ground on the opening morning as Sutcliffe took Tim Killick out to open the batting. The Middlesex student strode out under the experienced Yorkshireman's wing just as, five years earlier, Sutcliffe had stepped out of the same pavilion on his debut under the warm wing of Hobbs. Killick, destined for uniqueness as the only man to open in a Test at Edgbaston and later become vicar of Bishop's Stortford, comfortably assumed the mantle of Test cricketer as England eased to 59 without loss in less than an hour. After Killick sliced to slip, however, the innings lost its way. Hammond gave 22-year-old debut quickie Neville Quinn the thrill of his young life by missing a straight one as England limped to a tatty 128 for six. Hendren and Tate counter-attacked to add 87 in 50 minutes but when they departed to successive balls - Tate sending up a skier then Hendren surprised by an in-ducker - England were doomed to an unsatisfactory total on a good wicket.

In the final session of the opening day, the cricket began to get dull. South African openers Bob Catterall and Bruce Mitchell played Larwood and Maurice Tate with understandable caution then strangely, when Hammond and White took up the attack, retreated into total defence. Seventeen overs from the change bowlers yielded four runs off the bat as South Africa inched a joyless course towards a position of strength - 59 without loss - at the close.

On the second morning, Catterall and Mitchell resumed their safety-first, second and third policy and extended their partnership to 119. When the breach was finally made, Larwood quickly widened it by uprooting James Christy's off-stump and flattening Taylor's middle peg with a full-toss past a crass cross-bat heave. Tate then ousted Denys Morkel and South Africa had listed to 130 for four. Under pressure, they retreated into virtual inertia. Confusion and boredom enveloped the crowd as

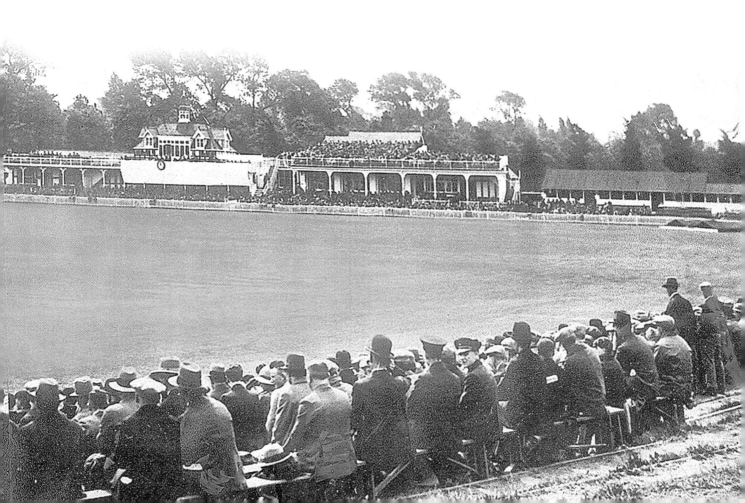

giants at the crease the cricket was tame. Runs arrived far too slowly to allow White to contemplate a credible declaration.

South Africa were finally set an impossible target of 304 in less than three hours. Catterall showed some adventure but Mitchell haunted the crease for a further 155 minutes for 61 runs (575 minutes for 149 runs in the match) and the contest petered out in front of 3,224 paying punters, most of whom stayed stoically to the end. Other potential customers had read the runes and neglected the final day's play in favour of visiting the Shrewsbury and West Midlands Show (featuring the inaugural Shrewsbury Chamber of Commerce Challenge Cup for the best Cheshire Cheese from a Shropshire Maker). They had chosen wisely.

Harold Larwood, Nottinghamshire and England

over after over was blocked out. Mitchell crawled his way to 88 in seven hours. The spectators made their views known, some by cat-calling, others by departing and when Larwood finally lopped off the tail the innings, worth 250 runs, had spanned a mammoth 172.4 overs. South Africa led by five runs after batting for 445 minutes compared to England's 225.

The match was on a slab, its lifeblood drained. When, late on the second day, England began their second innings, Killick showed familiar eagerness to attack but to the fifth ball of the third morning, he attacked Quinn once too often. That brought Hammond in to join Sutcliffe but even with those

Chapter 5

1957

England v West Indies May 30 1957

If Warwickshire's pride in hosting the inaugural Test at Edgbaston in 1902 knew few bounds, it was no less substantial 55 years later when West Indies played their first Test there.

Twenty-eight years had elapsed since the previous Test at Edgbaston. A long absence during which, especially after the Second World War, the club's

memorable matches ever played at the ground. All five days (this was the first five-day Test at Edgbaston) were blessed by fine weather in which a splendid plot unfolded. This was the first Test on which the BBC carried live radio commentary. "Don't miss a ball, we broadcast them all," boomed the corporation. There was much to relate.

Test cricket back in Birmingham - let's celebrate with an ice-cream

officers had planned, budgeted, lobbied and generally worked their socks off to attract England back to Birmingham. In 1957, they were richly rewarded by what remains one of the most

This was West Indies' fifth Test tour of England. Their improvement since sustaining a 3-0 whitewash on their first, in 1928, was apparent from their fourth, in 1950, when John Goddard's

The end, at last, for Cowdrey, caught by Kanhai

side won an enthralling four-match series 3-1. Even if that historic triumph owed something to the England team's transitional state following the war, the fulminant talent in the Caribbean was clear.

England's subsequent series in the West Indies, under Len Hutton in 1953/54, was a compelling tussle which finished all square at 2-2. So in 1957, with Clyde Walcott, Everton Weekes, Frank Worrell, Gary Sobers, Sonny Ramadhin and Alf Valentine in the touring party the summer stage was set for a treat; it's opening act at Edgbaston. Sometimes, expectations can be a burden. This match, despite ending in a draw, exceeded expectations.

Edgbaston was ready. Over nine years, £150,000 had been spent on ground improvements, increasing its capacity to 32,000, equal to that of Lord's. All reserve seats had been rapidly snapped up, many by West Indians who had recently relocated to the Birmingham area from the Caribbean. With them they brought a new kind of atmosphere to English cricket matches. For the first time, calypso arrived on the Edgbaston terraces.

On the first day the calypso was silenced for a moment before play while the team news was digested. West Indies sprung a shock by omitting Valentine, thus splitting up his legendary spin alliance with Ramadhin. After an inspection of the pitch, the selectors decided instead to give a debut to fiery young fast-bowler Roy Gilchrist.

After England won the toss, Gilchrist soon collected his first wicket when Brian Close edged to the tourists' other debutant, wicket-keeper Rohan Kanhai. Peter Richardson and Doug Insole advanced the score to 61 for one before Ramadhin spun his web.

Insole, deceived by flight, was bowled. Richardson was pouched at forward short-leg. From 104 for two, the innings subsided to 130 for eight as the tiny Trinidadian, turning the ball both ways from the City End, wove a mesmerising spell of 8-4-9-6. Only some late blows from Fred Trueman and Brian Statham averted total capitulation and although Trueman rapidly bowled Bruce Pairaudeau when West Indies replied, by the close they had reached 83 for one, Kanhai having built a composed unbeaten 42 in his first Test innings.

On Friday morning, England started well. With the first ball of the day, Statham trapped Kanhai. Trueman then bowled Weekes but whilst a bowling armoury of Trueman, Statham, Trevor Bailey, Jim Laker and Tony Lock has few equals in the annals of Test cricket, here West Indies had batsmen to match them. Walcott, hobbling after twisting his knee turning for a second run early in the day, recruited Pairaudeau as his runner and struck a charming 90. Twenty-year-old Sobers stroked an elegant 53. When both perished in quick succession, Collie Smith and Worrell (the latter, also hobbling after pulling a muscle, inherited the busy Pairaudeau from Walcott) climbed into a tiring attack to add 119 in the final session.

The sixth-wicket pair another added 71 on Saturday morning before Worrell finally fell to Statham's in-ducker in the last over before lunch. If England's relief was great, scarcely less was Pairaudeau's. Out for just a single, he had spent the next eight and a half hours running for his colleagues!

With further support from Goddard, Smith powered on to 161 to ensure his side a mighty lead of 288. When England declined to 113 for three, with Richardson, Insole and Close already out, early on the fourth day, their first Test defeat at Edgbaston beckoned.

Cometh the hour, cometh the men. Peter May and Colin Cowdrey first retrenched watchfully then counter-attacked gloriously. Ramadhin and Denis Atkinson wheeled on and on - and on and on and on - but were met by sound technique and wise judgment interspersed with regal strokes. May's was the ultimate captain's innings - responsible but assertive. When, having established total control, he rested in the 190s late in the day, Cowdrey sparkled. In the final over, the Kent batsman unfurled the most glorious of cover-drives to the boundary off Ramadhin to round off a day of inspiring counter-thrust. By the close, May and Cowdrey had added 265. They sat down to supper that night on 193 and 78 respectively having taken the total to 378 for three.

With a full day left, the weather fine and England only 90 ahead there was still work to do. Unruffled, the two batsmen continued their rescue operation. When Cowdrey was finally caught off Smith for

154, the fourth wicket had added 411. Still May advanced. Ramadhin sent down 98 overs and Denis Atkinson 72 (without taking a wicket) before the England captain finally declared just 15 runs short of a personal triple century.

Fascinating stuff as Ramadhin wheels away

May received a standing ovation but there was still fascinating cricket ahead. West Indies' target was 296 in 140 minutes but, brains deadened by 258 overs in the field, they batted fallibly. Trueman removed both openers, Kanhai falling to a brilliant catch by Close from a miscued hook. As the wicket

Wonderful effort chaps; May and Cowdrey bring smiles to the pavilion

started to break up, May introduced spin for the fifth over and with Lock and Laker in tandem, the over-rate quickened. Pressure built on the tourists. Laker bowled eight successive maidens. Sobers edged to slip. Worrell bat-padded to short-leg. Walcott managed just a single before perishing to Laker. Smith, so destructive the day before, eked out five runs in an hour before falling lbw. Weekes resisted longest but then spooned a catch to Trueman off Lock. In a gripping finale, Goddard and Atkinson were hanging on desperately as West Indies crawled to sanctuary at 72 for seven off 60 overs.

England had failed to force victory on their return to Edgbaston but a terrific match included feats to grace the history-books. The partnership between May and Cowdrey was the highest for any wicket for England. May's unbeaten 285 remains the highest Test score at the ground while Ramadhin's 774 balls in the match are the most delivered by any bowler in any Test. Of 3,536 balls delivered during the five days by 13 bowlers, not one was a wide or a no-ball while in England's second innings Kanhai conceded 23 byes - still the most in any Edgbaston Test innings.

The match was triumphantly organised with 64,977 spectators watching from the popular side, joining 26,500 members over the five days. Edgbaston's case for inclusion in the select band of regular Test match venues had been hugely enhanced.

There was, inevitably, a complaint or two. Spectators who wanted to leave the ground during the lunch interval were aggrieved to find no pass-out system in place so faced being charged again for readmittance. A few grumbles were also registered about delays caused by movement behind the bowlers' arms although, after the match, Warwickshire committee chairman Alec Hastilow was quick to confirm that sight-screens would not be installed. They would take up too many seats.

Taken as a whole, the event was a resounding success and the last word went to England's chairman of selectors Gubby Allen. "The organisation has been first-class," he said. "The gates have been good, it was a first-class wicket and the spectators appear to have enjoyed themselves. Absolutely first-class in every way."

Edgbaston had done itself proud.

Chapter 6

1958

England v New Zealand June 5 1958

West Indies' first signature in the Test match visitors' book at Edgbaston, in 1957, heralded a wonderful occasion; a five-day feast of fine, fluctuating, sun-drenched cricket. Twelve months later, New Zealand signed in for the first time and the occasion was shorter, greyer and altogether less grand. England won at a canter at 2.48pm on the fourth day as the tourists, still searching for their first victory after 21 Tests against England, imploded in the face of a hostile seam attack led by Fred Trueman.

From ball one, plenty of help was afforded to bowlers and the first batsman to fall victim was, sadly for the home members, Mike Smith. To Warwickshire's delight, their captain had been selected for his Test debut on the ground he had

called home since switching from Leicestershire two years earlier. Three weeks before his 25th birthday, the bespectacled Smith took his place in an England batting order which could safely be described as not half bad. In amongst Peter Richardson, Tom Graveney, Peter May and Colin Cowdrey, the former Oxford University captain landed - and he duly launched his international career with a blob!

After May won the toss, MJK was soon padding up in the dressing-room he knew so well, ready to open with Richardson. His first ball in Test cricket, from Tony MacGibbon, was a wide. The next two he defended solidly. By the next he was beaten for pace, ball thumped into pad and up went umpire Charlie Elliott's gnarled Derbyshire digit. As Smith

New Zealand step onto the Edgbaston turf for the first time on Test business...

trudged back up the pavilion steps, the home members greeted their captain with a warm wave of sympathy. They had witnessed a modest preface to what would become a weighty tome of a Test career.

As the ball seamed and swung, Richardson and Graveney were soon back in the pavilion alongside the debutant. May and Cowdrey reconstructed the

31 overs to survive on a gloomy first evening and England hit back hard. Trueman trapped Lawrence Miller and Bailey pierced the defence of Noel Harford and John Reid to send New Zealand into the close at an uneasy 41 for three.

The innings deteriorated briskly on Friday morning. John D'Arcy, having resisted pluckily in the previous night's gloaming in his first Test innings, soon

...and out come England

innings with a partnership of 121 but theirs was the only alliance of substance. The persevering MacGibbon dismissed them both and John Alabaster's dismantling of the lower order was delayed only by a thrash or two from last pair Jim Laker and Peter Loader which hauled the total over 200. New Zealand's unexpected success left them

edged Trueman. In the face of Trueman's fire, another debutant Trevor Meale, an attacking batsman by nature, subdued his instincts to grind out seven runs in 85 minutes, exemplifying New Zealand batting which was, according to the Birmingham Post, "overawed and introspective." Bailey supported Trueman's pace with a spell which

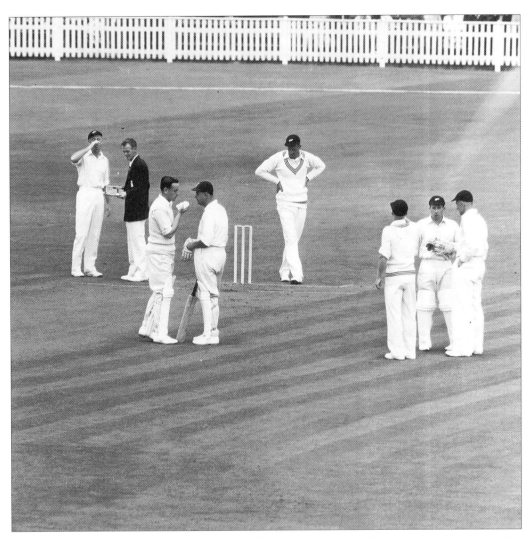

"Let's do it this way" - May and Cowdrey confer and so do the opposition

was parsimony itself and spinners Laker and Lock were left with largely a fielding brief as New Zealand, like Australia and South Africa before them, failed to reach 100 on their first Test innings at Edgbaston. It was left to numbers 10 and 11 Harry Cave and John Hayes to record the biggest partnership of the innings - 26 - but the deficit stood at 127, a significant margin on an untrustworthy pitch.

To the relief of all, Smith's second visit to the crease yielded his first Test run but he managed only six more before again falling to MacGibbon. A nick landed in Eric Petrie's gloves and the Warwickshire captain, having become the seventh player to be dismissed for seven in an Edgbaston Test, again departed to sympathetic applause. So many batsmen had played and missed during the match. Smith played and nicked. Graveney and May also missed out but Richardson made light of the difficult conditions. The Worcestershire captain advanced to 71 by the close of the second day when England were 131 for three, 258 ahead.

On Saturday, Richardson advanced to his fifth (and last) Test century in an alliance of 104 with Cowdrey before May's declaration left New Zealand a target of 343 in seven sessions. A draw, at this stage, was a tad unlikely, even more so after the tourists had declined to 69 for four by the close. D'Arcy was slickly picked up by Trueman in the gully. Meale reverted to type after his first-innings vigil and lofted Lock for four and six but then aimed to clear the ropes again and Smith sprinted 40 yards to take a wonderful catch at long-on.

On Monday morning the innings was ruthlessly asphyxiated. Noel Harford, 15 not out overnight, was hit in the face by a Trueman lifter and, badly shaken up, had to retire. He returned at 93 for five but Bailey bowled 39 balls without conceding a run and New Zealand succumbed quietly to defeat, shortly after lunch. The early finish left only the question of whether to hold an exhibition match to pad out the day for the spectators. Before the match the English Board of Control and the New

The unique atmosphere of an Edgbaston Test. Eric Hollies and Cyril Goodway (background) are among those chatting away

Zealand Cricket Council had agreed that some sort of entertainment should be arranged if three hours cricket, exclusive of intervals, remained in a day. Somehow the end happened to arrive, when Bailey pouched Hayes off Lock at 2.48pm, eight minutes after the exhibition deadline. There would be no crude limited-over thrash.

Despite its damp and one-sided nature, the match attracted 61,000 people. That figure included 39,549 paying spectators - almost 4,000 more than the total of 35,805 who paid to attend county cricket at Edgbaston during the entire summer. The £18,941 profit from the Test came in, to say the least, handy to Warwickshire. The importance of Edgbaston's Test match status to the club's financial health was growing.

Chapter 7

1960

England v South Africa June 9 1960

It was Edgbaston's turn to miss out in 1959 when India were the tourists but to Birmingham fell the first Test, in England, of the Swinging Sixties.

It wasn't quite the first Test anywhere in the Sixties. It was the ninth. Australia had played the last three of their series in India since the turn of the year and England a full five in the West Indies where, assisted by winning all five tosses, they won the series 1-0. The decisive victory arrived in the second Test at Port-of-Spain which was a blazing, vibrant contest. It included centuries from Ken Barrington, Mike Smith and Rohan Kanhai, a devastating burst from Fred Trueman, warnings to Wes Hall and Chester Watson for intimidatory fast-bowling and riots from the largest crowd ever assembled for any sporting event in the West Indies. A lively function.

Of the victorious team in that Trinidad cauldron in early February, seven players - Smith, Trueman, Geoff Pullar, Colin Cowdrey, Ted Dexter, Ray Illingworth and Brian Statham - were in the England side at sylvan and sedate Edgbaston to face South Africa five months later. Alongside them were all-rounders Bob Barber and Peter Walker, of Lancashire and Glamorgan respectively, included for their Test debuts. For the first time since 1949 England went into a home Test with no Surrey player.

Politics in cricket. Anti-apartheid protestors march on Edgbaston

South Africa arrived somewhat ring-rusty having not played a Test for more than two years since a 3-0 home defeat to Australia. Their most recent tussle with England, in 1956/57, was encouraging as 37 wickets from off-spinner Hughie Tayfield

proceedings, police with dogs were in attendance on the opening day but protests held outside the ground by Birmingham and District Anti-Apartheid Committee were orderly and dignified. While all remained quiet outside the ground, inside it there

Trueman counter-attacks at Tayfield's expense

underpinned their fightback from 2-0 down to square the series with wins in Johannesburg and Port Elizabeth. Three years on at Edgbaston, Derrick McGlew's side included three men new to Test cricket - fast-bowler Geoff Griffin, Kent left-hander (and Charlton Athletic footballer) Sydney O'Linn and Durban-born former Oxford double blue Jonathan Fellows-Smith.

The South Africans' visit was not universally welcomed. Warwickshire received letters from several members stating they would not attend the match as a protest against the visiting country's apartheid policy. In the light of threats to disrupt

was also little to excite as a disappointingly sparse gathering of 6,775 watched England make tortuous progress.

Neil Adcock soon ousted Cowdrey then a partnership of 61 in two hours between Pullar and Dexter ended when an Adcock bouncer shattered Pullar's left wrist. Only Dexter showed any aggression all day and when he perished with the total on 100, Raman Subba Row and Smith cloaked themselves in caution. They inched the score to 175 for three from 98 overs at the close. It was dull fare.

On the second morning, Subba Row and Smith both reached 50 but progressed little further. Thereafter only Jim Parks resisted Adcock and Tayfield for long and the innings concluded an hour after lunch. A total of 292 was nothing special but Trueman and Statham inflicted brisk damage on South Africa's reply. Trevor Goddard fell to a brilliant catch at short-leg by Smith to herald a collapse to 61 for five before John Waite found a worthy partner in O'Linn. The sixth-wicket pair ground out a half-century just before the close of a slow but more interesting second day which South Africa ended on 114 for five.

On Saturday, the cricket world celebrated Everton Weekes' receipt of an OBE in the Queen's Birthday Honours List and, at Edgbaston, Waite and O'Linn

pushing across the line and the querulous Fellows-Smith was tormented then trapped. England led by 106.

Second time around, with Pullar still in pain in the pavilion, Cowdrey took responsibility for facing the first ball. He was bowled by the second and with every run requiring extraction from a begrudging strip, England made uneven progress to 89 for four (Smith 18, Illingworth 6), 195 ahead at the close of the third day.

To the disappointment of the home members, Smith added only 10 more on Monday morning before lifting Tayfield to extra-cover. England stumbled to 118 for seven before Walker and Trueman, the latter striking 16 from a Tayfield over, lashed 45 for

Walker and Parks attempt to salvage a bat-pad from Griffin off Illingworth

resumed their diligent work. They added another 32 before Cowdrey's introduction of Illingworth into the attack sent the innings into decline. Warwickshire spin legend Eric Hollies had predicted on the first morning: "It will take spin on the third day" - and he was, just like his bowling for decades at Edgbaston, spot-on. O'Linn edged to slip, Waite was bowled

the eighth wicket. Statham then joined the debutant to add 39 for the ninth before Pullar - somewhat needlessly with his side already 308 runs ahead - strode out at number 11. He faced a single ball, one-handed, from Griffin before Statham, having scrambled a bye to gain the strike, sent up a skier next ball.

South Africa required 310 to win but Statham struck two early blows as McGlew edged to Parks and Goddard squirted to short-leg. Now the tourists showed their resilience. Tony Pithey and Roy MacLean added 53 for the third wicket and when Pithey was bowled by Illingworth, MacLean was joined in sturdy defiance by Waite. They took the score to 120 for three at the close and tucked themselves into their cosy pits on Monday night still harbouring ambitions of a dash at an historic victory. With seven wickets to fall, South Africa required another 190 runs.

Although the final day was full of possibilities, the club's officers were amazed and angered to see that, of 1,105,651 members of the human race residing in Birmingham at the time, only 1,074 elected to pay for admission to Edgbaston. In front of this select gathering, South Africa's victory hopes were seriously damaged by the second ball of the day, a speedy offering from Trueman which defeated MacLean's quixotic pull. Two hours later the last wicket had fallen. Waite fought valiantly for the second time in the match but Barber collected his first Test wicket when he bamboozled O'Linn and, as Cowdrey juggled his bowlers intelligently, England snuffed out the innings and the match. Victory reinforced their happy record at Edgbaston; played seven, won four, drawn three, lost none. Less happy was county secretary Leslie Deakins as he reflected on match receipts of £16,664 and a total attendance of 43,137, including members. "If Birmingham wants Test matches in the future then the city must give them far better support," Deakins said. "It is a major disappointment after all we have done to win back Test match status for Edgbaston."

Uniform on patrol - the protests all passed off peacefully

Chapter 8

1961

England v Australia June 8 1961

Twelve months later, Deakins was a much happier man and Edgbaston a much fuller arena. At last came the return of an Ashes Test to Birmingham. For only the third time - and the first since 1909 - England met Australia at Edgbaston and everyone connected to the county club was determined to seize their opportunity to impress the establishment. They succeeded. The match was immaculately organised and administrated.

What Deakins could not organise was the weather and unfortunately much of the event was conducted in bitterly cold winds accompanied by irritating showers. Still, the match unravelled intriguingly and

featured an English rearguard action redolent of that built by May and Cowdrey against West Indies four years earlier. Sadly the loss of seven hours and 40 minutes playing time ultimately forced it up a cul-de-sac.

The 1961 Australians, under the captaincy of Richie Benaud, were among the most popular parties ever to tour England. Upon their arrival, Benaud pledged that his men were committed to positive, attractive cricket and he was soon honouring his words with a series of bold declarations around the county grounds. This was not the greatest Australian side but their cricket was entertaining and their conduct

You can't trust the weather, even for Richie Benaud's most popular of Australian tour parties

Richie Benaud in the Edgbaston nets

exemplary. On June 8, the Ashes series dawned at Edgbaston amid high excitement and in front of a large, colourful, salivating throng.

England won their 11th successive toss but Benaud was not displeased to hear Colin Cowdrey choose to bat on a green pitch. Neither was he displeased by his seamers' use of the conditions as, on an opening day stripped of 90 minutes by rain and bad light, England limped to 180 for eight. Ken Mackay was the principal instrument of destruction, rarely erring in length or direction as he wobbled the ball about. The Queenslander's decisive burst arrived straight after a tea interval during which the wicket had been further freshened by a heavy shower. Mackay removed Ken Barrington, Mike Smith (caught in the gully second ball) and Raman Subba Row (who had resisted for 170 minutes) in the space of four balls.

Australia wrapped up the English innings in 20 minutes on Friday morning and then their top order, the sun on their backs, exploited more favourable

batting conditions. Fred Trueman laboured fruitlessly into the wind as Bill Lawry built a half-century in his first Test innings. Lawry perished when he bottom-edged a wide ball from Ray Illingworth to give John Murray his first Test victim but that was by no means the last wayward ball delivered by off-spinners Illingworth and David Allen and their profligacy was seized upon by Neil Harvey and Norman O'Neill. O'Neill ("the surest attraction since Bradman" according to the Birmingham Post) received a bruising welcome from Trueman - a short ball which reared into his ribs before he had scored - but fought through an uneasy start to unveil some glorious shots. He reached 82 before playing on to Brian Statham. Harvey progressed faultlessly to 97, was then reprieved when he lofted a short ball from Statham to cover only for Trueman to grass the catch, and soon passed his 20th Test century. Allen finally trapped him but Bobby Simpson, Peter Burge and Alan Davidson kept the board ticking over nicely to 359 for five by the close.

Australian joy as Cowdrey is bowled by Mackay

Australian treasurer Mr Steele with Brian Statham and Norman O'Neill

Heavy demand, as always, for Ashes tickets

Despite Australia's ascendancy, Saturday attracted a ground record crowd of 25,000 but they were 25,000 shivering souls. On a horribly cold, wet day, the tourists kept their concentration to continue piling up runs between the showers. Mackay slashed a vivid 64 but the loss of two and a half hours play delayed Benaud's declaration until after tea. Even then when England, trailing by 321, should have faced 50 awkward minutes batting, only two overs were possible before rain closed in yet again.

England faced an uphill struggle and on the fourth morning openers Subba Row and Geoff Pullar eschewed risk. They remained together until five minutes before lunch when Pullar wafted carelessly down the leg side and Wally Grout accepted the catch. That brought Ted Dexter to the crease, eager to terminate a run of seven Test innings without a half-century. He looked highly unlikely to end his barren spell as he made the scratchiest of starts. Twice he edged Davidson only for Mackay, at second slip, to lose sight of the ball in the dark background of the stand. With Dexter also groping uneasily at Benaud's leg-spin, England were leaning heavily on fortune as well as Subba Row (68 not out) when at

Ted Dexter's autographed bat from the game commemorating his record breaking innings against Australia of 180 with 31 fours completed in 345 minutes

2.30pm, the clouds opened and play was abruptly terminated for the day with England 106 for one. The rain which frustrated Archie MacLaren's side 59 years earlier, this time arrived to abet Cowdrey's.

On the final morning, Australia took the field with hopes still high of recording their first win at Edgbaston. England trailed by 215 and Dexter, five not out, had already required two reprieves. How he took advantage of his escapes! The sun came out, 10,000 people turned up - what a contrast to the paltry gathering for the final

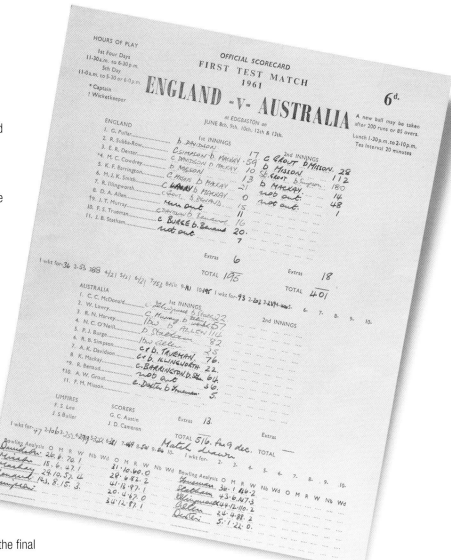

Four runs to point, for Statham off Benaud

Enjoying the day's cricket are Jim Laker, Bill Bowes and Ray Lindwall

throes of the South Africa Test 12 months earlier - and the pitch played easily. Subba Row and Dexter were straight on the offensive. They stroked 42 in the first half-hour to transform the mood from uneasy siege to bristling counter-offensive. Subba Row eased to a richly-deserved century before being bowled by Frank Misson for 112 out of 202. Cowdrey played on to Mackay with his team still 82 in arrears but by now Dexter's confidence was fully restored. Barrington dug in for more than three hours, content to hold up one end while his partner unfurled strokes at the other. Driving magnificently, the Sussex captain navigated England to safety then launched into scintillating overdrive. "The hour after tea," reported the Birmingham Post, "when Edgbaston's green was lit by a rare June sun, and Dexter, with England's arrears cleared, hitting

Simpson and Mackay tremendously to all points, was one of the most inspiring sights the ground can ever have seen."

Dexter struck 31 fours in his 180, which spanned 345 minutes and ended only eight minutes from the close. Then he supplied Grout with the first stumping in an Edgbaston Test since Dick Lilley ousted Monty Noble off Wilfred Rhodes in 1902 and spectators stood to salute the highest score by an England batsman against Australia at Edgbaston. There was just time for Smith to reach the crease and avoid a pair with a comparatively mundane but nevertheless steady-as-a-rock single.
An attendance of 83,000 paid ground record receipts of £38,000. Edgbaston had well and truly come of age.

Chapter 9

1962

England v Pakistan May 31 1962

On their second tour of England - their first having concluded in a 1-1 draw eight years earlier - in 1962, Pakistan paid their first visit to Edgbaston. They found it a bracing experience and were overwhelmed by an innings before tea on the fourth day. Conditions throughout the match were ideally suited to seam-bowling and totally alien to an inexperienced Pakistan team reared on the batsman-friendly pitches of the east. Javed Burki's talented but under-prepared tourists learned the hard way that dispatching the crimson rambler on the lifeless earth of Karachi and Lahore is rather different to dealing with a wildly deviating cherry on a Birmingham greentop.

England captain Ted Dexter knew all about the Pakistanis' vulnerability to seam. A week earlier he had skippered Sussex to a seven-wicket win, driven by the medium-fast armoury of Ian Thompson, Tony Buss, Don Bates and Dexter himself, over the tourists at Hove. The efficacy of seam in English conditions had, however, apparently still not fully dawned on Pakistan as they strangely chose to go into the opening Test with an XI including only two seam-bowlers - Mahmood Hussain and Antao D'Souza. That folly was briskly exposed as Dexter won the toss and England's batsmen filled their boots.

Colin Cowdrey, reluctantly pressed into service as an opener, and Geoff Pullar added 31 in 50 minutes

Tom Graveney gracefully sees off another boundary

Tom Graveney hooks another boundary on his way to record 97 in England's 1st innings

before Pullar played fatally across the line. From the moment that Dexter stepped out of the pavilion at number three the match began to accelerate away from the tourists. The two seamers plugged away nobly but their spin colleagues, their fingers cold and stiff as the sun struggled to inject warmth into a chilly day, extracted little turn. Cowdrey, after a slow start (dropped on 12 by Mushtaq Mohammed at first slip off D'Souza), blossomed while Dexter

twice lifted Nasim-ul-Ghani for six. The second-wicket pair put on 166 in 135 minutes before the captain perished in pursuit of a third six. That brought Tom Graveney, restored to the Test team after a three-year absence, to the crease.

Graveney had not represented England since the final, cyclone-affected Test of England's tour of New Zealand, in Auckland, in March 1959. As he eased

PAKISTAN ★ TEAM
1962

CAPTAIN—Javed Burki

VICE-CAPTAIN—Hanif Mohammad

Imtiaz Ahmad

Mahmood Hussain

Alimuddin

Wallis Mathais

Saeed Ahmad

Nasimul Ghani

Hasib Ahsan

Brig. R. G. HYDER (Manager)

Ijaz Butt

Antao DeSouza

Mushtaq Mohammad

Intikhab Alam

Munir Malik

Mohammad Farooq

Afaq Hussain

Shahid Mahmood

Asif Ahmad

Maj. S. A. RAHMAN (Asstt. Manager)

Buoyed by the ballast of their highest total for five years, England were able to attack and there were customary early wickets for Brian Statham and Fred Trueman, assisted by slick catches from Tony Lock and Graveney. Brothers Hanif and Mushtaq Mohammed batted skilfully to add 78 for the third wicket but the former edged Allen fatally and England then struck two heavy blows just before the close. Tony Lock enticed Mushtaq into an edge to Cowdrey at slip and Allen ousted Burki thanks to another fine catch close in, this time by Barrington.

off the mark with a gorgeous off-drive it seemed he had never been away. Cowdrey and Graveney put on 107 in 87 minutes before Cowdrey's polished innings concluded at 159 from 263 minutes with 21 fours. Ken Barrington missed out, trapped in front by a persevering Hussain who showed great heart by producing a fine spell at the end of a tiring day. Despite his efforts, England occupied the lofty perch of 386 for four at the close.

On Friday morning, Graveney was caught at short-leg without adding to his overnight score but Peter Parfitt and David Allen took up the cudgels with a partnership of 153 in 112 minutes. Parfitt collected his second successive century against Pakistan, following his 111 at Karachi in February, while Allen enjoyed himself hugely. The Gloucestershire player smote 11 fours before Pakistan's torment in the field was truncated by Dexter's lunchtime declaration. In 146 overs, wicket-keeper Imtiaz Ahmed had not conceded a single bye.

Pakistan resumed on 149 for five on Saturday when a crowd of more than 16,000 expected to see England briskly press home their advantage. For an hour, Imtiaz and Wallis Mathias kept out the spinners but Dexter's reintroduction of pace triggered a spectacular collapse. With his first ball of the day, Statham yorked Mathias. Trueman then took the new ball and sped it through Imtiaz's defence to hit off-stump. The off-stumps of Nasim and Mahmood were located with successive balls by Statham as Pakistan plummeted from 202 for five to 206 for nine. Faced with a hat-trick ball, D'Souza kept it out and then counter-attacked to add 40 in 35 minutes with Intikhab but Pakistan still trailed by 298 and, 10 minutes before lunch, followed on.

For much of the afternoon, openers Hanif and Ijaz Butt toiled admirably to lay a foundation. When Butt departed to a juggling catch by Trueman at deep square-leg Imtiaz, promoted to number three, continued his fine match by batting positively. He drove Allen for a towering six before slicing Lock to Graveney. Pakistan needed at least two batsmen to

Mushtaq Mohammad of Pakistan (C) is pictured with his brothers Hanif (L) and Sadiq (R) during a tour of England in 1967

play colossal innings if the game was to be saved but Hanif, limping heavily, fended into the slips and only Saeed Ahmed, unbeaten on 30 out of 158 for four at the end of the third day, passed 50. Early on Monday morning, he was removed by an alert catch by Parfitt at short mid-off and when Burki was castled by the new ball, England closed in on victory. Nasim and Hussain delayed the inevitable defeat with a ninth-wicket partnership of 50 but

Trueman returned straight after lunch to have them both caught in the cordon. England's emphatic victory was complete and, for the home members, happy tidings continued to arrive as news filtered through from Folkestone that Jim Stewart and Mike Smith had completed centuries to lift Warwickshire into a strong position in their county championship duel with Kent.

Chapter 10

1963

England v West Indies July 4 1963

The first nine Test matches to take place in Birmingham had all been the first of their respective series but in 1963 came a change. For the West Indies' visit, Edgbaston was allocated the third contest in the five-match series. The new spot in the tour itinerary only enhanced the appeal of the occasion as appetites were well and truly whetted by two dramatic and contrasting tussles preceding the game in Birmingham.

In the first, at Old Trafford, West Indies romped to a 10-wicket victory as the English batting folded in the face of off-spinner Lance Gibbs' match haul of 11 for 157. That thrashing stung an England side which had approached the series with confidence high after wintering well with a drawn Ashes series in Australia and a 3-0 whitewash of New Zealand. The second Test, at Lord's, was much more fiercely contested and much more even. In fact it could not

West Indies have always enjoyed plenty of support at Edgbaston

Charlie Griffith unleashes another express delivery

have been much more even, culminating in the most thrilling climax as Wes Hall delivered the final ball to David Allen with all four results still possible. England needed six to win and, having been undone by pacemen Hall and Charlie Griffith, were nine wickets down. To add pathos, at the other end to Allen was Colin Cowdrey, his left arm in plaster. Aware that his team could not afford to go two-nil down in the series, Cowdrey had heroically gone in to bat at number 11 despite a fractured arm. Eager not to waste such courage, Allen wisely elected not to attempt to hit the final delivery from Hall for six. He defended it for a draw - and so to Edgbaston. Hall and Griffith were again champing at the bit, only to be outbowled this time by Frederick Sewards Trueman.

Birmingham had not previously seen the best of Trueman for England. Five Tests there had brought him 23 wickets; a respectable return but including just one five-for, against New Zealand in 1958. Five summers on, he arrived in fine form having got among the West Indies batsmen at Lord's with 44-16-100-6 and 26-9-52-5.

Trueman's first task on an overcast Thursday morning was to rest his plates in the dressing-room as England, minus the stricken Cowdrey, won the toss and elected to bat. On a disjointed opening day, most energy was displayed by groundsman Bernard Flack and his team of mopper-uppers. Between the showers it was neither Hall nor Griffith who caused most damage. Instead the well-directed left-arm of Gary Sobers ousted Micky Stewart, Ted Dexter and Ken Barrington to peg the home side back. England closed a staccato day on 157 for five.

The second day brought just two truncated sessions of play - in the morning and evening. In the first, Brian Close's courageous innings ended when he shuffled across his wicket and was trapped by Sobers. Later, in a sunlit, 40-minute burst of activity, Fred Titmus eked out valuable runs but when he fended to short-leg two balls before the scheduled close, England, for the fifth time in five innings in the series, had failed to total 300.

On Saturday, there were 26,114 spectators present only for an ominous weather forecast to live down

Trueman is applauded from the field after his match-winning 12-119

to expectations. Only 160 minutes play were possible. Trueman soon plucked out Conrad Hunte's off-stump before Joey Carew, having hooked Derek Shackleton for six, attempted to do the same to the Yorkshireman but sent the ball looping back to the bowler. West Indies recovered to lay a foundation of relative promise at 108 for two, with Rohan Kanhai and Basil Butcher settling, before England struck a double-blow just before the close. Shackleton had Kanhai neatly caught, behind square, by Tony Lock

and Dexter trapped Joe Solomon to even the match right up again. West Indies closed on 110 for four.

The weather improved after the weekend and Monday at last brought a full day's cricket. England struck early as Butcher, who had scored a sublime 133 at Lord's, was snared by Dexter having adding just a single to his overnight score. The England captain also ousted Worrell while Sobers' promising innings was snuffed out by an inside-edge onto his

The Caribbean community turned out in force to watch the denouement. "West Indians from all walks of life had arrived at the ground expecting to see their heroes rapidly dispose of the remaining English batsmen and then bat their way to a hectic victory," reported the Birmingham Post. "There were bus crews' and postmen's uniforms, gaily-coloured shirts and wide-brimmed hats. Many of the womenfolk accompanied them to add to the gaiety and encouragement. Rolled newspapers were held to the mouths as megaphones and arms flung in the air in supplication."

The bus-crews were kept waiting as England's ninth-wicket pair added another 52 on the final morning before Lock's dismissal triggered the declaration. West Indies needed 309 in 280 minutes but lost Carew, third-ball, to Shackleton. In the next over, Hunte edged Trueman to second slip. 10 for two in the third over. Kanhai and Butcher briefly halted English progress but, when Dexter gave himself a brief spell, his second ball hit Butcher's middle stump. When Shackleton ousted Sobers (the ninth batsman to be dismissed for nine in a Test at Edgbaston), West Indies were 64 for four. Kanhai and Joe Solomon took the score to 78 for four before Trueman hit overdrive.

Kanhai mishooked and was caught at leg-slip. Worrell left the crease simmering with injustice after being adjudged caught behind. West Indies continued to attack and Trueman continued to take advantage. He finished with seven for 44, his last six wickets having arrived in 24 balls for just four runs (a boundary by Gibbs). England cruised to victory to leave their Test record at Edgbaston proudly reading won six, drawn four and lost none. Trueman's match analysis of 12 for 119 remains the best by any bowler in a Test in Birmingham.

Gary Sobers

stumps. Deryck Murray and Hall added 48 in 37 minutes for the eighth wicket but Dexter removed Hall with the assistance of debutant Phil Sharpe at slip and Trueman produced straight deliveries too quick for Griffith and Gibbs.

With a lead of 30 and no time to lose, England batted aggressively on the fourth afternoon. They zig-zagged to an uneasy 69 for four but were then lifted by Dexter, driving exquisitely straight and through the covers. With Sharpe, the captain added 101 then after a clatter of middle-order wickets Lock joined the debutant to gather 37 precious runs before the close to lift England to 226 for eight (256 ahead) going into the final day.

Chapter 11

1965

England v New Zealand May 27 1965

Hundreds of thousands of spectators have watched Test cricket at Edgbaston during the course of 100 years and most have thoroughly enjoyed the experience. Spare a thought, then, for those present on May 28, 1965, the second day of England's tussle with New Zealand. Watching Kenny Barrington becalmed in bitterly cold winds is about as tough as cricket-watching gets.

For New Zealand's visit of 1965, Edgbaston's Test regained its position at the front of a series. New

Zealand arrived as rank outsiders, having never beaten England in 31 Tests and, on their previous Test visit to Edgbaston seven years earlier, been thrashed with more than four sessions untouched. This time, defeat was again heavy although their stout second-innings resistance at least extended the match into its final day.

Mike Smith, having skippered England to victory in South Africa during the winter, led his country on his home county ground for the first time. It was to

Barrington spent more than an hour on 85 on his painstaking way to 137

Sinclair is out to Titmus, much to the approval of Cowdrey, Parks and Smith

be, not for the first time on home territory, a less than productive match for him with the bat. His team, however, outplayed the opposition for long periods.

Smith did contribute on the first morning - by winning the toss. He elected to bat and, in front of a weather-beaten audience of only 5,000, England logged unspectacular progress. At 11.30am, Geoffrey Boycott stepped onto the Edgbaston greensward for the first time on Test business and proceeded to add 54 thrill-free runs with Bob Barber. Boycott's laborious 23 spanned 105 minutes. Both openers got in then got out to Dick Motz and it was also Motz who ousted Ted Dexter to end a third-wicket partnership of 88 with Barrington. When Cowdrey joined the Surrey man, the tourists were given no glimmer of opportunity for the rest of the day. At the close, England stood at 232 for three; Barrington 61 in 195 minutes, Cowdrey 44.

On Friday, the nation's punters warmed to Lester Piggott's mount Meadow Court and heavily backed it to win the Derby. There was distress in Cheltenham where 29 people were struck by food poisoning from a batch of dodgy scotch eggs. At Edgbaston it was parky. Very parky. A bitter north-easterly knifed the ground - it was so cold that hot

drinks were served to the players on the field. Watching cricket was a pastime for the most ardent enthusiasts only and for those who did turn up, further misery was supplied in the form of boredom. Barrington became totally bogged down in the morning session. Four hours into his innings he reached 85 - and there he stayed for 62 minutes and 20 overs.

There was at least some movement at the other end. Cowdrey reached 85 before falling to left-armer Dick Collinge. That brought in Smith, determined to improve an Edgbaston Test record which read 0, 7, 54, 28, 0 and 1 not out. Next over he returned to the pavilion with another 0, having been trapped by Collinge. As Barrington plodded on, the suffering spectators at least enjoyed a late flourish from Somerset seamer Fred Rumsey whose unbeaten 21 figured in a last-wicket stand of 41. That concluded with the last ball before tea when Collinge finally terminated Barrington's vigil. The batsman's 137 had occupied seven hours and 17 minutes - a scoring rate which saw him dropped for the next Test.

In the evening session, Smith caught Bevan Congdon at short leg to supply Titmus's 100th Test wicket as New Zealand reached 59 for one at the close of a moribund day. On Saturday morning, the

Middlesex off-spinner hurried England into command. Graham Dowling, 30 not out overnight, added only two more before misjudging a looping off-break. From 63 for one, the tourists lost their remaining wickets for 53 runs. Titmus bowled Barry Sinclair. Trueman castled the captain and forced veteran Bert Sutcliffe, at 41 playing his 42nd and, it was to transpire, last Test to retire having taken a bouncer in his right ear. Warwickshire pair Tom Cartwright and Bob Barber spun their way through the lower order and although Sutcliffe re-entered the fray at 115 for nine, two minutes before lunch, he was unable to resume afterwards. England led by 319.

Early in their second innings New Zealand's problems increased when Congdon top-edged a sweep at Barber and retired with a split lip. By the time he returned, Barber had bowled Dowling and drawn Sinclair into a fatal forward grope. The middle order, however, showed much more substance, albeit in a hopeless cause, second time round. John Reid was assertive and lofted Titmus for six but perished at long-on trying to repeat the shot. The patched-up Congdon also fell to Titmus but fifth-wicket pair Ross Morgan and Arthur Dick added 70 by the close. New Zealand, at 215 for four, were still in deep trouble, requiring another 104 to make England bat again, but were putting up a fight.

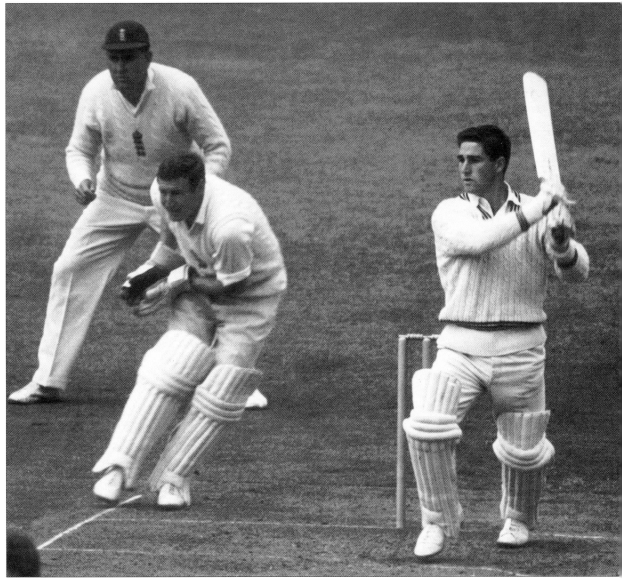

Pollard cover-drives as Parks and Cowdrey wait for an edge

England Captain Mike Smith

They continued to do so on Monday. It seemed the end might come quickly when both overnight batsmen were briskly removed. Barber bowled Dick and Morgan was pinned lbw by Trueman to send New Zealand to 249 for six - still 70 behind. The gallant veteran Sutcliffe then found a bullish partner in Vic Pollard, a 19-year-old student with only five months of experience of first-class cricket behind him. When Sutcliffe had made his Test debut, against England at Christchurch in 1947, Pollard, had been oblivious to the exploit - he was only one year old. Almost two decades later the old 'un and the young 'un combined admirably. They dealt carefully with the spinners and took their team into the lead with a stout alliance of 104 before Sutcliffe fell to Dexter and, a valiant valedictory half-century tucked under his belt, departed Test cricket forever. Motz gave Pollard further support but lobbed a

return catch back to Barber and when the labouring Trueman - "on this performance no longer a power in the land," accused the Birmingham Post - at last tidied up the tail, the teenager was left stranded 19 short of a richly-deserved ton.

Requiring 95 to win, England were eight without loss overnight and coasted to victory on the final day in a ground which remained near-deserted despite the offer of half-price admission. Barber passed 50 then holed out in search of the winning runs. Boycott duly pocketed those and a not out into the bargain and England's record at Edgbaston was further strengthened; won seven, drawn four, lost none.

Chapter 12

1967

England v India July 13 1967

July 13, 1967. Coal-miners at Cannock Wood Colliery, having been on strike, went back to work in the morning and then downed tools again in the afternoon in a row over bonuses. Hugh Bogle was selected in the British team for the Ryder Cup in Houston. Eire international Theo Foley joined the coaching staff of Northampton Town and India began their first Test match at Edgbaston.

England's summer of 1967 was split into two three-match series, against India and Pakistan. To Birmingham fell the third and final Test against an Indian side already 2-0 down and demoralised. Life didn't get any better for them at Edgbaston. Remarkably, India joined Australia, South Africa and New Zealand on the list of countries to fail to amass 100 in their first Test innings at the ground.

Heads-or could it possibly be tails? Pataudi and Close debate

Runs for Brian Close

Murray can only watch as Kunderan connects with a sweep

The Indians arrived in Birmingham engaged in a largely face-saving exercise at the end of a one-sided series. They lost the first Test, at Headingley, by six wickets having encountered Geoffrey Boycott at his most adhesive. The Yorkshire batsman ground out an unbeaten 246 in 27 minutes short of 10 hours (his first 100 occupied almost six hours, an excessively cautious rate of knots which led to him being dropped for the second Test). India hit back with 510, their highest total against England, but having already followed on 386 behind, could not save the game. They never looked like saving the second Test at Lord's which England, fuelled by the runs of Ken Barrington and Tom Graveney and the wickets of Ray Illingworth, won on the fourth afternoon by an innings and 124 runs.

For the third Test, England reinstated Boycott in place of John Edrich. Colin Milburn also came in at the top of the order as Basil D'Oliviera dropped out. Warwickshire pair Dennis Amiss and David Brown played their third and 11th Tests respectively and their first on their home ground. India's team was far from devoid of ability. The Nawab of Pataudi junior and Ajit Wadekar had made runs in the series while there were high class bowlers: Bishen Bedi, Bhagwat Chandrasekhar, Srinny Venkataraghavan and Erapally Prasanna. They were, though, spin bowlers, unlikely to revel in English conditions.

England won the toss and out went the blocker and the basher. Boycott and Milburn were little troubled by India's opening attack of Venkat Subramanya and Budhisagar Kunderan who soon gave way to the spinners. After an hour, Boycott was stumped, bringing in Barrington to one or two ribald messages from supporters who recalled his most recent offering in an Edgbaston Test. This time his work was fully appreciated though as he stood between England and top-order collapse. Milburn and Graveney, surprised by bounce, were taken at short-leg and Amiss edged the last ball of the morning to slip to leave England precariously placed at 112 for four.

Skipper Brian Close dug in alongside Barrington who hit Venkat and Prasanna for six but after Prasanna prised them both out and David Brown ran himself out, India had far exceeded their expectations by trimming England to 191 for eight. The tail held up their charge. As the spinners tired, Middlesex wicket-keeper John Murray added 50 for the ninth wicket with John Snow and 57 for the tenth with Robin Hobbs to lift the total to a respectable 298.

In five overs before the close, India reached nine without loss but Friday brought a torrent of wickets. Twenty fell in all with India's first innings hoovered up in less than 37 overs. Brown struck the first blow, bowling Kunderan with the third ball of the morning and the Indians' technique then failed a rigorous examination. Wadekar was caught by Amiss off Snow, Pataudi was bowled by Brown and

Murray is bamboozled and bowled by Bedi

Ouch - Boycott rubs his head after getting in the way of a throw from the boundary

after the fast-bowlers unzipped the top half of the order, the spinners took care of the rest.

England led by 206 but Close, perhaps mindful of the fact that £1,300 worth of advance bookings had been taken for Saturday's play (when MCC president Sir Alec Douglas-Home also planned to attend) declined to enforce the follow-on. So England went in again and Boycott overshadowed Milburn in an opening stand of six before, to his considerable pique, missing a straight one from Subramanya. This time Pataudi took the new ball himself but only for two overs before the spinners were wheeling away. They made England work hard for their runs but with such a commanding first-innings lead behind them there was too little pressure on the batsmen. A fifth-wicket stand of 78 between Amiss (whose dreary 45 occupied 140 minutes) and Close took the game right away from the tourists. Close clubbed Bedi for two sixes and, in the last hour, Brown swept lustily so that when Robin Hobbs fell to the final ball of the day, India faced a target of 410 in exactly three days.

On Saturday, Farokh Engineer (batting with a runner) and Kunderan started solidly but failed to develop their innings. Still, when Wadekar and Pataudi joined forces to lift India to 178 for three at tea, there appeared a grain of hope for the tourists but England knew that they were effectively one wicket away from a very long tail. Sure enough that next wicket prompted a startling collapse. The last seven wickets fell for 92 runs as Illingworth, Hobbs and Close (the captain bowling his 21.4 overs in nine spells to keep the batsmen thinking) rushed their team to victory. The Indian spinners indulged in some thrashing with the bat with Chandrasekhar, one of the most renowned rabbits of all-time, scaling the unimaginable heights of 22 before he attempted to advance to 28 by launching Close into orbit. Boycott completed a splendid diving catch in front of the sight-screen and the match was over at 6.18pm on the third day. Spectators who had planned to attend on Monday or Tuesday had to reconsider their diaries - a state of affairs which was to become rather too familiar at Edgbaston decades down the line.

Chapter 13

1968

England v Australia July 11 1968

Johnny Gleeson to Geoffrey Boycott. Boycott sweeps. Fails to connect. Ball strikes pad. Bowler appeals. Umpire assents. Boycott departs, shaking head. Seconds later a figure familiar and dear to all cricket followers emerges from the home dressing-room and 18,000 spectators inside Edgbaston rise, as one, to their feet. Striding through the bright Edgbaston air is Colin Cowdrey in his 100th Test match. The first cricketer to reach that milestone, Cowdrey doffs his cap almost diffidently. He is cheered all the way to the crease. The Australians, too, applaud him warmly. Everybody present enjoys the historic moment.

That Cowdrey went on to commemorate his century of Tests with his 21st Test century in the 201st Test between England and Australia was sweet and stylish. The achievement was, however, an isolated highlight of an unfulfilling and watery occasion.

Groundsman Bernard Flack prepares his beloved plot

Tails - or might it be heads? Colin Cowdrey and Bill Lawry find out

Australia arrived in Birmingham for the third Ashes duel leading the series 1-0. They won the opening match at Old Trafford by 159 runs. The second, at Lord's, was ruined by rain, a climate-form with which the tourists had become depressingly familiar. Their traditional tour opener against Worcestershire at New Road had been totally washed out and Australia went on to lose 49 of their first 60 hours of scheduled cricket. The Lord's Test was stripped of half its allotted playing time by the weather. It was horribly frustrating for the tourists. Everywhere, they were haunted by rain although that constant grey cloud at least had a silver lining of a sort. With the summer apparently

doomed to stay wet, the Australians, having established their early lead, appeared well-placed to complete a decade in possession of the Ashes.

Then, on Wednesday July 10, the weather took a turn for the worse. Early in the evening a storm of biblical proportions arrived over the West Midlands - and settled in. All night the deluge hammered down. Three quarters of an inch fell. All main roads into Stratford-upon-Avon became impassable. In Kineton, Rubery and Nether Whitacre, soft-water barrels filled to the brim. The elfin glades of Stoneleigh became sodden and Edgbaston Cricket Ground was a lake. At 10am next morning the field

Freeman's leg stump is bent by Illingworth

was so drenched that umpires Charlie Elliott and Hugo Yarnold decided play would not be possible all day. Those optimistic supporters, who had turned up at the ground in vain hope, made their way instead, depending upon their priorities, back home, to work or to the nearest public house.

Mercifully the sun shone on Friday when England, 1-0 down in the series and a day down in the match, had to hurry. They chose to bat but, on a virgin wicket not played on since part of the square had been relaid three years before, openers Boycott and John Edrich were forced to defend as seamers Graeme McKenzie, Eric Freeman and Alan Connolly relished the damp conditions.

A painstaking first-wicket partnership yielded 80 runs in 56 overs before Boycott fell to Gleeson - and that's where we came in. Enter Cowdrey, cheered all the way to the crease by the crowd and Australian team. Unaffected by the ovation, he was

Exit Cowper, also bowled leg stump by Snow

Four to square leg for Boycott

soon into his stride, piercing the covers and picking gaps on both sides of the wicket. Edrich, after 280 minutes batting, was well taken by Brian Taber down the leg-side and Ken Barrington was defeated by a break-back but Cowdrey was impossible to unsettle even after, on 58, he pulled a muscle and was forced to recruit Boycott as his runner. At the close he was unbeaten on 95 - just five short of the most popular of centuries.

On Saturday morning, that milestone did not come quickly. Hobbling badly, Cowdrey required 20 minutes to gather the five remaining runs and then the resultant ovation had hardly died away before he perished to Freeman. Graveney's elegant innings closed when he tried to reach three figures by lifting Connolly over mid-on but lost his leg-stump instead. After a late-order collapse it was left to last pair John Snow and Derek Underwood to lift England over 400.

Australia suffered two early blows in reply. David Brown hurried one through Ian Redpath and Bill Lawry retired with a little finger fractured by a ball from Snow. With both openers in the pavilion, only 10 runs on the board and a big, excited crowd baying, here was a big test of temperament for Bob Cowper (24 years before he became the first man to officiate as referee in an Edgbaston Test) and 24-year-old Ian Chappell. They rose to the challenge. Both were troubled by Brown but drew the sting of England's pacemen to steer their side to 109 for one at the close. With just two days remaining the match appeared destined for a draw.

On Monday, there was bad news for smokers. While fags went up - a packet of 20 could now cost as much as 4s 5d - Cowper's middle-stump soon went down, courtesy of Snow. Chappell, however, fresh from an unbeaten 202 against Warwickshire on the ground a month earlier, was unflappable. He held England up for 195 precious minutes before losing his leg-stump to Barry Knight. At 195 for four at lunch, the tourists were set fair for safety and they duly reached the follow-on figure without further mishap. A collective loss of concentration followed from the lower order as Underwood and Ray Illingworth took the last five wickets for just nine runs. The avoidance of that follow-on, however, meant that only something sensational could now unlock victory for the home team.

England desperately needed quick wickets on the final morning but Redpath and Cowper denied them and when Snow eventually trapped Redpath, Chappell soon knuckled down again. The left-handed Cowper took responsibility for dealing with Underwood, while Chappell faced Illingworth and Australia were hauling themselves towards safety when they were saved the trouble by that familiar substance from above. Drizzle sent the players scurrying from the field at 12.30pm, then firmed up into steady rain. The lush grass, which could have

That hurt; Edrich feels the pain after taking a Freeman lifter on the glove

England led by 187 with nine hours play left. They had no time to lose but Boycott and Edrich again scored slowly against accurate bowling. Graveney, having taken over the captaincy from the injured Cowdrey, employed a more positive approach. This enabled him to set Australia a target of 330 in six hours 10 minutes but the tourists safely negotiated a late-evening workout from Snow and Brown to reach nine without loss overnight.

housed a fascinating denouement, instead spent the afternoon, morose and unobserved, absorbing water. All that remained was to present the Horlicks Awards for best batsman and bowler from each side. Cheques for £100 were welcomed by Cowdrey, Underwood, Chappell and Freeman.

No let-up; 68 for one it remained as rain continued to fall on the final day

Chapter 14

1971

England v Pakistan June 3 1971

After a three-year absence, Test cricket returned to Edgbaston in 1971 with the second visit of Pakistan. Their first, nine years earlier, had highlighted the fallibility of their batting technique against the moving ball in English conditions. Their second was rather different. They dominated the match, thanks principally to the sublime skills of a slender, bespectacled young batsman on his first tour of England. Hitherto barely known outside his own country, Zaheer Abbas used the Edgbaston stage to step smoothly from anonymity into the history books.

England approached the summer's first Test - the 687th ever - with confidence high. Under Ray Illingworth they had enjoyed a productive winter having regained the Ashes then beaten New Zealand, in a two-match series, 1-0. Reasonably enough, for the opening tussle with Pakistan, they selected a team drawn substantially from the

Ray Illingworth leads out his men

Another sublime boundary for Zaheer Abbas

successful touring party. The XI included 10 of the tourists plus Dennis Amiss, recalled on his home ground for the seventh Test of an international career still in uncertain infancy. The Harborne-born 28-year-old settled into an impressive batting order of John Edrich, Brian Luckhurst, Colin Cowdrey and Basil D'Oliveira. Even deprived of the injured Geoff Boycott and John Snow, England expected victory. They ended the match heavily in debt to the weather for helping them salvage even a draw.

Before his arrival with the 1971 tourists, little was known in England about Zaheer. Worcestershire's members were the first to observe his quality as the 23-year-old announced his talent in his first innings in England, a fluent 110 in the opening tour match at New Road. This young product of the dust and heat of Sialkot possessed the eye and co-ordination to adapt to the damp English early summer. His 138, in late May, on a wet pitch at Gravesend against a Kent side including Derek Underwood, earned him selection for the opening Test - only his second Test appearance.

Zaheer was soon at the crease. After Pakistan captain Intikhab Alam chose to bat, Aftab Gul was struck on the head by Alan Ward's third delivery and retreated to have six stitches inserted in the wound.

Passing his bleeding and shaken colleague on the way, Zaheer sauntered out to face England's quickest bowler and was immediately at home. On an easy-paced pitch, he lost one partner, Sadiq Mohammed playing too early at Peter Lever, but no more on an opening day which shook any shred of complacency out of England. D'Oliveira was accurate and bowled 16 overs for nine runs between lunch and tea but quickies Ward, Lever and Ken Shuttleworth were entirely subdued while there was little turn for Underwood or Illingworth. After tea, Zaheer struck three fours in an over from Underwood to trigger an evening strokefest. In alliance with Mushtaq Mohammed, Zaheer treated the crowd to an orgy of boundaries, with the plunder of 82 runs in the first hour of the third session. Pakistan closed the day on 270 for one, Zaheer 159 and Mushtaq 72.

On Friday morning, they extended their partnership to 291 and when Mushtaq departed to Cowdrey's last catch in a Test match in England, Zaheer motored on. Finally, he was dismissed for 274 from 467 balls in 544 minutes including 38 fours. It remains the highest score by a Pakistan batsman against England and the highest by any batsman in his first innings against England. And what style. "Never really a dull moment," wrote the Birmingham

Post. "Even when he was kept quiet on the first afternoon it was by short of a length bowling. Twenty-three is an early age to join the immortals but this is company Zaheer deserves to enter."

After the newly-immortalised Zaheer finally perished, attempting to sweep Illingworth, Asif Iqbal continued the carnage. Eighteen-year-old all-rounder Imran Khan, on his Test debut, ran himself out trying to give the senior batsman the strike and, with Iqbal 98 not out at the close on Friday, Intikhab extended England's punishment into the third morning to allow completion of an aggressive century. Pakistan's 608 for seven was the highest total in Tests between the two countries and with leg-spinners Intikhab and Mushtaq ready to rock and roll if the pitch started to turn, the tourists were in a powerful position.

As so often when a team has been fielding for more than two days, there were early casualties when they at last batted. Edrich, a foundation stone of the recent Ashes victory, was caught by, who else, Zaheer off Asif Masood's second ball. Cowdrey fatally offered no stroke and Amiss' middle stump was plucked out by a searing inswinger to reduce England to 46 for three.

Luckhurst and D'Oliveira dug in to begin the rearguard action. Imran's first spell in Test cricket failed to yield a wicket but spinners Intikhab and Pervez Sajjad took up the attack to good effect. They winkled out Luckhurst, Illingworth and D'Oliveira to send England six wickets down and still 440 runs behind.

Alan Knott's response was typically positive and inventive. Using his feet nimbly he wrested the initiative from the spinners. With diligent support from Lancashire pair Lever and Shuttleworth, the Kent man kept England in the match with a vivid

Emphatically out - Amiss's middle-stump is sent flying by Masood

The old Thwaite scoreboard makes tough reading for England

counter-attack to brighten a dank, grey Saturday afternoon. Knott hurried to a century in 123 minutes with 21 fours and was unbeaten on 114 out of 320 for seven (still 288 behind) at the close.

Knott's brisk dismissal on Monday morning by another inswinger from the big-hearted Masood sentenced England to follow on for the first time against Pakistan. The visitors sensed victory. Edrich again went cheaply to Masood but the bowler then had to retire with stomach and thigh problems. In his absence, Luckhurst and Cowdrey added 80 to steer England towards safety in the hope that the clouds, which had resided over Birmingham throughout the game, would unload themselves. England's need for help from above became more urgent when Masood returned to the field and

bowled Cowdrey with his first delivery back. Luckhurst gritted on with support from Amiss, who made 22 in an hour before mishooking Masood to mid-on. Luckhurst reached 84 by the close of the fourth day when England were 184 for three, still 71 behind.

English prayers were answered. It rained all night and long into the final day so that play could not commence until 5.06pm. Pakistan needed to rattle through the middle and lower orders to harvest the victory they deserved but, observed only by serried ranks of empty seats, Luckhurst was immovable. After 89 deliveries, bad light closed in again to administer the last rites upon a match which had known its share of gloom but also the coruscating glory of Zaheer.

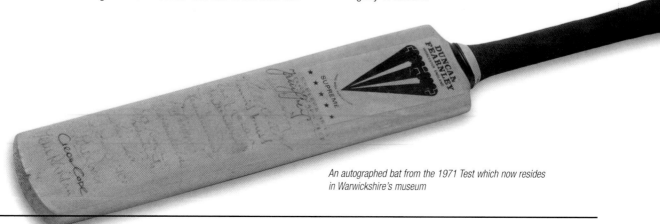

An autographed bat from the 1971 Test which now resides in Warwickshire's museum

Chapter 15

1973

England v West Indies August 9 1973

Having missed out on hosting an Ashes Test in 1972, Warwickshire welcomed the West Indies to Edgbaston the following season for the second instalment of a three-match series. The match was graced by some wonderful cricketers among a vastly talented, if under-achieving, West Indies team but was to register on sports and news bulletins for all the wrong reasons. This was Edgbaston's ugly Test.

Under the captaincy of Warwickshire batsman Rohan Kanhai, West Indies had caused a surprise in the series opener at The Oval. They lodged an

emphatic 158-run victory - their first win since 1969 - to earn a significant advantage in a short series. Kanhai's men arrived at Edgbaston well aware that even a draw would mean they could not lose the series. Avoidance of defeat, therefore, became top priority and their safety-first policy included a detail or two to which exception was taken by a lot of people, most of all veteran umpire Arthur Fagg.

The friction and fuss lurked unseen around the corner when an exuberant crowd of 13,500 gathered on the opening morning. The spectators

West Indies touring party of 1973

Derek Underwood

from the crowd. While Illingworth sent down 27-18-18-0, the spectators alternated between sleep and abuse towards the left-hander but his concentration never wavered.

The tone was set for a match of high tedium and bad temper. On the second morning, Deryck Murray drew 35 runs out over 210 minutes. Fredericks reached 150 and, far from at last accelerating, stayed at that figure for 30 minutes. Even the slow-handclappers had surrendered to apathy by the time he finally deemed it appropriate to attack Underwood and Amiss completed a splendid catch at long-on. After 510 minutes of remorselessly single-minded batting, Fredericks returned to the pavilion to a reception of less than total warmth but it was when England began their reply after lunch things really turned sour.

Geoff Boycott had reached 12 when he appeared to edge a delivery from Keith Boyce. It was clear to most people in the ground that Boycott had hit the ball but the batsman stood his ground and Fagg's finger stayed furled. The West Indians, feeling robbed of England's prize wicket, became openly hostile. Led by Kanhai, there was much staring, simmering and gesticulating and the resentment only festered as Boycott avoided further mishap to lay a solid foundation with Amiss. England were 96 without loss at the close.

Faced with such dissent, Fagg started to wonder whether his £125 match fee was worth all this hassle. On Friday night he threatened to withdraw from the game and next morning supported his threat with action. Fagg stayed in the umpires' room while Harold Bird, officiating in only his second Test, was accompanied to the middle by Warwickshire coach (and former first-class umpire) Alan Oakman. As play got underway, England chairman of selectors Alec Bedser and West Indies' manager Esmond Kentish urged Fagg to resume and, after one over, he did venture out but a tense, unattractive session followed. When Fagg took the field, Kanhai tossed a bowler's sweater at him without a glimmer of recognition, never mind apology, and the cricket continued amid an atmosphere of thinly-concealed scorn. Boyce and Julien delivered a barrage of bouncers to Amiss, Brian Luckhurst and Frank Hayes and repeatedly ran down the pitch as the tourists slowed the game

were closer to the action than usual because the boundary was not marked with the customary rope. The perimeter fence itself was deemed the boundary in an attempt to prevent a repeat of pitch-invasions which had interrupted the Oval Test. It proved to be a successful move. The spectators' behaviour was fine; it was that of some players which left much to be desired

After Kanhai won the toss and chose to bat, West Indies devoted the next five sessions to the acquisition of 327 runs. Roy Fredericks, an aggressive batsman by nature, did not peep from his shell during an opening day which saw the tourists crawl to 190 for five from 98 overs. Fredericks' caution was most extreme against Ray Illingworth. The Glamorgan player scored only three singles from the first 98 balls he faced from the off-spinner to provoke derision and slow-handclapping

down to a crawl. Only 26 overs were bowled in the session.

At lunchtime the tourists' salad sandwiches were accompanied by a warning from the umpires. It was heeded - in the first hour after the interval Gary Sobers and Lance Gibbs sent down 24 overs. England's run-rate, however, was no more appealing than their opponents' had been and at the end of a day which few of the 20,000 crowd would remember with affection, England were 265 for seven - 62 behind - from 128 overs with Keith Fletcher on 37 and Geoff Arnold 3.

The diplomats got busy during Sunday and, drained of its malice, the match petered out in banal fashion. It was heading firmly for the dullest of draws anyway but Fletcher and Arnold supplied it with a hefty further shove in that direction by wringing just 23 runs from the first 19 overs on Monday. When Fletcher was finally out, Boycott, who had twice retired hurt on Saturday, reappeared

for a third time but Underwood soon perished and England's innings closed on 305 from 156.4 overs. Two innings had brought 632 runs from 306.1 overs and the match was ready, nay crying out, to be embalmed.

Kanhai and Clive Lloyd at last provided some sparks of enterprise with half-centuries to extend West Indies' advantage, at the close of the fourth day, to

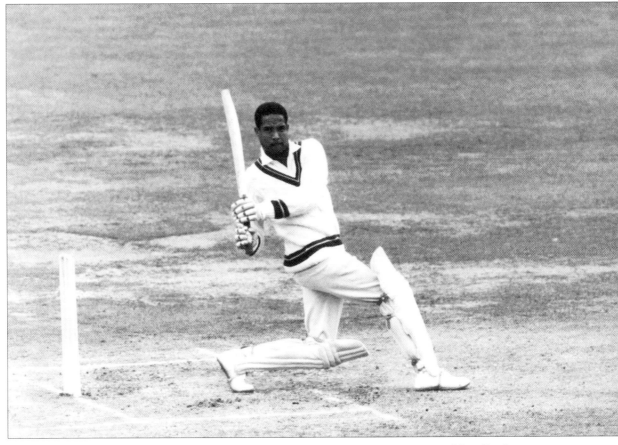

Sobers drives four

Flying the flag; but there was little for this England supporter to enjoy during an unpleasant Test match

227 with five wickets still to fall. Theoretically they were in a position to push for victory but Kanhai's objective remained wholly to deny England the slightest sniff of levelling the series. With Boyce unable to bowl due to a heel injury, the tourists batted on and on, simply challenging England to bowl them out. Julien gathered 11 runs in an hour. Murray dug in again before becoming the first batsman to be dismissed hit wicket in an Edgbaston Test. Sobers resisted skilfully so that England were finally set a notional target of 325 in 227 minutes. There was no attempt to prise a spectacular victory. Frank Hayes, having scored a century on his Test debut at The Oval two weeks earlier, offered no stroke to his Lancashire team-mate Lloyd to sample his first taste of succulent Test duck while Amiss, dropped by Kanhai at slip on 15, helped himself to an unbeaten 86 achieved, in its final stages, against the less-than-fearsome bowling of Fredericks and Kanhai.

Chapter 16

1974

England v India July 4 1974

If England had begun to consider themselves impregnable at Edgbaston - played 15, won eight, drawn seven there so far - nothing that happened between July 4 and 8, 1974, did anything to alter that view. On India's first Test appearance in Birmingham, seven years earlier, they lost inside three days. Second time around, their defeat occupied even less playing time as England completed one of the most emphatic of all Test triumphs at 4.10pm on the fourth day - even after the entire opening day was lost to rain.

A heavy victory for England was predictable enough. India arrived 2-0 down in the three-match series and reeling from a drubbing of rarely paralleled magnitude in the second Test at Lord's. England won there by an innings and 285 runs after piling up 629 (Dennis Amiss 188, Mike Denness 118, Tony Greig 106) and then rifling India out for 42 (Geoff Arnold 8-1-19-4, Chris Old 8-3-21-5) in their second innings. Ten days and an uninspiring draw with Nottinghamshire later, India lined up at Edgbaston and swallowed another deep dose of embarrassment. For only the third time in history, a Test was won by a team losing just two wickets along the way.

While England, for the first time in eight years, fielded an unchanged XI, India adjusted their batting line-up from the Lord's debacle. In came Sudhir Naik (for his debut) and Ashok Mankad at the expense of Brijesh Patel and all-rounder Madan Lal. There was also a shift in spin personnel as Srinny Venkataraghavan replaced Bhagwat Chandrasekhar. For all these people, selected or deselected, there was little to do, as the rain fell on Thursday, except discuss the appointment of Don Revie as England's football manager but when play started on time on Friday it took just seven seconds for the match to start hurrying England's way. That was the timespan of Arnold's run-up before delivering the opening ball to Sunil Gavaskar. The Indian maestro nicked, Alan Knott claimed the catch and, as Gavaskar waited, Bill Alley, officiating his first Test, was called upon to make an adjudication from his very first ball. Having

removed Gavaskar with one that nipped away, Arnold nailed Naik with one that nipped back in and, with his side 17 for two in the seventh over, India captain Ajit Wadekar's decision to bat first had the makings of a clanger.

For a while, Wadekar led from the front but Arnold and Mike Hendrick probed away waiting for errors which came along regularly enough to propel England into swift and full control. Lancashire wicket-keeper Farokh Engineer pulled savagely and with some success but was badly let down by a feeble lower-order. The last five batsmen mustered only nine runs between them as India were all out for 165 just before tea. By the close, England were heading for an ascendancy as great as that of the previous Test. The Indian bowlers managed just a single maiden as Amiss and David Lloyd, playing only his second Test, eased to 117 without loss.

Amiss was now at his peak as an international cricketer. During the previous winter he had become the first man to score three centuries in a rubber against the West Indies. His unbeaten 262, in 570 minutes, to shepherd his team to a draw at Sabina Park, was a monument of concentration, courage and technique. With scores of 56, 47 and 188 already behind him in this series, and now 57 not out overnight, here, surely, a Test century on his beloved home ground beckoned. But no. On Saturday morning he added another 22 before an attempt to chip Prasanna over the leg-side infield found only the hands of Mankad at mid-wicket. The landmark of a Test ton on his home patch was to elude Amiss forever.

His departure was only a momentary interruption to England's progress. To the delight of most of the 10,000 crowd, captain Denness joined Lloyd in a second-wicket partnership of 211. India's bowlers, woefully weak in the seam department, unerringly located the middle of the bat as Denness collected his third century of the summer against the tourists. When the skipper chipped back to Bishen Bedi, Keith Fletcher took advantage of tiring bowlers to

Sunil Gavaskar - India's biggest hope was removed first ball

collect a breezy half-century. Lloyd kept his snout in the trough to conclude with an unbeaten 214 which included, due to the slow outfield, only 17 fours from 455 minutes batting. As the innings' lowest dismissed scorer, with 79, Amiss qualified for the time-honoured duty of packing the bag when Denness, his side 294 ahead, declared to allow his bowlers a chance to inflict damage before the close. They obliged. Chris Old found Gavaskar's edge and Arnold bowled nightwatchman Syed Abid Ali before India closed a grotesquely one-sided day on 12 for two.

After the debacle of India's second innings at Lord's, there was little hope of interesting cricket on Monday so the crowd was sparse. Wadekar was trapped by the 18th ball of the day but the tourists did summon up some defiance. Naik and Mankad, neither of whom had shared in the Lord's humiliation, played and missed copiously but survived to add 87 for the fifth wicket before the latter was dismissed in unfortunate fashion. He leaned out of the way of a short ball from Old only to lose his cap which fell onto the stumps, dislodging the leg bail.

Lloyd cuts Bedi to the boundary on his way to an unbeaten 214

Naik battled on for three and a half hours before missing a sweep at Greig. Engineer again hit hard but again the tail was appallingly timid - in the three Tests only four double-figure scores had been lodged by India's batsmen seven to 11 - and England cruised to a 3-0 series whitewash which earned them a prize of £1,800. The last act of the match belonged to Alley, who raised the finger of doom when Engineer played across the line to Mike Hendrick. In his first Test, Alley had activated dismissals from the first and last deliveries.

Bishen Bedi who brought his unique spin-bowling charm to Edgbaston

So much for impregnability. In 1975, 73 years and 42 days since MacLaren and Darling had ventured out of the Edgbaston pavilion to toss that historic coin, Australia arrived equipped with Dennis Keith Lillee, Jeffrey Robert Thomson and Maxwell Henry Norman Walker. England's proud unbeaten record in Birmingham was swept away by an innings by the fourth afternoon and while English supporters were dismayed by their team's timid surrender, they could only admire their conquerors. An ageing England side was simply overwhelmed by fiery, focused and disciplined fast bowling, coupled with brilliant catching.

You didn't have to be Nostradamus to see it coming. Australia had romped to a 4-1 victory in the previous winter's Ashes series as Sydney-born 24-year-old Thomson introduced himself to the Poms with 33 wickets at 17.93. Lillee and Walker shared 48 wickets between them and England's only victory arrived in the irrelevant sixth Test when injuries ruled Thomson out completely and restricted Lillee to only six overs.

Four months later, the teams met again on the other side of the globe, in a World Cup semi-final at Headingley. Lillee and Thomson mustered a mere one wicket between them but left-armer Gary Gilmour chipped in with six for 14 from 12 overs as England were routed for 93. It was hardly surprising, then, that when, three weeks later, England won the toss before the opening Test at Edgbaston, there was not a dressing-room clamour to pad up. Mike Denness, under severe pressure as captain after that winter drubbing, read the mood of his men and chose to field - the first England captain to do so in a Birmingham Test. His decision simply delayed the inevitable.

Australia included 10 of the XI which had beaten England in the World Cup. Gilmour was the unlucky man omitted, replaced by off-spinner Ashley Mallett. England, meanwhile, stuck principally with the players who had been routed down under. Nine of the winter tourists were selected along with recalled

fast-bowler John Snow and Essex batsman Graham Gooch, given his debut two weeks before his 22nd birthday. The temptation to call up Kent's highly promising all-rounder Bob Woolmer (who a week earlier had scored 55 and 85 and taken a hat-trick against the Australians for the MCC at Lord's) was resisted.

On Snow, Geoff Arnold and Chris Old did English hopes hang as Australia, put in by England for only the 10th time in 215 Tests between the countries, began their innings on an overcast morning. To Denness' dismay, however, the ball hardly swung and the sight of the dear old Thwaite scoreboard reading 77 without loss at lunchtime was a morale-sapping one for England's followers.

They found the second session a little more productive. Alan Turner, on his debut, skied a pull to mid-on off Snow. Rick McCosker, playing his first Test in England, was deceived by Arnold's slower ball and when Greg Chappell played across a full-toss and perished without scoring, English hopes stirred. They rose further when Doug Walters and Ian Chappell edged into the slips to leave Australia 186 for five, but an abrasive counter-attack by Rodney Marsh retrieved the initiative for the tourists. As Ross Edwards dropped anchor, Marsh pulled and cut with abandon to score 47 out of 57 runs and lift his side to 243 for five when rain arrived to lop off the last 17 minutes play.
If England had not exactly dominated day one, they at least ended it on a relatively even footing. On day two, however, came the moment when their batsmen had to finally contend with Lillee, Thomson and Walker and, as widely feared, the innings briskly assumed the shape of an old English pear.

First, Australia's last five wickets delivered another 116 runs. Marsh's ebullient innings (a six and eight fours in 100 minutes) ended, much to his ire, when he edged Arnold's first delivery after a five-minute delay while the state of the ball, only eight overs old, was debated. Edwards' four-hour occupation of the crease, an excellent effort for his team, was

Lillee celebrates the dismissal of Amiss

Lillee hurries England towards their first defeat at Edgbaston

ended by Gooch's catch but Thomson compiled a free-spirited 49 before holing out to Underwood. Thomson, the middle man of Woolmer's hat-trick eight days earlier, became the first batsman to fall one short of 50 in an Edgbaston Test.

At 2.45pm, John Edrich and Dennis Amiss began

England's reply on a surface which was slow and easy-paced. After one over, rain stopped play and then, during a 100-minute stoppage, freshened up the pitch nicely to the disconcerting sound of Aussie pacemen revving up in the dressing-room. Soon they were unleashed and by the close, England were 83 for seven. Arthur Fagg's armpits got some

Greg Chappell survived only seven balls before falling for a duck

Greg Chappell, Doug Walters, Rod Marsh and Ian Chappell

air as Thomson, over-excited, fired down five wides in his first two overs and was withdrawn from the attack but Lillee and Walker unveiled an immaculate display of perfectly-directed pace and movement. Amiss fended to backward short-leg and Keith Fletcher and Denness were taken in the gully. At 46 for three, Gooch arrived for his first Test innings. To his third ball, angling away down the leg side, he aimed a glance which landed cruelly in Marsh's gloves. Tony Greig lifted the crowd by driving Walker for two meaty fours but then edged fatally. Alan Knott succumbed to Lillee and, five minutes before the close, Edrich's gallant effort ended when he was beaten by an in-ducker. The back of England's resistance had been shattered as Lillee's figures read 12-6-13-3 and Walker's 15-5-35-4.

England's tail was removed in 25 minutes on Saturday morning when, following on 258 behind, their higher-order colleagues attempted to impose themselves second time round. Further distress was quick to arrive when, in the fifth over, Amiss was struck on the left elbow by a Lillee lifter and forced to retire hurt. Edrich failed to set down roots a second time as he edged to Marsh. This time it was Fletcher who carried the fight but his young Essex colleague completed a pair on his debut. Gooch's seventh delivery from Thomson, now finding his range to add to England's problems, reared off a length to take the edge. Fletcher completed a valiant half-century but was almost immediately caught in Lillee's thickly-populated cordon. Only the arrival of rain, which caused two delays, extended the match beyond the weekend as England tumbled to 93 for five by the close with four specialist

batsmen out and the other harbouring a badly
bruised elbow.

On Monday morning, Prime Minister Harold Wilson
outlined his "total will and determination" to grapple
with inflation but England's grappling with the
Australian bowling remained wantonly devoid of will
and determination. Showers again affected play but
only a total deluge could save Denness' team.
Amiss returned, but after he quickly gloved a rising
delivery into the leg-trap, only some frivolous death-
throes remained. Snow drove Mallett over long-off
for six but then edged to Marsh to supply Thomson
with his fifth-wicket. At five past three, Mallett finally
intruded on the festival of top-class pace-bowling
by flighting an off-break past Underwood's forward
grope to seal victory.

 "I have never been in a match," said Denness,
"where one side was so badly caught out by
changing conditions." Sympathy from the press was
thin, though, and Greig, Boycott and even 43-year-
old Ray Illingworth were all touted as his successor.
What the journos, in their frenzy of scapegoat-
hunting, did not know was that Denness had
already offered his resignation to the selectors
during the Edgbaston trouncing. For the second Test
at Lord's, Greig was in charge.

Chapter 18

1978

England v Pakistan June 1 1978

Before June 1978, Yorkshire seamer Chris Old had registered only peripherally on the Edgbaston Test match spectrum. Three appearances there for England had brought him 10 wickets with a best analysis of three for 52 against India in 1974. As a Yorkshire player he had happy memories of the ground. Ten months earlier, Old had thrashed the second-fastest century in history (in 37 minutes, albeit against the Pembertonesque bowling of John Whitehouse and Rohan Kanhai) against

Warwickshire but, in Test terms, Edgbaston had so far yielded only middling returns for Christopher Middleton Old.

Bob Willis, meanwhile, had not figured on that spectrum at all. Although the Warwickshire fast-bowler entered the 1978 season with 35 Test appearances already behind him, none had been on the ground he had called home since switching from Surrey six years earlier. That situation changed

Joy in the cordon as Old ousts Wasim Raja, caught by Taylor, at the start of his historic over

for the visit of Pakistan in 1978. Willis played, so did Old and each left a heavy - and very different - imprint on the occasion.

The two teams were familiar with each other having met the previous winter in Pakistan where they slugged out one of the dreariest of all series. The three Tests were almost secondary to a backdrop of debate about whether the home country would and should select their "Packerstanis" (Majid Khan, Zaheer Abbas, Imran Khan and Mushtaq Mohammed who had signed contracts with Australian tycoon Kerry Packer's World Series Cricket). In the end, the quartet in question did not participate but, amid a plethora of statements, claims, counter-claims and speculation, the cricket

itself took a back seat. In fact, it did little to draw attention to itself as three stalemates extended the sequence of draws between the teams, in Pakistan, to 11. For connoisseurs of tedium, bickering and crowd disturbances, it was a series to cherish - for anyone else, it was one to forget. When the teams reconvened in Birmingham six months later, there was more to appreciate - some memorable cricket, sadly overshadowed by one controversial and bloody moment.

First came the excellence. An interesting opening day was just starting to tilt England's way as Pakistan, from a decent foundation of 91 for two, declined to 125 for five when Old, in the space of a single over, wrote himself into history. The 29-year-

A nasty taste; Pakistan nightwatchman Qasim is led away after taking a Willis bouncer in the mouth

Brearley is dropped by Mudassar off Sarfraz

old had been bowling for 75 minutes since lunch but was being held up by Wasim Raja and Sarfraz Nawaz who had added 22 for the sixth wicket. Then, at 3.25pm, Old launched into his rhythmic, quick-stepping run-up from the City End to begin his 19th over.

The first ball was straight and defended by Raja. The second brought the breakthrough, taking the outside edge to nestle in Bob Taylor's gloves. Captain Wasim Bari arrived, took guard, assessed the field, crouched into his stance and played inside his first ball which knocked out off-stump. Old was on a hat-trick.

The hat-trick ball, to Iqbal Qasim, was a no-ball but Qasim's reprieve was short-lived. Old's next offering found the edge and Bob Taylor scooped up a brilliant catch inches from the ground. Three in four balls. Mightily did the crowd roar Old in to bowl next to Sikander Bakht. The batsman, having padded up in a hurry, was soon padding down again as he who edged low to second slip where Graham Roope accepted the catch. Four in five balls. Ecstasy in the

Rea Bank Stand. Another hat-trick opportunity. Liaquat Ali defended solidly and took a single to send a sensational over into history as 0-w-w-nb-w-w-1. In the space of five minutes Pakistan had plummeted from 125 for five to 127 for nine. Few overs in the history of the universe have received a valedictory ovation as long or as loud.

Sarfraz and Liaquat halted the landslide and steered a safe course through to 162 for nine by the close but, refreshed overnight, Old located yet another edge, Liaquat's, after five minutes on Friday morning and captain Mike Brearley accepted the catch to wrap up the innings.

Old's Test-best figures of seven for 50 had won England time to bat with care. Barry Wood departed early (and forever from the Test scene) but Middlesex pair Brearley and Clive Radley took the total beyond 100 before the captain perished in pursuit of a non-existent second run. His self-destruction brought David Gower to the crease for his first Test innings. The 21-year-old Leicestershire batsman took guard, adjusted his pads and fixed

Javed is caught by Brearley off Edmonds as England speed to victory

his sight upon the distant figure of left-arm seamer Liaquat. Gower's first ball was a long-hop which he pulled to the boundary as though it was the most natural thing in the world to do. The first four of his 8,231 Test runs was safely banked. Given a life on 15, when the obliging Liaquat grassed a straightforward chance at mid-on off Mudassar Nazar, Gower advanced serenely. He added another eight boundaries on his way to his maiden Test half-century, overhauling Radley in the 50's despite having reached the crease 100 minutes after his partner.

Gower's departure to the persevering Sikander was Pakistan's last success of the day. Radley, 34 years old but playing only his third Test, tucked and scampered and nurdled away to 95 (in 279 minutes) by the close at which Roope was 22 and England, already 92 ahead, were 256 for three.

Early on Saturday, Radley completed a century which, while an offering of little beauty, had established an excellent platform for his team. From the crowd's viewpoint, it was not entirely awful news that Radley and Roope both then fell to Sikander because that brought in Ian Botham. In only his sixth Test match, the young Somerset all-rounder was immediately on the offensive. As Geoff Miller played the straight man, Botham, full of bravado, went through his repertoire of hefty drives, square slashes and quick-eyed clouts. The ball sped to all parts of the playing area. This was the sort of rumbustious Saturday afternoon entertainment for which county committees yearn as Botham powered to his century in 170 minutes with 11 fours. Having exploited a persevering but punchless Pakistan attack, England declared at tea with a lead of 288.

After Old's exploits, a Gower cameo and a Botham century, what more feasting could be laid before England's happy supporters? Well, not a lot on Saturday as Pakistan declined to roll over. In the final session, Mudassar Nazar and Sadiq Mohammed were little troubled and within touching distance of stumps when Mudassar was bowled by left arm-spinner Phil Edmonds. In came Pakistan's slow left-armer Iqbal Qasim who duly fulfilled his objective as nightwatchman as Pakistan closed at 95 for one, still trailing by 193. England were set fair for a commanding victory but it was to be tainted.

On Monday morning, Willis roared in with the benefit of a strong breeze behind him. In his first

Roope pounces, to the delight of Botham beside him

over, he dug in a lifter which flew over Qasim's head. As the nightwatchman continued to defend steadfastly, Willis twice more tested him with rapid, rising deliveries, a tactic which appeared askew to the playing condition which states; "Captains must instruct their players that the fast, short-pitched ball should at no time be directed at non-recognised batsmen".

When Willis switched his attack to round the wicket, Pakistan's fears came true. Another delivery reared from the pitch but this time defeated Qasim's retreat and thudded into his mouth. The batsman crumpled to the ground and had to be led, dazed, from the pitch to have his lip stitched. Pakistan were angry at such hostility directed towards a batsman who usually bats at nine but, in defence of their strike bowler, England drew attention to the grey areas in the rules. Should a nightwatchman who is batting successfully at number three in the order enjoy the protection afforded to tail-enders? Qasim was certainly no mug with the bat. On his Test debut at Adelaide he had defied an Australian attack led by Dennis Lillee long enough to add 87

for the last wicket with Asif Iqbal. He was, however, clearly no specialist either. The incident was to trigger months of debate and reflected little credit on an England side already well-placed in the match.

The incident's immediate effect was to accelerate England's passage to victory. Sadiq, clearly upset by hearing the ball crunch into his partner's face, lasted only two more balls before being trapped half-forward by Old. Mohsin Khan and Javed Miandad added 53 for the third wicket but when Miandad was caught sweeping, just before lunch, Pakistan trod a hasty path to defeat. With the pitch offering turn, Edmonds and Miller hurried through some irresolute batting. When Willis propelled the new ball into Liaquat's stumps, seven wickets had fallen for 55 runs, Qasim was not sent out to resume his innings and the 825th Test match to take place on planet Earth was won by England by a margin of an innings and 57 runs.

Chapter 19

1979

England v India July 12 1979

If the Edgbaston spectators were, in 1978, the first to get a glimpse of David Gower's ability in a Test match environment, those in 1979 witnessed the full Monty. India arrived with a bowling attack comprising rookie fast-bowlers, ageing spinners and anodyne dibbly-dobblies and Gower, in his 13th Test, led England in a fulsome process of boot-filling. During the first six sessions they piled up 633 for five, the highest total in a Test at Edgbaston. It was England's highest Test score since their famous fourth-innings 654 for five, chasing 696, against South Africa in Durban in 1939 - a "timeless" Test on which time had eventually to be called after 10 days because England had to get back to Cape Town to catch the ship home.

When Wally Hammond's side finally trotted up that pre-war gangplank, Geoffrey Boycott was still 19 months away from being born in the fair south Yorkshire town of Fitzwilliam. Almost 40 years later, Boycott was in Birmingham to join Gower in taking full advantage of perfect conditions (innocuous bowling, firm track, sunny weather). Both men passed personal milestones. Gower's double-century was his highest innings in first-class cricket. Boycott's 155 took him past 6,000 runs in Tests and completed his set of centuries on each of England's six regular home grounds.

On the opening morning, before a crowd of less than 7,000, Mike Brearley and Derek Randall missed out on the runfest. They both fell to catches behind the wicket off Kapil Dev, an all-rounder of huge promise from Chandigarh, already participating in his tenth Test at the age of 20. After lunch, though, any trace of assistance from the pitch for Dev and fellow seamer Karsan Ghavri dissipated and the serious run-harvest began. Boycott was joined by Graham Gooch, back for his first Test appearance at Edgbaston since his debut pair against Australia in 1975. The Essex batsman, now well-established in England's top order, found the likes of Ghavri and Mohinder Armanath considerably less exacting than he had, as a callow

debutant, found Lillee and Thomson. Gooch dominated a third-wicket partnership of 145, hammering a six and 13 fours in 83 in two hours before offering debutant wicket-keeper Bharath Reddy his third catch off Dev. Boycott was in for the duration though, a fact outlined early on by his consumption of 94 minutes to reach double figures - even on a classic Bernard Flack flat-track. He chugged serenely onward (19 at lunch, 71 at tea) and reached his century before the close at which Gower was 43 and England placed handsomely at 318 for three.

During the first two sessions on Friday, Gower took merciless toll of the bowling. India's problems mounted as Armanath and Bhagwat Chandrasekhar collected injuries and with the off-spin of captain Srinny Venkataraghavan ineffective, Kapil Dev and Ghavri bore a huge burden. Kapil won an lbw decision from Barrie Meyer against Boycott (even after 476 minutes batting the Yorkshireman, well forward to the ball which dismissed him, hated to go) but Gower, driving and pulling with grace and force, remained until beyond tea. Botham bashed 33 in 39 minutes and Gower's partnership with Geoff Miller reached 165, a sixth-wicket record for England against India, before the left-hander's arrival at 200 prompted the declaration. Gower had batted for 365 minutes, faced 279 balls and struck 24 fours. Kapil Dev, Ghavri, Chandrasekhar and Venkat all conceded more than 100 runs while extras contributed 60, an Edgbaston Test record which included 27 leg byes, still the most in any Test innings at the ground.

During 75 minutes batting on Friday evening India lost two wickets, both to fine close catches by Gooch. First he accepted a difficult low chance at third slip when Cheten Chauhan gloved a Botham lifter. Then from the last ball of the day he pounced at silly-point to oust the dangerous Dilip Vengsarker. India closed at 59 for two; 574 behind.
On Saturday, the contest was, for a brief period, more equal as brothers-in-law Sunil Gavaskar and Gundappa Viswanath showed technique and

Geoff Boycott leans back out of the way of a bouncer

patience to keep England's varied attack at bay. They defied the pace of Willis, the range of Botham, the accuracy of Mike Hendrick, the flighted left-arm spin of Edmonds, the flatter off-spin of Miller and the prosaic slows of Boycott. Thirty-five minutes before tea, though, Gavaskar pressed the self-destruct button. He turned Willis to leg and embarked on a single. Not the first man to underestimate the speed of Randall at mid-wicket,

Gavaskar was sent back but arrived after Taylor had broken the wicket with Randall's throw. The opening batsman's diligent innings, which included just three fours in three hours, was needlessly ended. Viswanath continued to defy and Anshuman Gaekwad clung on unconvincingly for two hours but when Viswanath was caught off bat and pad by Botham, the innings buckled in the face of England's seam and swing attack. Gavaskar was

(L-R) Umpire Barrie Meyer shares a joke with England captain Mike Brearley during a drinks break

back at the crease before the close as India, following on 336 behind, reached seven without loss.

With the pitch still playing flawlessly, Gavaskar and Chauhan batted soundly on Monday morning and were still together at lunch. Their alliance reached 124 before Chauhan lifted a drive at Willis to Randall in the covers. Hendrick then struck the crucial blow when he extracted some shock lift from the begrudging strip and Gavaskar edged to Gooch at third slip. When Gooch accepted another chance

in the cordon to dismiss Gaekwad, India's resistance caved in. From 227 for four, they lost their last six wickets for 26 runs in 10.1 overs as Botham obtained considerable swing with the new ball. Four wickets in the space of five overs took the Somerset all-rounder's Test tally to 94 in two years. Hendrick trapped Reddy and forced Ghavri to loft to cover to complete impressive match figures of 44.5-17-81-6 for the Derbyshire man and secure victory shortly before 6pm on the fourth day - just in time to catch 'Crossroads' on the goggle-box.

Boycott on his way to a first innings score of 155

Chapter 20

1981

England v Australia July 30 1981

Many "I was there" achievements have been recorded at Edgbaston during its first 100 years. Exploits which those fortunate enough to have witnessed recall for years ahead, smiling nostalgically, hitching up their trousers and proudly asserting; "I was there, y'know". Wilfred Rhodes rattling through the Australians in 1902. The heroic alliance of Peter May and Colin Cowdrey in 1957. Cowdrey hobbling to a century in his 100th Test in 1968. Chris Old's sensational over in 1978. All capital "I was there" fodder. Top of the list, however, is England v Australia, 1981, and the inspirational Ian Botham wrapping up victory on a mesmeric, sun-drenched Sunday afternoon.

To Edgbaston fell the challenge of hosting the Test immediately following Headingley, 1981, one of the most sensational contests of all time. In Leeds, England won by 18 runs after following on. Botham 149 not out. Bob Willis eight for 43. The stuff of legend. Nine days later in Birmingham, anti-climax surely beckoned. After the Lord Mayor's Show. But no. Remarkably, the contest sped to a finish if not quite as unlikely then just as thrilling as at Headingley.

To the astonishment of most onlookers the match, which took place on a good pitch, was dominated by bowlers. All 22 players batted twice yet nobody scored a half-century - the first time since England

Marsh shows his delight at catching Boycott behind for 29

faced West Indies at Bridgetown in 1935 that not a single 50 was registered in a Test. The only half-century was from no balls which contributed 51 to a match total of 91 extras.

As is often the case when batsmen struggle, the plot fluctuated and fascinated from ball one. That initial delivery brought together two great cricketers; Dennis Lillee propelled it towards Geoffrey Boycott after Mike Brearley, in his second match back as England captain, elected to bat. There was little in the pitch to encourage bowlers yet by 5.30pm England had been dismissed for 189. Brearley, restored to open the batting as Graham Gooch dropped to number four, resisted longest. His 48, in just under four hours, was to prove the highest score of the match but Terry Alderman, deriving generous swing from the City End, was most pleased with his opening day's work having added five wickets to the 20 he collected in the first three Tests.

More Marsh joy as Gower goes

Botham bowls Kent as history sensationally unfolds

Before the close, Chris Old ousted John Dyson and Allan Border but on Friday Graeme Wood, nightwatchman Ray Bright, Kim Hughes, Graham Yallop and debutant Martin Kent applied themselves to move Australia into the lead with five wickets in hand. As Willis (plagued by no balls), Old and Botham plugged away with limited success, it was left to off-spinner John Emburey to peg the tourists back during a long spell in the afternoon. The tourists led by 69, of which England had erased 49 for the loss of their captain, trapped by Lillee, before the close.

Marsh goes...

the Australians handle another low target? Ten thousand people, including plenty of Aussies, attended on Sunday to find out. Warwickshire's supporters, their county team almost falling off the bottom of the championship, harboured the most urgent need of a fillip.

Willis struck two early blows. In the third over he softened Dyson up with three short deliveries then pitched the next one up and watched it burst through the batsman's defence. Captain Kim Hughes then brainlessly lifted the ball straight to John Emburey who had been placed deep in the leg side field by Brearley in case of just such an aberration. 29 for three. On a slow pitch, Willis had taken two for 15 in 11 overs of sustained aggression.

... and so does Alderman. It's all over

There were 15,000 people in on Saturday to see several batsmen get a start but fail to build. Ray Bright struck a succession of telling blows, ousting several of England's main men as they sought to accelerate. Boycott, after squeezing 29 runs from more than three hours, Gower, Gooch and Willey all fell to the left-arm spinner. Gatting showed commendable patience but at 167 for eight, only 98 ahead, England were in trouble and even after Emburey, sweeping profitably, and Old added 50 for the ninth wicket, Australia's victory target of 151 appeared, if certainly no formality, accessible. Before the close, England removed Wood, trapped by Old, and Australia resumed at noon on Sunday on nine for one, Dyson five, Border two.
 With the humiliation of Headingley, where they failed to chase 130, so fresh in mind, how would

Botham grabs a souvenir stump after taking Australia's last five wickets to secure victory

As the sun beat down on a boisterous crowd, tension was almost palpable in the air but the unflappable Border and Yallop steadied the innings. They quietly increased the score to 87 for three. With seven wickets in hand, just 64 more runs were needed for Hughes' men to take a 2-1 lead in the series and reclaim the initiative. All those Headingley heroics from Botham and Willis would go down in the history-books as a miracle in a losing Ashes cause.

Even when Emburey prised out Yallop, Kent joined Border to eke out another 18 runs and take Australia to within 46 of victory with six wickets in hand. Then came the first real tingle of anticipation among England's supporters. Emburey produced a fiendish delivery which spat up at Border. The left-hander could only glove it to Gatting and by far the biggest obstacle to English success was removed. With the ball starting to turn, Brearley toyed with the idea of using tandem spin and signalled to

The celebrations are underway - what a way to spend a quiet Sunday afternoon!

Ian Botham gets the first taste of champagne after being voted 'Man of the Match'

Peter Willey to loosen up. On an impulse he threw the ball instead to Botham. It was a colossal gamble. Yes, the all-rounder was a wicket-taking bowler but sometimes at a price. Two loose overs here and the match was lost. Instead, Botham delivered a classic spell of straight fast-medium bowling which brought him five wickets for one run in 28 balls.

The dangerous Marsh plumped for aggression and was bowled past a cross-bat hoik. 114 for six. Bright fell lbw first ball. England's supporters were in overdrive now. The noise in the ground, Brearley was to acknowledge, was unlike anything he had heard before. Amid an atmosphere of almost gladiatorial intensity, Lillee edged and Taylor took a tumbling catch at the second attempt. Kent, in a maelstrom of a climax on his debut, was yorked. 120 for nine. When Botham powered another perfect yorker through Alderman's hopeless defence there was an explosion of sound that will remain forever with anyone fortunate enough to be present. England had won by 29 runs and, for the second time in a fortnight, their supporters tasted levels of excitement and joy rarely experienced by sports fans once in a generation.

Chapter 21

1982

England v Pakistan July 29 1982

For the 21st Test at Edgbaston, against Pakistan, added to the cast list of cricketers to have played Test cricket there were the names of Chris Tavare, Allan Lamb, Ian Greig, Eddie Hemmings, Tahir Naqqash, Mansoor Akhtar and Abdul Qadir. Warwickshire seamer Gladstone Small very nearly joined the list. With injury worries in England's squad, the 20-year-old seamer was called away from his county's championship match against Lancashire in Southport as cover. In the end, he was released back to the north-west coast to participate in one of the championship's most sensational games (Warwickshire, having closed the

first day at 523 for four, lost by 10 wickets!) and another four years were to elapse before Small finally did make his Test debut.

England went into the opening Test in good form. Already during the summer they had won a Test series with India 1-0 and recorded convincing wins in both Prudential Trophy one-day matches against Pakistan. The tourists, however, under Imran Khan, were an experienced side and particularly well-endowed with batting talent. In warm-up county games they had beaten each of Sussex, Glamorgan and Worcestershire by an innings.

No heroics this time from Botham as Imran flattens his off-stump

Willis, skippering his country on his home county ground for the first time, won the toss on a sunny morning and chose to bat. To the surprise of many of the 11,000 crowd, the jaunty figure of Derek Randall ventured out to open with Chris Tavare. The Nottinghamshire maverick duly christened the occasion with a volley of strokes which brought 16 runs from the first nine balls but then offered no stroke at all to Imran and his bails flew like sparks. Lamb was caught playing away from his body but Tavare and David Gower escorted England to the promising territory of 164 for two. Either side of tea, however, Imran hurried his team into control. In the space of 10 balls before the interval, he took out the opposition's two principal pillars, finding Gower's outside-edge and beating Botham through the gate. Tavare's 245 minutes of endeavour was terminated early in the evening session after which only Geoff Miller offered meaningful resistance. Imran's return of seven for 52 was the best by a Pakistan bowler against England. In a single over's batting before the close, Pakistan lost Mudassar

Nazar when Botham won a debatable lbw decision. Friday brought news to gladden the heart of every right-thinking Englishman. Beer prices, it was announced by the region's major brewery, were to be frozen for the foreseeable future at 52p a pint. While these happy tidings was digested and exploited around the city, at Edgbaston every Pakistan batsman from two to nine got a start but most perished to ill-judged attacking shots. Javed Miandad moved promisingly to 30 but when Hemmings was brought on for his first bowl in Test cricket Javed obligingly lifted his fourth ball to Willis at mid-on. "Block, slog, block, slog, out - it was beach cricket at its worst and only Javed knows what he was attempting," related the Birmingham Post. Mohsin Khan and Imran both perished hooking and only Mansoor Akhtar was patient enough to pass 50 as Pakistan's carelessness cost them a first-innings deficit of 21.

With Imran's pace reduced by a groin strain, Randall and Tavare advanced England to 51 without

Agile work from Taylor to catch Naqqash off Greig

Wasim Bari slices over the slips

loss by the close. On Saturday, to the delight of the English spectators among a cosmopolitan crowd, Nottinghamshire's finest rode his luck in outrageous fashion. Bamboozled by Qadir, Randall simply kept larruping him to leg and, to the leg-spinner's massive irritation, getting away with it. It was just as

Zaheer, double-centurion at Edgbaston 11 years earlier, is caught by Taylor for just four in Pakistan's second innings

Randall pulls Qadir for four (above) to reach his century but moments later (below) marches away, bowled by Imran

well that he did because England's other batting crumbled. Tavare became Imran's eighth victim of the match. Lamb, ill at ease in his fourth Test, played too late at Tahir who, also playing his fourth, embarked upon the performance of his career. While Randall's eccentric progress continued, Tahir removed Gower and Mike Gatting and then Botham first ball. When he castled Miller, the 23-year-old from Lahore had captured five wickets fr 20 runs in 45 deliveries. Still there was Randall who, to the warmest of ovations, passed 100 but when he fell to Imran for 105, in 249 minutes, out of 188, England were still only 209 ahead with two wickets to fall.

On Saturday evening came that most endearing of all sights, a spot of tail-wagging. Hemmings, born just 30 miles away in Leamington Spa, connected with a few swings to add 24 with Bob Taylor before Willis arrived to supply the main act. The captain walked out bristling with confidence, having struck a championship-best 63 not out against Gloucestershire at Nuneaton a week earlier. To stir his ossocks still further as he approached the crease, he became the first specialist fast-bowler to

Tavare turns for the pavilion as Javed claims the catch at silly point

Willis wields the willow in his record-breaking innings

play 100 innings in Test cricket. His celebration took the form of some lusty blows in his highest Test score of 28 not out. When Taylor departed for a canny 54 in the final over of the day, the last wicket had added 79 to raise Pakistan's target to a much more challenging 313.

Miandad is cleverly run out by Gatting from short leg

Sunday morning was cloudy and clammy; ideal swing-bowling conditions which Botham wasted no time in exploiting. With his second delivery he won another lbw decision (no doubt this time) to leave Mudassar nursing a pair. His sixth induced an edge from Mansoor. Javed was scuppered by the quick thinking of Gatting. He played Botham to Gatting's left at short leg then wandered out of his crease only for the fielder to transfer the ball from left hand to right and throw down the stumps. Pakistan had two days at their disposal but batted as though the target had to be reached in two sessions. Mohsin, having charged to 35, was trapped offering no stroke by Botham. Eleven years earlier, Zaheer treated the Edgbaston crowd to a ten-hour masterclass - this time he reached only four before flashing inappropriately at Willis. Wasim Raja carved to fifth slip and perished for an even-numbered score for the seventh time in 11 Test innings in England as Pakistan listed to 98 for seven. As his ship went down, Imran defied robustly and deposited Hemmings for two sixes in an over but when his last mow at Miller proved fatal, a sixth successive Edgbaston Test had failed to reach a fifth day.

Chapter 22

1984

England v West Indies June 14 1984

Hopes were never high of the 22nd Edgbaston Test reaching a fifth day. In the summer of 1984, Clive Lloyd's West Indies squad arrived in England as indisputably the pre-eminent force in world cricket. Joel Garner, Michael Holding and Malcolm Marshall led a fast-bowling pack of unprecedented depth. Viv Richards and Gordon Greenidge headed a batting unit of explosive talent. They were also a fielding side of rare athleticism and skill.

And in the blue corner... England, fresh from the most appalling of winters during which they were beaten, for the first time over a series, by each of New Zealand and Pakistan. The lowest point arrived in early February. Four months before facing the mighty West Indies in Birmingham, England registered arguably their most inept performance. They were beaten in three days by an innings and 132 runs by New Zealand in Christchurch. A rabble would have played better. The prospects for the 1984 series against Clive Lloyd's magnificent 'Windies' were less than rosy.

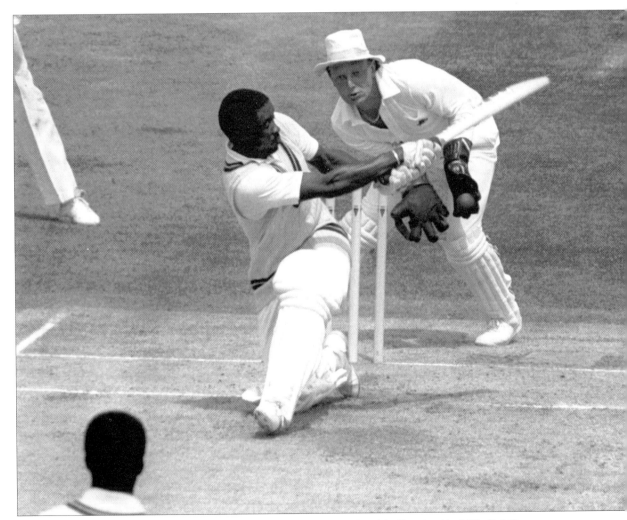

Baptiste sweeps four during his partnership of 150 with Holding

More runs for Holding

Following the New Zealand defeat, David Gower replaced Bob Willis as captain with the thankless mission of squaring up to the world's best in a five-Test series. On the first morning of the first contest, at Edgbaston, he won the toss - so far so good. He chose to bat. Just over half an hour later, two batsmen were in the pavilion nursing blobs and another was in an ambulance nursing a head injury. Welcome to Blackwash City!

Out to open the batting went left-handers Graeme Fowler and, making his debut, Warwickshire's Andy Lloyd. As Marshall and Garner took up the West Indies attack, Lloyd, to the home members' delight, showed no trace of nerves. He looked solid and composed despite two partners failing to score. Fowler gloved Garner to Jeffrey Dujon down the leg side and Derek Randall, optimistically employed at number three, was bowled off bat and body but Lloyd moved solidly to 10 out of 20 for two. Then Marshall scurried in again and let fly a ball which was only slightly short but reared at the batsman. Lloyd tried to sway out of the way but the ball did not rise as much as he expected and, to a gasp of horror from the stands, crunched into the earpiece of his helmet. The unfortunate batsman, concussed and with blurred vision from a detached retina, was escorted from the field to hospital where he was to remain for more than a week. Within the space of 33 minutes on a sunny June morning, Lloyd's entire Test match career had been discharged.

With a buzz of concern at the stricken Lloyd still audible among the 10,000 crowd, West Indies got on with the merciless business of dismantling the rest of the English batting. Gower and Alan Lamb took the score to 45 for two but departed in quick succession to catches behind the wicket. Botham arrived with a plan; to attack any red, round item that happened to pass close to him. He was dropped on nought then bowled by a Garner no-ball and for a while his luck held against the quick bowlers. Botham crashed 10 fours in 64 from 82 balls but his luck ran out when Lloyd turned to off-spinner Roger Harper who immediately inveigled him into sending up a catch to mid-off. Paul Downton defied nobly for 112 minutes but fears of England's inability to cope with the tourists' pace attack proved well-founded. 191 all out.

When West Indies replied, Willis trapped Greenidge and Desmond Haynes in his sixth over but West Indies were steered through to 53 without further loss at the close by Larry Gomes (four) and Richards (14). During the next five sessions the tourists truly asserted their superiority. The correct and selective Gomes and the increasingly aggressive Richards added 206 in 205 minutes for the third wicket. Richards, feeling under the weather and batting sketchily at first, settled himself with a withering burst of four boundaries off Derek Pringle and went on to gather 17 fours and a six before driving left-arm spinner Nick Cook to Randall at extra-cover. England were left to regret their decision to omit Neil Foster in favour of a second spinner. Bizarrely, first spinner Geoff Miller was not used until West Indies were 260 for three as Botham and Cook toiled away to little effect. Gomes added 53 with Jeffrey Dujon and 124 with Lloyd who kept the momentum high with a powerhouse 71 in 89 balls. By the close on Friday, West Indies had reached 421 for seven, 230 ahead, but if the English bowlers thought that the wickets of Gomes (for 143, with 16 fours, in 384 minutes), Lloyd and Marshall in the closing overs meant their suffering was over, they were wrong. Saturday morning brought total humiliation.

Harper was soon bowled by Pringle to bring Holding loping to the crease to join Eldine Baptiste. To the unconfined joy of their supporters, the numbers nine and ten proceeded to lash 150 runs in 114 minutes. Holding, in particular, revelled in England's disarray, clubbing four sixes and eight fours and taking with particularly relish to England spearhead Willis. Gower appeared lost for a plan, the fielding became ragged and resigned and Willis, Botham, Pringle and Cook each conceded more than 100 runs. The record ninth-wicket partnership finally closed when another lavish Holding hit landed in Willis's hands. Pringle quickly dismissed Garner to secure one of Test cricket's more bracing five-fors but England, with Lloyd still hospitalised, required 415 to make the West Indies bat a second time.

It didn't look too good when they imploded to 65 for four. Downton, taking Lloyd's place at the top of the order, again showed laudable determination and judgment but Fowler was trapped lbw and Randall, Gower and Lamb all contributed to their own downfall by fencing outside off-stump. It was left to

Lloyd is felled by a Marshall lifter and is escorted out of the Test arena forever

The sun shone for Richards, though, as he struck a superb century

Botham, more restrained second time around, to join Downton to see England through to 112 for four at the close.

Whenever Botham was about, hope existed for England but this was a hole from which even he could not exhume them. He added only eight on Monday morning before failing to deal with a vicious in-ducker from his Somerset team-mate Garner. While, across the city, there were casualties at Villa Park as Deadly Doug Ellis sacked management team Tony Barton and Roy MacLaren, at Edgbaston the England batsmen continued to fall like nettles before a scythe. Downton's defiance was ended after 280 minutes - more than six and a half hours in the match - by a catch at silly-point. There was some irrelevant fiddling and flashing from Pringle and Willis before the latter edged Garner (taking the bowler's haul to nine for 108 in the match) to close the curtains on England's embarrassment.

Chapter 23

1985

England v Australia August 15 1985

England's demolition by West Indies at Edgbaston in the opening Test of 1984 triggered a joyless summer in which they lost the remaining Tests by nine wickets, eight wickets, an innings and 64 runs and 172 runs respectively. A late-summer draw in a one-off Test with Sri Lanka extended England's winless sequence to 12 matches, over the last eight of which David Gower had presided as captain. English cricket was at an appallingly low ebb yet during the following winter, still led by Gower, they shocked the cricket world by fighting back from 1-0 down to beat India 2-1. That unprecedented feat

stirred hopes of an Ashes victory in 1985 against an Australian side which had spent the first half of the winter suffering a beating by West Indies scarcely less emphatic than England's had been. For their Ashes tour, Australia were also without key players, notably fast bowlers Terry Alderman, Rodney Hogg and Carl Rackemann, who were not considered for selection due to their involvement in the unofficial tour of South Africa.

When England won the opening Test, at Headingley, by five wickets their success-starved supporters

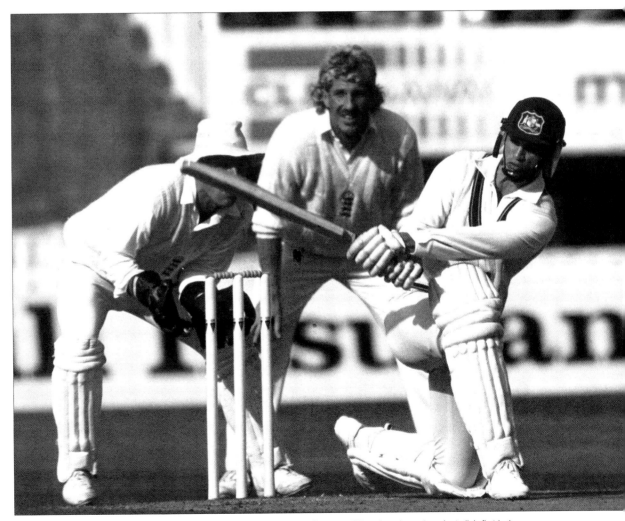

Wessels sweeps Edmonds as he anchors Australia's first innings

Lawson evades an Ellison bouncer on the way to 53

grew excited. Feet were kept on the ground, however, by Australia's four-wicket victory at Lord's, followed by draws at Trent Bridge and Old Trafford. Level at 1-1, the series was fascinatingly poised for, in calendar terms, the latest Test match to take place in Birmingham. As the next twist to a fluctuating series was eagerly awaited, everything came right for Gower's side. They beat Australia and eluded the weather in thrilling style. Big runs, sensational bowling, controversy - this game had the lot, all in England's favour.

When, after two rain-affected days, the first innings of the match was still not complete, a decisive result appeared out of the question. Kepler Wessels' diligent 83 in 228 minutes underpinned Australia's sketchy progress to 218 for seven. Fast-bowlers Geoff Lawson, Craig McDermott and Jeff Thomson then lifted the total to 335 for eight (Lawson on 53, Thomson 28) at the close on Friday. In front of a big Saturday crowd, the finely-balanced match and series lurched England's way.

The lurch began from the first ball of the day from which Lawson attempted a quick single. Gower swooped to run him out, Bob Holland lasted just two balls and Graham Gooch and Tim Robinson headed off to pad up. Before lunch, Gooch supplied Thomson with his 200th and last Test wicket but, on a glorious Saturday afternoon, Robinson and Gower put the bowling to the sword. The Nottinghamshire and Leicestershire batsmen batted for the rest of the day, first establishing control then

greedily taking advantage of wilting, wayward bowlers. Ten years earlier, Thomson had torn England apart on this Brummie turf but now he was punished for more than five runs per over. Holland hardly turned a ball while the pacemen served up sufficient loose deliveries for the batsmen to score quickly without risk. At the close Robinson was 140 and Gower 169 and England, 355 for one, were 20 in front.

When, early on Monday, Robinson played on to Lawson for 148, the second-wicket partnership had added 331 in 343 minutes, the second highest stand for any English wicket against Australia. Gower went on to amass 215 - the highest score for England against Australia at Edgbaston and his personal highest in all cricket - from 314 balls with a six and 25 fours. Mike Gatting then indulged in a spot of callous kicking of the opposition when they are down. He blazed to a merciless century from 125 balls while Botham, reaching the crease in the

Gower collects one of 25 fours in his glorious 215

Keep it going - Gatting and Gower confer as the runs pile up

Key moment - Phillips is about to perish caught by Gower off the boot of Lamb

pressure-free scenario of 572 for four, added a tinge of breathtaking arrogance to the onslaught by casually lifting his first delivery, from 20-year-old pace protege McDermott, far back over the bowler's head for six. After Botham was acrobatically caught by Thomson at deep mid-wicket, Gower waited for Gatting to reach his century before finally, at 595 for five, bringing the party to a close. Or so it seemed. By the close on Monday, Australia, trailing by 260 on first innings, had collapsed to 37 for five.

They progressed calmly enough to 32 for the loss of only Andrew Hilditch, who bafflingly helped a Botham long-hop straight to long leg. Wood and Wessels survived to within half an hour of the close of a day which had already provided more than enough for England followers to savour. Then those fans' cups truly began to runneth over. Richard Ellison, the Kent swing-bowler, unleashed a spell of four wickets for one run in 15 balls. Wessels flashed at a wide one. Holland, the nightwatchman, played fatally across the line first ball. A score of 32 for three would have represented a tasty evening's work but there was more. Wood sent a leading edge looping to Robinson at cover and then came the ultimate prize of Border's wicket, the left-hander bowled through the gate.

All over - McDermott is caught by Edmonds off Botham and victory is England's

The shell-shocked Australians returned to their hotel. Up in their sombre rooms they pondered a choice of EastEnders (Den plans a night on the tiles), The Des O'Connor Show (with guests Pia Zadora and Wall Street Crash) or Brookside (a distraught Harry takes his anxiety out on Sandra) to divert them from the stark fact that they remained 223 behind with half their second-innings wickets down.

If, during the interval of The Des O'Connor Show, Border and his chaps fitted in a few prayers for rain it appeared that they were answered on Tuesday morning. Drizzle prevented play before lunch and when Greg Ritchie and Wayne Phillips reached the crease at 2.30pm, they harboured a glimmer of hope. For 26 overs, with Ritchie rock-solid and Phillips more assertive, they denied the English attack. Then Lady Luck parked her cheeks squarely on England's bench. Phillips leaned back to cut a short ball from Phil Edmonds and made clean contact. The ball slammed into the heel of the boot of Lamb at silly point and travelled in a gentle arc to

the hands of Gower. England celebrated. Phillips hesitated. Umpire David Shepherd vacillated. He consulted his colleague David Constant at square leg. Out, said Constant and Australia's principal hope, glowering with a sense of injustice, trudged away.

There was more for Gower's men to do. Three wickets were still required as the last 20 overs began but with England cramming overs into the disappearing time, their pressure told. Botham returned to remove Simon O'Donnell and McDermott and England' victory was secured with 11.5 overs to spare. An eighth successive Edgbaston Test had concluded in less than four days of playing time.

Chapter 24

1986

England v India July 3 1986

After their eclipse of Australia at Edgbaston in 1985, England went on to regain the Ashes in style. In the final Test, at The Oval, David Gower and Graham Gooch scored big centuries and Ian Botham and Richard Ellison shared 13 wickets as England lodged successive innings victories over the Aussies for the first time since 1956. Les Taylor pouched a return catch from Murray Bennett to seal victory and bring thousands of English supporters pouring onto the turf to celebrate in front of the pavilion. Champagne flowed. Hugs and handshakes were exchanged. Sweetness and light oozed from every orifice of The Oval yet less than a year down the line, when India visited Edgbaston for the third and final Test, they were opposed by an England side which had completed the quantum leap from delirium to disarray.

Winter brought a 5-0 evisceration by the West Indies. Gower's team, unpicked by pace quartet Joel Garner, Malcolm Marshall, Patrick Patterson and Michael Holding, was beaten by the less-than-

What's the score...

...ah yes, 0 for 2 as England hit early trouble

trifling margins of 10 wickets, seven wickets, an innings and 30 runs, 10 wickets and 240 runs. Early summer of 1986 brought further grief with heavy defeats in the first two Tests against India - this time England's batsmen failed to deal with the rather less explosive armoury of Chetan Sharma and Roger Binny. India won the first Test, at Lord's, by five wickets to trigger Gower's removal as captain. Mike Gatting took charge for the second, at Headingley, where England were simply outplayed. Bill Athey's first-innings 32 was the top score for his team as India won by 279 runs - their biggest victory over any opposition by a margin of runs - early on the fourth day.

Striving to avoid an eighth successive defeat, England made five changes. Gower, missing at Leeds due to a shoulder injury, returned and there were recalls for Phil Edmonds and Neil Foster. Kent opening batsman Mark Benson and Worcestershire seamer Neal Radford made their debuts. Out went Graham Dilley, suffering from a tooth abscess, while

culled from the XI which played at Leeds were Wilf Slack, Chris Smith, Allan Lamb and John Lever. Slack, Smith and Lever never played Test cricket again.

The air of resignation among home supporters quickly thickened on the opening morning as England, having won the toss, hastened to nought for two in 13 balls. India captain Kapil Dev ousted Gooch and Athey with perfect outswingers to deposit England into a familiar pit of despair. Captain Gatting, however, a true trench-fighter, led his team's excavation from trouble. First came an elegant cameo from the demoted Gower who stroked 49 before becoming the first English batsmen to be dismissed for that score in an Edgbaston Test. His dismissal by Sharma left England uncomfortably placed at 88 for four with only one specialist batsman - the captain - left. The captain, at last abetted by some worthy support, responded.

French and Gatting celebrate as Armanath is bowled by Edmonds

Prizes don't come much bigger; Gavaskar's wicket, caught by French off Foster

Gatting added 96 with Derek Pringle, 94 with John Emburey, 49 with Neil Foster and 40 with Phil Edmonds as the men of Middlesex and Essex supplied England's batting with a degree of almost-forgotten backbone. When Radford's first Test innings yielded a duck, Gatting remained unbeaten after 387 minutes of resistance. His innings of 183, which included two sixes and 20 fours, was exactly the injection of defiance that England's flaccid confidence required.

His bowlers, however, struggled to back him up. Sunil Gavaskar, making his 115th Test appearance to overtake Sir Colin Cowdrey's world record, and Krisnamachari Srikkanth gave India's reply a flying start. Radford conceded 35 in five overs as the openers thrashed 53 in 39 minutes before departing in quick succession. Srikkanth steered to slip, then Gavaskar offered no shot to Pringle's fourth ball which darted back in to hit off-stump. Still, on Saturday morning, at 228 for three, with Mohinder Armanath and Mohammad Azharuddhin ticking along nicely, India appeared set for a healthy lead. Azharuddhin fell to the deserving Foster and Armanath was bowled by Edmonds but Kiran More and Binny added 68 for the eighth wicket to again conjure visions of a useful advantage. Again the innings was reeled back in as Emburey dismissed both and, for only the second time in a Test match involving England (South Africa v England at Durban in 1910 the only precedent), both teams lodged the same first-innings scores.

England's second innings opened at the start of the fourth day and advanced pleasantly to 152 for two. For the second time on his debut, Benson got a start but did not develop it - culpable, perhaps, for an opening batsman but surely not deserving of his subsequent eternal banishment from Test match cricket. Benson's valedictory ball in the Test arena was delivered by Ravi Shastri but it was Sharma, skidding in full of purpose and aggression at fast-medium who removed Gooch (for a spectacular 40 off 43 balls), Athey (a rather less flamboyant 38 in three hours), Gower (to Gavaskar's 100th catch in Test cricket) and Gatting. Although Emburey batted cussedly for the second time in the match India were set only 236, in a minimum of 84 overs, to win; a chaseable target, if far from straightforward on a wearing pitch.

Again Gavaskar and Srikkanth provided a spectacular launchpad. They galloped to 39 in only three overs and after Edmonds lured Srikkanth into a fatal sweep into Pringle's hands at square leg, Armanath helped Gavaskar ease the total along to 101 for one. A startling collapse rushed England back into the game. Edmonds, extracting turn from the City End, dismissed Armanath, Vengsarker and Shastri and as Foster prised out the plum wicket of Gavaskar, four wickets tumbled for four runs in 38 balls before Azharuddin and More halted the slide and took the score to 126 for five at tea.

A fascinating finale beckoned - 110 runs or five wickets for victory - but bad light and rain caused a

Shastri departs, caught by Emburey, but India, assisted by the weather, held on for a draw

The joy of cricket; young supporters of both sides watch together

48-minute delay. When a resumption was possible India, their victory hopes obliterated, simply defended for the draw - the first such result in an Edgbaston Test since 1973 - and the match was put gently to sleep, as was the unfortunate Benson's fledgling Test career.

Chapter 25

1987

England v Pakistan July 23 1987

July 1987. Environment Minister Nicholas Ridley unveils another round of tight public spending. The Soviet Union's deputy foreign minister Yuli Vorontsov considers the 72 American nuclear warheads attached to Pershing missiles ready to wing their way towards the USSR at a moment's notice and describes them, understandably enough, as "no joke". Peter Holm tells a Los Angeles divorce court that he still loves Joan Collins, a 61-year-old Cheltenham man receives a suspended three-year jail sentence for falsely claiming that his cello was destroyed by fire and Edgbaston's Test throws up one of its most gripping finales.

For four days of England's tussle with Pakistan, batsmen were in control. Critics of captain Mike Gatting were not slow to point this out after he had flown in the face of history by inserting the opposition. Gatting anticipated early assistance for his seamers from dampness in the wicket. It did not materialise - indeed the strip turned out to be a flat-track of the Edgbaston old school.

Only one Pakistan wicket fell in the first session - and that to a spinner. Shoaib Mohammed was adroitly caught by Neil Foster over his left shoulder at deep extra cover but all day the seamers toiled against the broad bat of Mudassar Nazar. The opener added 135 for the third wicket with Javed Miandad and although the latter's attractive 75 from 145 balls was terminated by a Graham Dilley yorker late in the day, Mudassar reached a patient century from 298 balls and was unbeaten on 102, out of 250 for three, at the close.

The tourists, already 1-0 up before this fourth Test of five, were well-satisfied but it had been a barren day for Warwickshire members in the crowd and, as they headed to the bars for solace, further grim news arrived. Warwickshire, trapped on a bunsen at Southport, had lost to Lancashire by 10 wickets in two days.

Day two at Edgbaston brought those Warwickshire and England fans anguish of a different kind as

Down comes the rain

Runs for Gatting...

increased as disorganisation turned to farce. While the umpires waited, the light closed in again and, after consulting their meters, off again went the officials, to howls of derision.

When cricket finally resumed, further frustration was supplied to England's supporters by Pakistan's garrulous and gritty wicket-keeper Salim Yousuf. His team having faltered to 317 for seven, Yousuf

...and for Broad in the thrilling final session

professional cricket's sporadic ability to needlessly needle its paying punters went into overdrive. A murky day brought several interruptions for rain and bad light and after one of these, a five-minute delay, umpires Alan Whitehead and Barrie Meyer strolled out at 2.38pm ready for play to resume. This development was noted with approval and relief by the 9,000 crowd who responded with ironic cheering. Unfortunately, no member of the English team was bothering to keep an eye out for such an eventuality. The BBC beamed to the nation live pictures of the umpires waiting in the middle but the goggle-box in England's dressing-room was tuned to a different channel. The spectators grew agitated as the umpires waited in the middle, peering hopefully into the distance like twitchers on a vacant moor. The agitation in the stands only

Imran battles to keep his team afloat

(dropped on four by Botham off Dilley) compiled a Test-best unbeaten 91 as the last three wickets generated 122 runs.

After England, led by Gatting's third successive century in Tests on the ground, replied with a resounding 521 the match seemed destined for a draw. In 15 overs late on the fourth day, Pakistan made untroubled progress to 38 without loss so they began the final day 44 runs behind with all second-innings wickets standing. Tuesday was, surely, a one-way ticket to Draw City calling only at Tediumville and Banal Springs.

Far from it, although there was nothing in the morning to hint at excitement ahead. Dilley ousted Mudassar but Shoaib and Mansoor Akhtar steered Pakistan to 74 for one, eight runs behind at lunch. Then Foster sparked the match into life by trapping Mansoor and forcing Javed to edge to first slip. Ian Botham took up the baton with a brilliant return catch to dismiss Salim Malik. Foster sentenced Shoaib to become the first batsman, during Edgbaston's 25 Tests, to be dismissed for 50 and when Botham bowled Ijaz behind his legs, suddenly, with Pakistan 116 for six, just 34 runs in front, it was 'game on'.

Excellent, tough cricket followed as captain Imran Khan fought tigerishly. Abetted by the dogged Yousuf and Abdul Qadir and a small but significant 13-minute interruption for bad light, the captain defied for 27 overs to delay England's charge. When Pakistan's last wicket finally fell, England's target for a sensational victory was 124 from 18 overs which began at the start of the final hour.

With several players vastly experienced in one-day cricket, the task appeared manageable, especially after Nottinghamshire openers Chris Broad and Tim Robinson added 37 in five overs. Broad raced to 30 from 23 balls but his departure to a looping catch in the gully unhinged the run-chase. Imran, exactly 731 weeks after his first bowl at Edgbaston had yielded six for 63 for Oxford University against Warwickshire, and Akram bowled fast, straight and often short to defensive fields, forcing the batsmen to take risks.

Robinson holed out and Botham mishooked to deep fine leg but England were still on target at 62 for three from nine overs. Halfway to the total, half the overs used and fast-scorers Gower and Gatting at the crease. The two great bowlers rose to the occasion. Imran defeated Gower and then, with pressure increasing, Gatting, sent back by Bill Athey, was beaten by Ijaz's throw. Emburey thrashed Imran over extra cover for six in an over which went for 15 but the required run-rate edged upward. Thirty were needed off three overs. 24 off two. 17 off one. Athey's longevity dealt a severe blow to England's hopes. The Gloucestershire batsman collected just 14 runs in seven overs and after Emburey and Edmonds were run out in the final over the two sides - 15 runs and three wickets short respectively - accepted the draw with two balls remaining.

The attendance over five rain-affected days was 42,500. Match receipts were £287,080, a figure eroded by the costs of increased policing to prevent a repeat of crowd misbehaviour which had marred the one-day international between the countries on the ground two months earlier. Peace reigned this time and those supporters who took a chance on a final day which had looked like a dead duck were rewarded with a pulsating finish. Even though England's claims to be the dominant force in world cricket were becoming ancient history, their record at Edgbaston remained formidable. Played 25: won 14, drawn nine, lost two.

The covers are rolled on as rain stops play once more

Police presence was heavy as tensions were raised

Wasim Akram smothers the life out of England's run chase

Chapter 26

1989

England v Australia July 6 1989

Of seven tests played by Australia at Edgbaston before 1989, they had won just one, the Lillee, Thompson and Walker-driven innings victory of 1975. Fourteen years after that triumph, their superiority over England was equally vast but a weather forecast of "sunshine with outbreaks of thundery rain" (rain in Nassau, cloudy in Beijing, clear in Honolulu) came savagely true to rob them of the victory they fully deserved.

Much had changed since the Australians' two most recent visits to Birmingham, in 1981 and 1985, each of which brought embarrassing defeat. Under the inspirational leadership of Allan Border, they had begun to turn the corner which was ultimately to lead to their domination of world cricket. England,

meanwhile, were on the crest of a slump with only a single victory (over Sri Lanka in a one-off contest at the end of 1988) to show for 21 Tests.

That wretched sequence included the first two contests of the 1989 Ashes series. Under the management of Ted Dexter, and with David Gower reappointed captain, England were thumped by 210 runs at Headingley and six wickets at Lord's. Two-nil up with four to play, Australia were ready to reclaim the Ashes. And so to Edgbaston where only the most partisan England supporter harboured much optimism. The realists were proved right but so, unfortunately for Border's men, were the weather-forecasters.

Refreshments are a welcome break in the hot weather

Four more for Steve Waugh

While Australia selected an unchanged side, England's planning was chaotic. Robin Smith, Allan Lamb and Neil Foster were lost to injury and Mike Gatting withdrew following a family bereavement. Back into the team came Chris Tavare (recalled for his first Test in five years), Ian Botham (after two years) and Tim Curtis. Paul Jarvis, originally dropped, received a last-minute recall when Foster reported a bleeding blister on his bowling hand. Middlesex seamer Angus Fraser made his debut.

After Australia won the toss and batted, Jarvis bowled like a man in whom the selectors had no confidence. With Graham Dilley also misfiring, the tourists were put under no early pressure, despite sultry, bowler-friendly conditions, and Geoff Marsh and Mark Taylor added 88 for the first wicket. Although they, along with Border who offered no stroke to a ball which hit leg stump, departed in the space of eight overs, David Boon and Dean Jones were soon playing with assurance. Boon was unluckily ousted when a drive from Jones flicked off Jarvis's fingers and shattered the stumps at the non-striker's end. That brought in Steve Waugh, not short of confidence with scores of 177 not out, 152 not out and 21 not out so far in the series and he quickly settled alongside Jones. At the end of a day truncated by a post-tea storm, Australia were 232 for four.

Get it - the flying Russell

Treatment for Botham

The next two days were badly affected by those thundery showers (still cloudy in Beijing, still clear in Honolulu). On Friday the cricket amounted to 59 minutes during which Fraser collected his first Test wicket, that of Waugh bowled through the gate for a sprightly 43 from 54 balls. The felled batsman could at least console himself by reflecting upon a series average of 393. On Saturday, Aston Villa manager Graham Taylor arrived back from holiday armed with £2million to rebuild his team - ah, those were the days - and, between further showers, Jones' concentration remained total. Having arrived at the crease on Thursday afternoon, he was finally dismissed, caught in the deep by Lancashire's Ian Folley, fielding as substitute, on Monday morning. Jones' 157 from 293 balls with 17 fours was the highest innings by an Australian in a Test at Birmingham. Border's side were all out for 424, a decent total but still representing the best effort by England's bowlers so far in the series, Australia having amassed 601 for seven and 528 in the first innings of the earlier Tests.

England began their reply at noon and their reshuffled top order quickly folded. Curtis battled hard for 41 but when he and Kim Barnett fell in successive overs, England were 75 for five and,

Jones advances to a classy 157

Dilley delivers

with the follow-on figure 150 away, vulnerable to another defeat. Botham, displaying much greater caution than usual, and Jack Russell consumed valuable crease time but both fell just before the close. Botham was bowled through a big drive and Russell cut hard and perished to an exceptional slip-catch, via the wicket-keeper's gloves, by Taylor. England went into the final day still 40 adrift of the follow-on figure with only the tail left.

Fortunately, that tail wagged. From the fourth ball of the day Fraser was run out after Emburey was

Not much for Gooch to celebrate

caught snoozing when a big single beckoned. The spinner expiated his error by slashing four boundaries off Merv Hughes and, with the determined Dilley, taking England to within 10 runs of the follow-on figure. That target was reached after Dilley's diligent defence, which spanned 87 minutes, was supplemented by some uninhibited swinging from Jarvis.

Not that the Aussies were too bothered. Two-nil up with three to play was a groovy situation and nothing during this soggy spectacle had suggested England were capable of mounting any sort of fightback. Border allowed his batsmen to shepherd the match to a draw. Botham completed a satisfactory return to Test cricket with a spectacular slip catch to dismiss Taylor while Tavare's international career meandered to its conclusion during a dull session enlivened only by the thrill of watching Curtis deliver his only three overs in Test cricket. It remained cloudy in Beijing and had, by now, also clouded over in Honolulu while evidence of the enduring appeal of the Australian tourists was that, despite the rain, the Test generated £683,372.

Chapter 27

1990

England v New Zealand July 5 1990

Archie MacLaren, Arthur Gilligan, Peter May, Colin Cowdrey, Ted Dexter, Mike Smith, Brian Close, Mike Denness, Mike Brearley, Bob Willis and David Gower all captained England to Test victories at Edgbaston. In none of that esteemed list, however, was there a greater sense of relief at the achievement than that experienced by Graham Gooch when his England side defeated New Zealand in July 1990.

Of 25 home Tests since their Ashes triumph of 1985, England had won just one - against Sri Lanka at Lord's in 1988. Of the remaining 24 they had, under Gower, Mike Gatting, John Emburey, Chris Cowdrey, Gooch, Gower again and Gooch again, drawn 12 and lost 12. It was a home record of a risibility to compare with that of Woolwich Arsenal in the Football League Division One in 1912/13 but, in 1990, England hit back. They registered back-to-back series wins over New Zealand and India and the revival began in Birmingham.

England press for victory as Hemmings sets an attacking field

Greatbach out, caught in the slips

The match was historic for another reason. Sir Richard Hadlee, for so long the driving force of New Zealand cricket, who had just been knighted in the Queen's Birthday Honours List, played his 86th and last Test. To Hadlee went the honour of bagging Devon Malcolm as his 431st and final Test victim but despite rounding off his career in appropriate fashion, with his 36th haul of five or more wickets in an innings, he could not lift his team to victory. Never mind. Hadlee was hugely applauded anyway. Of success, at this point, England's need was much the greater.

The third and final contest in the series was the decider, the first two having been sentenced to draws by rain. England started the match at least consoled by the knowledge that it could not go to penalties - during the previous evening their players shared the frustration of the nation as their football counterparts lost a nerve-shredding World Cup semi-final penalty-shootout to Germany. Gooch - like all men of true perspicacity a West Ham supporter - and Michael Atherton vented their frustration on New Zealand's bowling next day.
 Rain delayed the start until 2.45pm after which England, surprisingly put in on a firm track by New

Zealand captain John Wright, prospered. Gooch and Atherton put on 170, the highest opening stand for England in Birmingham, and although Atherton was trapped by Martin Snedden half an hour before the close, England had established a position of rare promise at 191 for one, with Gooch 95, at stumps.

The captain's resolve was required next morning as he passed his ninth Test century, only to see the rest of the specialist batsmen fall around him. They were bailed out by the lower and middle order. After Gooch's 394-minute vigil was ended by Hadlee's catch, Jack Russell, Chris Lewis (on his debut), Gladstone Small (at last playing an Edgbaston Test eight years after so nearly doing so) and 41-year-old Eddie Hemmings prolonged the innings into the second evening. In reply to 435, the tourists reached nine without loss from eight overs before the close.

On Saturday, with an alarming quantity of empty seats in evidence - takings for the Test were to amount to £390,000, some £28,000 less than projected - Hemmings bowled his side into command. Malcolm also took important wickets, including that of the obdurate Wright, to break a

Gooch on his way to his ninth Test century

Hadlee trying to see off the England batsmen

promising opening stand with Trevor Franklin. The Derbyshire quickie also ousted Mark Greatbatch who became over-adventurous just as he was seizing the initiative. Lewis's first Test victim was Martin Crowe who departed in a sulk having at first declined to observe umpire Barrie Meyer's lbw verdict. Hemmings, meanwhile, on what many Warwickshire supporters believe should never have ceased to be his home ground, ended Franklin's stolid 270-minute defiance and worked his way through the lower order to nurture hopes of enforcing the follow-on. New Zealand avoided that

Hemmings probes away

with two wickets to spare but Hemmings then briskly mopped up those to harvest a Test-best six for 58.

England began their second innings, leading by 186, at the start of Monday and again Gooch and Atherton supplied a solid start before Gooch was gated by Snedden for 30 from 32 balls. At 99 for three at lunch, England had no time to lose and their commendably positive approach brought a clatter of wickets in the afternoon. Only Atherton, who batted for 190 minutes before chipping to mid-wicket, passed his captain's score as the last seven wickets crashed for 29 runs in the face of Hadlee's farewell five-for. The crowd relished their final opportunity to see this craftsman at work and after Hadlee wrapped up the innings with the hallowed wickets of Hemmings and Malcolm, he led his side off the field to a generous ovation.

New Zealand's target was 345 - the fifth highest score to win a Test - in eight and a half hours. Again, Malcolm inflicted early damage, trapping the potentially adhesive Franklin. Lewis added the wicket of Wright before the close at which New Zealand were 101 for 2: Jones 37, Crowe 10. "England in position to win Test" boomed the TV news headlines on Monday night prompting

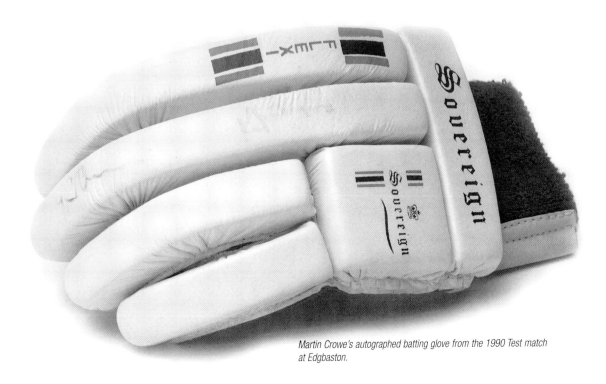

Martin Crowe's autographed batting glove from the 1990 Test match at Edgbaston.

Hadlee leaves the field for the last time to generous applause

delivery of the day, a looping off-break, took Greatbatch's edge and progressed in a gentle arc to Atherton at slip. When Ken Rutherford also fell in the slips, Hadlee walked in. A fairytale end to a mighty career? No. Shackled by his former Nottinghamshire team-mate Hemmings, Hadlee eked just three singles from 44 balls before, on 13 from 51 in total, missing an extravagant drive at Malcolm. The Derbyshire fast-bowler steamed in, in search of the coup de grace, and when he wrecked Danny Morrison's wicket, England's long drought was over. Other home grounds had proved fickle in recent times but the national team's love-affair with Edgbaston continued. Played 27: won 15, drawn 10, lost 2.

Warwickshire's Small on familiar home territory for England

widespread fainting, spluttering into pints and dropping of jaws accompanied by rueful cries of: "They'll cock it up." Could England grasp the opportunity?

Yes. On Tuesday morning, Jones added only three more runs before Gooch accepted a stinging catch, high at slip, off Small. That united Crowe and Greatbatch - two men with the explosive ability to snatch victory, never mind stave off defeat. Crowe was trapped by Malcolm and then Hemmings' third

Chapter 28

1991

England v West Indies July 25 1991

Few love affairs, however, could survive the interference of 11 big, hairy West Indians and sure enough in 1991, even Edgbaston's happy influence upon the national side was blown apart. To the Caribbean pace onslaught, there was, still, simply no answer.

When the West Indians arrived for their 14th Test tour of England, the home supporters braced themselves for further punishment. They received an early surprise, however, as England won the first Test (their first victory in 24 home tussles with West Indies) and, to the amazement of many, when the two teams fetched up in the Birmingham for the fourth Test they were still all square at 1-1.

England's initial victory, by 115 runs at Headingley, owed everything in a low-scoring match to captain Graham Gooch's unbeaten 154, batting through England's second innings of 252. After a rain-ruined second Test at Lord's, the third, at Trent Bridge, brought a restoration of normal service as West Indies coasted to a nine-wicket victory thanks to the customary fast-bowling barrage of Curtley Ambrose, Malcolm Marshall and Courtney Walsh. England's early success in the series was starting to appear redolent of a Third Division side sneaking an early goal against Premiership opposition in an FA Cup tie. At Edgbaston, sure enough, class soon told. West Indies were used to beating England and England were used to bowing to Caribbean brute

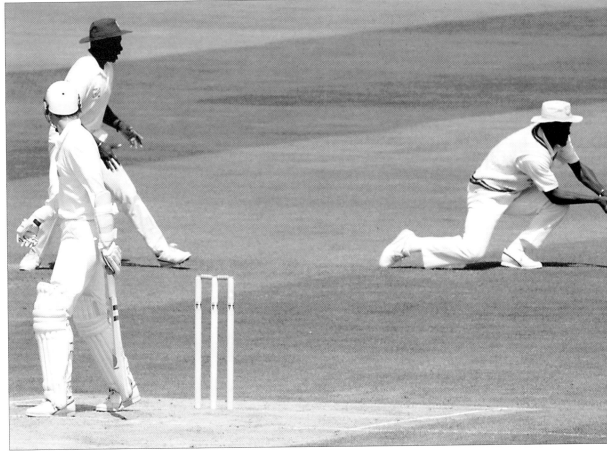

Atherton caught by Hooper off Patterson

strength. In the fourth Test, to use an analogy from the Beano, Bully Beef was about to address Chips in the usual way.

In front of 15,000 people on the opening day, a familiar tale of English woe unfolded. Viv Richards won the toss and gleefully gave his bowlers first use of a helpful pitch. When play started 65 minutes late Gooch, passed fit to play only at the last moment after recovering from tonsillitis, took debutant Hugh Morris out to open with him. The captain was reprieved first ball when Carl Hooper grassed a chance in the slips but there was no such luck for Morris. He edged the 12th ball of the match, from Patrick Patterson, and Jeffrey Dujon made no mistake. The doughty Michael Atherton joined his captain to add 47 before falling to a wicked break-back in a wonderful over by Walsh. That brought in Graeme Hick. Pitched into Test cricket in this toughest of all series, Hick had so far gathered 55 runs from five innings. With a modified stance, the Worcestershire batsman hinted at comfort for a while but never became confident.

After hitting just three fours in 149 minutes he fell, for the fifth successive innings, to Ambrose, this time courtesy of a catch at first slip.

After Gooch was bowled off and middle by Marshall, the burden of resistance was carried by Mark Ramprakash. Since his debut in the opening Test, the young Middlesex batsman had shown courage aplenty in making 27, 27, 24, 13 and 21, with sturdy if strokeless defiance and here was the same again. He gritted out 29 before mishooking his 84th delivery. West Indies simply pounded away and waited for batsmen to buckle. "If it is painful to bat against," related the Birmingham Post, "it is sheer torment to watch. There is such a monotonous repetitiveness to it all. Like an automatic grinding machine, the West Indies bowlers get through 12 overs an hour. There has got to be more to the game than fast bowling."

England's innings, 184 for nine overnight, was completed after 11 balls on Friday and then West Indies' batsmen asserted themselves. England

House full for the West Indies visit

Defreitas is caught by a diving Richardson bowled Marshall

Bob Wyatt and Prime Minister John Major

opening bowlers Phillip DeFreitas and Chris Lewis (fellow former pupils of Willesden High School) failed to extract the venom from the pitch that the West Indian quicks had done. Phil Simmons and Desmond Haynes were not parted until 52 were on the board and Richie Richardson then showed that, along with ineffable timing and strokeplay, he possessed technique and guts. Despite suffering from a virus, he dealt skilfully with the moving ball and combined patience with punishing strokes. "De sun is shinin'" a West Indies supporter informed members of the press box, "and de runs are bein' made".

To England's relief, Hooper and Richards both gave it away after getting a start but Richardson passed his first century in three tours of England just before the close. England had moved no nearer a solution to their seemingly endless search for a satisfactory spinner, Richard Illingworth having delivered 17-2-75-1 as West Indies took supper on 253 for four (65 ahead) with Richardson 103 and Gus Logie 24. On Saturday morning, England's bowlers, led by

Lewis, fought back. The Leicestershire all-rounder's second ball was cut by Logie into Atherton's hands at gully. He won an lbw shout from David Shepherd to oust Richardson (for 104 from 229 balls with 13 fours) and then brushed aside the tail to claim his first five-wicket haul in Test cricket. Having restricted the first-innings difference to 104, England had every right to be pleased with their morning's work but, when their second innings staggered to six for three, that lead appeared more than enough.

Patterson promptly pinned Morris and found Atherton's edge. Ambrose yet again did for Hick. De sun was still shinin' but de runs were certainly not bein' made. The gallant Gooch got stuck in with Allan Lamb to add 65 but, as so often in recent times against West Indies, when one England wicket fell, there was a cluster of casualties. Patterson bowled Gooch, Lamb edged Walsh and Jack Russell snicked before he had scored, to leave England 96 for six - still eight runs away from avoiding an innings defeat. Ramprakash again hung on with grim fortitude, without ever threatening to take the initiative and after he and Defreitas departed, England were 144 for eight, still only 40 ahead. The game was up, it seemed - but the plot still had a wrinkle or two left.

Derek Pringle and Lewis survived through to 156 for eight on Saturday night then on Sunday stood up to the pacemen to extend their ninth-wicket alliance to 92 in 33 overs. Pringle's 45 spanned more than five hours while Lewis pulled and drove magnificently to add a maiden Test half-century to his first five-wicket haul earlier in the match. Lewis finally lifted a catch to substitute Clayton Lambert at extra cover after an ebullient 65 from 94 balls with 10 fours. A wonderful Test career, surely, lay ahead.

Atherton hooks

Richardson caught at slip by Hick off Defreitas for 0 in the West Indies second innings

Pringle supplies England with a crumb of hope

Guyana-born Lewis had delayed the West Indies but they still required only 152 for victory. Simmons and Haynes eased to 23 without loss before the match exploded back into life as Dominica-born Defreitas struck three times in six balls. Haynes and Richardson fell to splendid slip-catches by Hick and when Simmons shuffled fatally in front, the tourists had plunged to 24 for three. Was this to be a 1981 v Australia scenario? Was Edgbaston to rescue England yet again?

Not a bit of it. Hooper and Richards climbed into England's attack with a measured but destructive partnership of 133 from 32 overs. Hooper's 55 included eight fours while Richards passed 50 for the 68th time in his 120th Test on the way to 73 from 97 balls with a six and nine fours. His six was the winning blow, delivered just before 6pm when, having blocked 10 deliveries, the West Indian captain liked the look of the next, from the hapless Illingworth, and deposited it over long-on. It was a final thrust of real panache to a fascinating Test, thoroughly enjoyed by 59,917 spectators.

Chapter 29

1992

England v Pakistan June 4 1992

During 100 years, many and varied spectators have attended Test matches at Edgbaston and most have thoroughly enjoyed the experience. A few, however, have had cause to assume a grumpy state of mind.

Those whose coats were muddied by the City End scramble of 1902 were certainly touched by the grumpy stick. So, too, those forced to watch Ken Barrington in underdrive in the bitter cold in 1965 and those who witnessed Alan Whitehead and Barrie Meyer hanging around in the middle like spare parts in 1987. It was the class of 1992 however, at least those present on the second day, who take the grumpy biscuit.

Pakistan were the visitors for the opening Test of an eagerly-awaited series. It was the first between the countries since England's 1987 tour when the Shakoor Rana/Mike Gatting kerfuffle soured the countries' relationship so bitterly that it took five years for the rancour to become latent enough for them to meet again. It was to prove worth the wait; an intoxicating series with excellent, exciting cricket laced with controversy. Sadly for the Edgbaston audience, all the excitement arrived in the later Tests - in Birmingham there was just controversy and even that was not directly cricket-related.

An hour before the scheduled start on Thursday, rain arrived to wash out the first day's play. Not a single delivery was bowled so the 8,500 ticket-holders were disappointed. Disappointed but not disgruntled because, as there had been no play at all, they at least received a full refund of their admission price. They were the lucky ones.

On Friday, 15,000 people turned up hoping that a dull, grey morning would brighten. There was no play before lunch but the multitude waited patiently and just after 1pm came an announcement that play would start at 2.45pm. The sky continued to glower but no more rain fell so, at 2.42pm, out went the players. Phillip Defreitas marked out his run and turned to deliver the first ball. Eighty-two seconds later he had propelled two, one each to

Part of the Test Match Special team; David Lloyd, Asif Iqbal, Brian Johnston, Bill Frindall and Trevor Bailey

Miandad escapes as Botham makes a great effort to take a catch at slip

debutant Aamir Sohail and Ramiz Raja, when, to the crowd's dismay, on came the fourth light on the scoreboard. That denoted bad light and off went the players. Sohail and Raja turned to the pavilion after shaking hands, evidently overjoyed at having survived such a taxing session unparted. The spectators, who had paid ticket-prices of up to £26 were, of course, less than chuffed. Only later, however, when play was abandoned for the day, did a sense of injustice begin to bite and tempers start to rise.

At 5pm came tidings from the Test and County Cricket Board. As there had been some cricket no refunds would be made, it announced, before adding generously; "All holders of today's tickets will be entitled to admission on Monday."

That gesture (with the final day's play already doomed to irrelevance, the first two having been obliterated by rain) was greeted with the cynicism with which it was offered. Spectators on all sides of the ground, not least those who had waited, cold and damp, in the uncovered Stanley Barnes Stand, were united in contempt for the TCCB who knew that full refunds would have cost more than £200,000. The board was playing fast and loose with the crowd's tolerance. Would the audience at

an opera be satisfied if, having paid £26 for a ticket, they heard two notes warbled in their direction before everybody left the stage? Not really. An angry mob gathered near the pavilion as officials of both TCCB and Warwickshire were escorted from the ground in clandestine fashion. It had been one of the most spectacular public-relations gaffes in English sporting history.

Amid all the furore, the match had been, barring batting calamities, sentenced to stalemate and when cricket at last resumed on Saturday it soon became clear that no such calamities were likely. On a benign wicket, Defreitas ensured England a measure of control by ousting Sohail, Asif Mujtaba and Ramiz by early afternoon. Thereafter the 17,000 crowd could only admire the quality of Javed Miandad and Salim Malik. England were soon regretting their decision to leave out leg-spinner Ian Salisbury, (included in the squad in place of the injured Phil Tufnell but left out of the XI) as their seamers found nothing in the pitch and Graeme Hick's off-spin was milked. Warwickshire's Tim Munton, like Salisbury omitted when the team-sheets were handed in, was left to reflect that this would have been a daunting debut as the two high-class batsmen lifted their side to 290 for three by the close, Javed 99, Malik 80.

Malik drives Hick during his innings of 165

Stewart pulls on his way to 190

On Sunday, Miandad moved well into his 23rd Test century, an innings of considerable charm, while Malik plundered more forcefully. When Malik was finally trapped by Defreitas, the fourth-wicket partnership had yielded 322 - a record for any wicket in Tests between the two countries. Malik's 165 from 297 balls included a six and 19 fours. There were 19 fours, too, in Javed's unbeaten 153 from 336 balls. On the bland pitch England's attack had, DeFreitas apart, been rendered helpless. Only the Lancashire all-rounder took wickets in the innings' 137 overs.

Without the injured Wasim Akram, Pakistan's bowlers found the going equally tough. Gooch bat-padded to short-leg off Aqib Javed but Alec Stewart underlined his growing stature by hurrying to his fourth century in five Tests. Hick collected his maiden half-century in his eighth Test but, having reached 51, in 102 balls with seven fours, failed to build further. Remarkably, he had faced just three deliveries from Waqar Younis on the way to 50 but, when the pace spearhead came back, Hick immediately steered a catch tamely to gully.

Robin Smith was more durable. He helped Stewart to add 227 - the highest third-wicket partnership in Tests between the countries - and as soon as England passed the 297 required to avoid the follow-on, any spark of interest in the match faded. Stewart's sparkling 190, including 31 fours mostly pulled, cut and driven with venom, was finally ended by debutant quickie Ata-ur-Rehman. The youngest man to play Test cricket in Birmingham, Rehman, just ten weeks beyond his 17th birthday, then blew away the unfortunate Mark Ramprakash whose second ball rose sharply from a length, one of only a handful of deliveries in the match to misbehave.

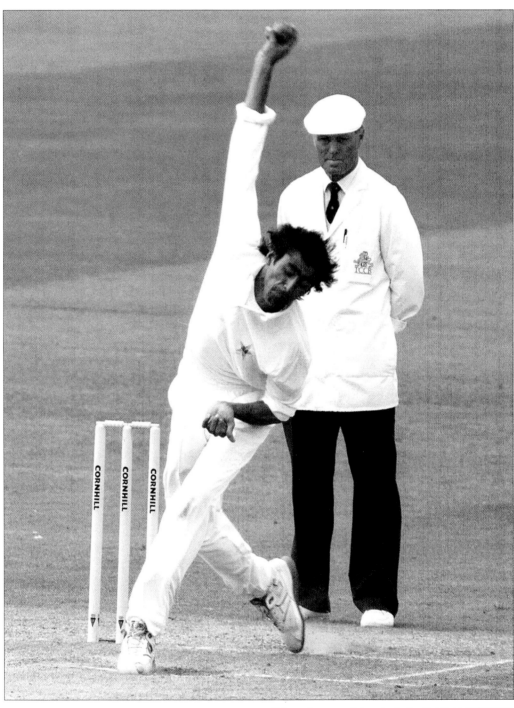

Rehman, the youngest player to play in a Test Match at Edgbaston

Miandad hooks Lewis

The match was ended half an hour early, appropriately, by a thunderstorm. This skeleton of a Test match will be remembered only for the storms of temper generated by Friday's two-ball fiasco and, most poignantly of all, by the unfortunate spectator who was in the gents while those expensive balls were bowled.

Chapter 30

1993

England v Australia August 5 1993

Over the years England had handed out some heavy punishment at Edgbaston while taking relatively little in return. In 1993, the chances of them handing out heavy punishment to anyone (other than supporters daft enough to back them to win) were remote in the extreme.

The Edgbaston Test was the fifth contest of an Ashes series in which England were already 3-0 down. After the fourth Test - an innings-and-148 run rout at Headingley - Graham Gooch resigned the captaincy and Michael Atherton became his country's 71st captain. Since the thraping at Leeds, which ensured the Ashes stayed with Australia for the third successive series, there had been much navel-gazing, brow-beating, finger-pointing and scapegoat-hunting. England fetched up at Edgbaston with a new captain and a much-changed team. The result of the reshuffling; they took further punishment of the heavy variety, culminating in another high-profile casualty when Ted Dexter resigned as chairman of selectors. Receipts from the match amounted to over a million pounds but England, in terms of inspiration, were bankrupt.

Slater is caught by Smith to the delight of the fielders who rush to congratulate the bowler, Such

Emburey is finally caught by Healy for 37 after a stand of 104 with Thorpe

First the scapegoats. Somerset batsman Mark Lathwell's Test career was consigned to history. He was dropped, along with county colleague Andrew Caddick whose 0 for 138 off 42 overs in Australia's only innings at Leeds was deemed unacceptable.

Martin McGague's 0 for 115 off 28 at Leeds was apparently considered the right side of acceptable but he was ruled out by injury so Steve Watkin and Devon Malcolm were called up. However, when it emerged, two days before the match, that the pitch

A crucial moment as Stewart misses stumping Steve Waugh

was likely to turn, the selectors vacillated and hurried John Emburey, 17 days short of his 41st birthday, into the squad. England finally went in with arguably their most anaemic attack of any of the 695 Tests they had played. A pace attack of Martin Bicknell (one for 155 on his debut at Leeds) and Mark Ilott was supported by spinners Peter Such and John Emburey. This was the armoury which the new captain had to wield against a batting unit of Mark Taylor, Michael Slater, David Boon, Allan Border and Mark and Steve Waugh.

Atherton, an intelligent man, knew that the first hand dealt to him as captain was hardly over-endowed with trumps, but his immediate response took the form of assertive leadership. After winning the toss, he led England's resistance on the opening day. In fact he was virtually England's only sustained top-order resistance, defying for 192 minutes as partners came and went. Gooch edged a bouncing outswinger, Robin Smith missed an

attempted back-foot force off Mark Waugh and then Matthew Maynard, recalled for his second Test five years to the week after his first, bat-padded to silly point. Alec Stewart offered his skipper more staunch support and smote Shane Warne for six and four off successive balls but when both fell in three balls - Stewart caught and bowled off a leading edge and Atherton stitched up by a shooter from Paul Reiffel - England were in familiar disarray at 156 for five. "You make my life hell," the Princess of Wales had bawled, that morning, at a photographer as she emerged from a screening of Jurassic Park with her two sons. England's batsmen knew the hunted feeling.

Twenty-five-year old Nasser Hussain had, since his recall for the third Test at Trent Bridge, offered a ray of hope with 71, 47 not out, 15 and 18 not out from numbers seven and eight. This time he failed, bowled by one from Reiffel which pitched off and held its line. Graham Thorpe and Emburey, with

The dynamic Shane Warne

differing amounts of recourse to the text-book, partially rebuilt the innings before Thorpe got the thinnest edges to an attempted drive. Reiffel, intelligently harnessing a strong breeze from the City End, took out the tail to become the first Australian to harvest a six-wicket haul in an Edgbaston Test.

England's cadaverous bowling attack was then sent to work and at first Australia, perhaps complacent, meandered to 80 for four. Slater was surprised by one from Such that turned big on him and ballooned a catch to short-leg. Boon was trapped by Emburey's 10th ball, Taylor was run out by Maynard's throw from long-leg and Border perished to a smart slip-catch by Hussain. When Steve Waugh was deceived by his second ball, from Such, for a split second 80 for five beckoned, but Stewart made a porridge of the stumping. A gilt-edged

chance had been missed and the Australians joyfully got on with imparting some of that heavy punishment. With Mark Waugh at his most elegant, the twins added 153. Waugh (M) stroked 18 fours in 137 from 219 balls before steering a catch to backward square-leg shortly before stumps. Australia closed at 258 for five, just 18 in arrears.

Early wickets on Saturday would have kept England in the match but, after Steve Waugh quickly edged Bicknell, Australia's middle and lower order made hay. Ian Healy, Merv Hughes and Reiffel counter-attacked, in turn voraciously, agriculturally and gratuitously, to net their team a lead of 132. By the close on Saturday, England had erased 89 of those for the loss of their new captain. They were still clinging on in the match but a horrible Sunday morning sent them tumbling headlong to defeat.

High-class spin did them in. Smith fell trying to cut a flipper and Maynard edged a straight one. Gooch attempted to pad away a Warne delivery only to be bowled behind his legs as it spun massively out of the rough. Somebody needed to play a long, long innings but Stewart was adjudged lbw and Hussain was pouched at silly mid-off. Again Thorpe and Emburey defied admirably and remained undefeated between lunch and tea but their partnership of 104 was a mere pocket of delay to Border's invincibles. When Tim May switched to the Pavilion End his first ball found Emburey's edge to

...his rearguard action ends as he is stumped for 60 off Warne

trigger the loss of three wickets for no runs in 12 balls. Bicknell was taken at short leg and Thorpe became the first man to be dismissed for 60 in an Edgbaston Test. Ilott connected once or twice with hefty swings but, when he missed with another mow at May, the Australian spinners had taken five each and Australia required 120 to win from a day plus six overs.

England needed to inflict damage on the fourth evening but Taylor and Slater survived without alarm. Both got out, early on Monday, to catches at silly mid-off but the adamantine Boon knuckled down and Mark Waugh treated Such and Emburey with little short of contempt as he cruised to 62 from 87 balls. Australia's 12th victory in 18 Tests against England was completed just after lunchtime.

Thorpe acknowleges his 50 in the second innings. Then...

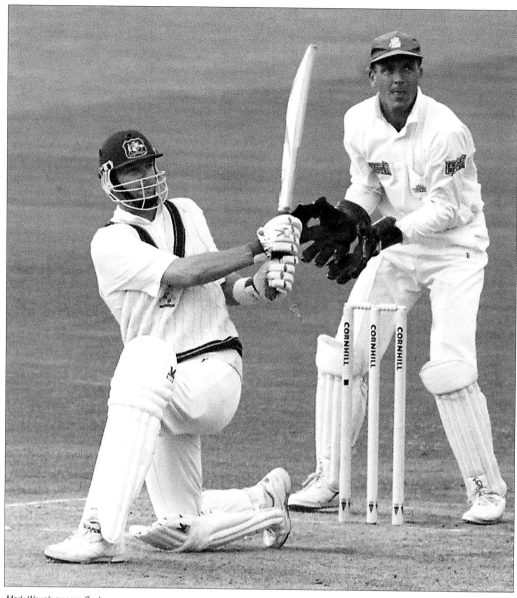

Mark Waugh sweeps Such...

By then the public address system had imparted the news of Dexter's resignation. The chairman had fallen on his sword, having steered England to just nine victories in 44 Tests. The announcement triggered a warm round of applause from the spectators but Dexter was not there to hear it. He was attending a junior tournament in Manchester allowing news of his departure to be made public at lunchtime which was, curiously, the first that Atherton knew about it.

... and duly went on to receive the Man of the Match award from Brian Johnston

Chapter 31

1995

England v West Indies July 6 1995

June 26, 1995. Lord's. Dominic Cork bowls from the Nursery End. Courtney Walsh wafts, wicket-keeper Alec Stewart accepts the catch and England have beaten West Indies by 72 runs. Cork's match-winning analysis of seven for 43 in the tourists' second innings is the best by an England player on his debut. After suffering a nine-wicket drubbing in the first Test at Headingley, Michael Atherton's team had hit back, watched by 111,938 enthralled people over the five days, at Lord's to level the series. Cork, Darren Gough and Angus Fraser had outbowled Walsh, Curtley Ambrose and Ian Bishop.

Since that defeat, the West Indians had lost by an innings to Sussex. Were the first cracks in West Indies' long-held hegemony in world cricket starting to show? Was the gulf between them and England at last starting to close? The third Test, at Edgbaston, promised to be a cracker.

That was the alluring theory. Instead, from every perspective other than that of the most partisan West Indies supporter, it proved to be a disaster. From the first ball, short of a length, from Ambrose, which steepled away down the leg-side for four wides, it was clear that here was a pitch unsuitable for Test cricket. England were swept to defeat before lunch on the third day - their quickest defeat in a home Test since they were blown away by Australian quicks Jack Gregory and Edgar McDonald inside two days at Trent Bridge in 1921. England's revival was stunted, several players were hurt, Warwickshire's credibility as a Test host was tarnished and spectators who had looked forward to a day's cricket-watching on Saturday, Sunday or Monday were denied.

England had resisted the cliché of not changing a winning side and dropped Mark Ramprakash who

Opening of the new RES Wyatt stand by Molly Wyatt

The rot sets in as Atherton is caught behind by Murray off Ambrose in the first over

bagged a pair at Lord's. Lancashire's Sydney-born batsman Jason Gallian was given his debut and the 24-year-old, along with the 20,000 crowd, watched with interest on Thursday morning as Ambrose's opening salvo from the Pavilion End exploded over Atherton's shoulder. Three balls later Ambrose's line was spot-on and Atherton edged fatally. So did Hick, to his fifth ball, which Carl Hooper fumbled in the slips only for Richie Richardson to accept the rebound.

Graham Thorpe could have been excused some caution - during the Lord's Test he spent a night in hospital after taking an accidental Walsh beamer on the helmet - but the Surrey batsman instead lifted the crowd with his positive approach. He struck five handsome fours in 46 minutes before Ambrose produced an unplayable lifter which left Thorpe with a badly bruised thumb before diverting into Sherwin Campbell's hands in the gully.

After Stewart's courageous innings ended playing across the line, in went Gallian. There have been more comfortable first Test innings. After much ducking and diving, he was rapped on the glove by another spiteful lifter at the cost of a hairline fracture of the middle finger of his right hand.

Before he had time to dwell on that pain he was bowled off bat and foot by Kenny Benjamin. Smith was at his most gutsy and stuck at it for 144 minutes but even with Ambrose forced off the field by a groin strain, this was neither a fair nor an entertaining contest. The West Indian pacemen took greedy advantage and when the innings met its early grave, extras had contributed more than eight batsmen combined.

Having mustered just 147 - their lowest score against West Indies in Birmingham - England needed to strike back quickly but Fraser, Gough, Cork and Peter Martin could not match the Caribbean fast-masters. West Indies closed on 104 for one and the one wicket that did fall owed more to the presence of two naked intruders on the field than anyone wearing whites. The streakers' presence loosened Hooper's concentration and he was caught, leg-glancing, next ball.
 Brian Lara fell immediately next morning but Campbell compiled a bracing 79 from 140 balls with 16 fours. When he was bowled by Cork, West Indies were 156 for four, only nine ahead, but, just as he had during West Indies' previous Test at Edgbaston, Richardson displayed his quality. The captain marshalled the lower order expertly and by

Richardson builds a true captain's innings

England were 63 for six. Cork, Martin (optimistically employed at number six) and Gallian were briskly turned round to chants of "What a load of rubbish" from the crowd. Smith's tenacity knew no bounds and he, along with Gough, edged the score along to 88 for six but then the final three wickets arrived in a familiar cascade. The pitch had one last souvenir to donate. Richard Illingworth had just time to sustain a broken knuckle before falling to Bishop as England, for the second time in the match, lowered their lowest score against West Indies at Edgbaston. Smith and extras combined had provided 117 out of England's pitiful match tally of 236 runs.

The inquest that sprung into immediate overdrive was two-pronged. It focused upon England's spineless batting performance but also, significantly for Warwickshire's peace of mind in terms of retaining their Test status, that pitch.

the time he was last out for 69, he had steered his side from 141 to three to 300 all out, a lead of 153. That advantage appeared more than sufficient, especially with Stewart unlikely to bat. The folly of employing a front-line batsman as wicket-keeper was manifested by Stewart damaging a finger as he dealt with a bouncer from Darren Gough.

With 17 overs to face on Friday, England promoted Smith to open and the Hampshire batsmen responded with more sturdy, if solitary, defiance. Walsh plucked out Atherton's middle stump. Ian Bishop, still obtaining steep bounce, took out Hick who retreated from a lifter and gloved it into the slips. Thorpe slashed at a wide one and, although Cork held on as night-watchman, the match was speeding to an outrageously early conclusion. On Friday night, England dined on 59 for three (Smith 33, Cork 15) - still requiring 94 to avoid an innings defeat.

Before the occupants of the Rea Bank Stand had downed their first two tinnies on Saturday morning,

A rare success for England as Campbell is bowled by Cork for 79

Poised for the next victim...

Michael Hurst, chairman of the county's grounds committee, insisted that Warwickshire had nothing to reproach themselves for. "We were asked by the England selection committee, through Ray Illingworth, to induce as much pace and bounce as we could," he said. "Ray asked us to do it and we obliged." Atherton had a different view. "The fault for the game ending in this brief period is in the hands of the Edgbaston club for producing such a pitch," said the captain while West Indies manager

...and another one falls as Atherton loses his middle stump

The gallant Smith avoids another bouncer

Edgbaston becomes a large picnic area as the match finishes early on the third day

Wes Hall responded with the confidence of a man who knows his armoury is superior. "You prepare the pitches," he said, "and we'll play on them. We'll play in the car park if necessary,"

It was left to BBC commentator Richie Benaud to look beyond the pitch and pinpoint the bitter truth that England did not want to hear. "England's batsmen," said Benaud, "with the exception of Robin Smith, were pathetic in both innings."

Chapter 32

1996

England v India June 6 1996

After the 1995 debacle, Warwickshire were under pressure to provide a surface suitable for Test cricket when India visited for the first Test of the summer of 1996. There was a partial improvement. Two weeks before the match, a strip originally earmarked for use was rejected as unsatisfactory.

While the second choice transpired to be better than the 1995 vintage, it was a long way from perfect. Again, the match failed to reach a fifth day or even a fourth afternoon but, while the Edgbaston square only partially regained its credibility, Nasser Hussain seized the opportunity to give his an enormous boost.

Azharuddin is bowled by Mullally for 0

Srinath takes the attack to England

34 months and 27 Tests after his Test career had been consigned to limbo following a duck against Australia at The Oval. Nick Knight was back for his third Test and first on his home ground. Back too came Chris Lewis while there were debuts for Ronnie Irani, Alan Mullally and Min Patel. India, also in deep transition, included four debutants - Sunil Joshi, Paras Mhambrey, Venkatesh Prasad and Vikram Rathore. Of the two stranger-filled dressing-rooms, England ended the match much the happier - and happiest of all was Hussain.

Against the country of his birth, the 28-year-old was allocated England's troublesome number three slot, something of a poisoned chalice having failed to yield a century in 32 innings. However, all Hussain had to do on the opening day was field as England dominated from the moment that Mohammad Azharuddin unwisely chose to bat on a pitch offering assistance to the seamers. By 5pm, India were dismissed for 214 following a catalogue of careless work from their top order. None of the top eight batsmen reached 25, with the biggest bonus arriving for England when the crown prince of Indian cricket, Sachin Tendulkar, perished uncharacteristically playing across the line, to Dominic Cork. Azaruddhin was ousted by Irani's fifth delivery in Test cricket, a leg-stump half-volley which the batsman flicked crisply off his legs only for Knight to execute a stunning catch as the ball seared beyond him. Only a violent 52 from 65 balls from Javagal Srinath averted complete capitulation to England's reshaped attack. The home side closed the day in command after Knight and skipper Michael Atherton eased to 60 without loss in 19 overs.

When Knight fell straight away on Friday morning, Hussain's chance to kick-start his staccato Test career had arrived. Early on he scratched about desperately and appeared perpetually about to perish but fortune was on his side. He had scored only three when, in one Srinath over, he was dropped at short-leg then narrowly survived a mishook to fine-leg. Doggedly, the Essex batsman struggled on, scoring from only seven of his first 60 balls, and then at 14 came his big slice of luck. He appeared to glove a leg-side catch to wicket-keeper Nayan Mongia, again off the impressive Srinath but, to the Indians' disbelief, survived. Hussain ignored his unjust escape, stayed focused and, fortified by

The England set-up, both on and off the field, was in a state of considerable flux. Ray Illingworth was still chairman of selectors but had resigned as manager in March following England's ignominious World Cup quarter-final defeat to Sri Lanka in Faisalabad. David Lloyd was newly installed as coach and had begun promisingly. Galvanised by his infectious enthusiasm, a much-changed England team opened the summer with a 2-0 Texaco Trophy triumph over the Indians.

For the opening Test, England's XI showed sweeping changes from that humiliated by 10 wickets by South Africa in the final Test at Cape Town at the start of the year. Out went Alec Stewart, Robin Smith, Angus Fraser, Devon Malcolm, Peter Martin and Mike Watkinson. Hussain was recalled

INDIAN TOURING TEAM TO ENGLAND 1996

M.Azaruddin Cpt

S.Tendulker

N.Hirwani

V.Rathau

A.Kumble

B.Prasad

J.Srinath

S.Raju

A.Jadeya

S.Manjrekar

S.Ganguly

R.Dravid

P.Mahbry

N.Mongia

England celebrate Tendulkar's first-innings dismissal by Cork

the lunch break, began to middle the ball. In the afternoon, an ugly duckling of an innings matured into a very fine knock indeed. It was just as well for England that it did because meaningful support was slow to arrive.

Valuable assistance was supplied only by the debutants. Irani thrashed 34 from 34 balls then after Jack Russell, Lewis and Cork were removed in the space of eight balls, Patel batted stoutly for 13 overs in a ninth-wicket partnership of 49. When Patel became Anil Kumble's belated first victim,

Hussain celebrates his maiden Test century

Hussain still required seven runs to reach his maiden Test century. Mullally played straight and stayed patient though and Hussain's watershed century arrived from his 193rd ball. He had advanced to 128 in 309 minutes, from 227 balls including 18 fours and a six, when he finally hooked Srinath into the hands of substitute fielder Rahul Dravid at long-leg. The tenth wicket, like the ninth, added 49 to assure England a lead of 99.

That advantage rapidly increased in value as India, five without loss overnight, collapsed to 68 for five on Saturday morning. The exception to another clueless batting display was Tendulkar who expiated his first-innings lapse by compiling one of the great Test centuries at Edgbaston. Having taken early care on a difficult, deteriorating surface, the 23-year-old announced his demand for the initiative with five fours in two overs from Irani. The 18,000

Mullally ousts Mongia

Irani catches the eye on his debut

crowd were then treated to a masterpiece. Tendulkar compiled a glorious century – his ninth in Tests – brimming with exquisite strokes while his team-mates floundered against Cork, Mullally and Lewis. Tendulkar finally perished, for 122 from 176 balls with 19 fours and a six, to a mishook neatly pouched by Thorpe running back from mid-wicket and by Saturday night the match was done and dusted. England, chasing a target of 121, were 73 for the loss of Knight, adjudged lbw by umpire Darrell Hair, although the ball appeared to be travelling too high.

Hussain joined Atherton to ensure there would be no Saturday evening collapse and, although the Essex batsman added just a single on Sunday before hooking Prasad to long-leg, Thorpe joined his captain to ease England to victory before Sunday lunch. India's away record – just one victory in 29 away Tests – continued to dive, England were optimistic that, under Lloyd, their fortunes were about to soar and Warwickshire had, pitch-wise, bought themselves some time.

Tendulkar acknowledges his century, one of the finest innings of Edgbaston's Test history

Chapter 33

1997

England v Australia June 5 1997

Test cricket has dimensions and depths that no other sport can match. At its best it offers the audience hour after hour, day after day of twists, quirks, nuances and complexities laced with feats of skill, strength, spirit and fortune from members of both winning and losing sides. The best Tests are tales unparalleled in sport; epics brimming with pathos and permutation as big issues thrillingly unfold, surrounded by dozens of fascinating minor issues.

Australia's visit to Edgbaston in 1997 was such a story. It had everything. Surprise by the barrowload. Heroics from members of the victorious team. A truly uplifting innings in defeat. Great theatre. Great sport.

Edgbaston's was the opening Test of the Ashes series and the reconvening of the old adversaries attracted 19,000 people on the first morning. England's supporters arrived in a state of familiar resignation. Australia were firm favourites. The home country's followers could only hope that their team would at least put up a fight this time - at least bloody Australia's nose before declining to defeat. Logic suggested that it would be another Ashes series, another tale of Australian domination, but England's supporters lived in hope.

They must have been good hopers. Twenty overs into the first day, Australia were 54 for eight. If that left the home supporters suspecting that a collective fantasy was unfolding, their delirium only

Two of the greats Thomson and Lillee coaching would-be fast bowlers

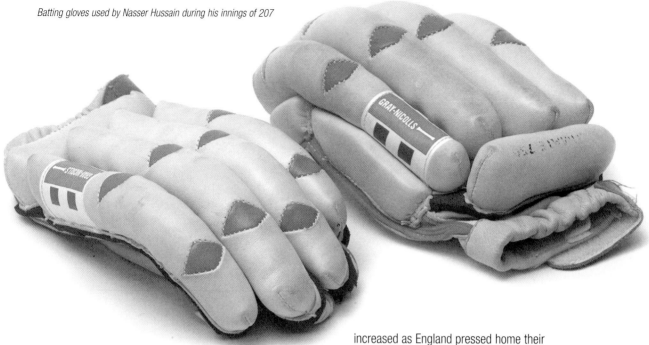

Batting gloves used by Nasser Hussain during his innings of 207

Stewart hurries England to victory

increased as England pressed home their advantage. By the close of the first day England, having dismissed the Aussies for 118, were 200 for three. Dreamland, surely - the real McCoy would start tomorrow. In fact England were to see the job all the way through.

The first day will forever stand as one of the most mesmeric and memorable instalments of Test cricket at Edgbaston or anywhere else. After Australia won the toss they were devastated by disciplined and aggressive work by seam-bowlers obeying the golden rule; pitch it up. The strip offered some help but, in overcast conditions, it was swing that did the damage.

Matthew Elliott was its first victim as a big inswinger from Darren Gough seared through his gate in the fifth over. In the next, captain Mark Taylor's horrible sequence of form – 20 Test innings without a half-century – continued when he sliced Devon Malcolm to debutant Mark Butcher at second slip. Gough bowled Mark Waugh with another inswinger then turned his attention to Greg Blewett. A perfect off-cutter bowled the South Australian middle and off only to be called no-ball. The next delivery was an equally good leg-cutter which was edged to Nasser Hussain at third slip.

Caddick got busy from the Pavilion End and successive deliveries leapt from a length to induce edges from Steve Waugh and Ian Healy. Michael Bevan sent a looping catch off Malcolm to Mark Ealham in the gully and when Jason Gillespie was trapped by Caddick it was 12.36pm. About that, England's ecstatic supporters cared not a fig. They cared rather more that Australia were an

A vital wicket in the second innings as Steve Waugh is lbw to Gough

astonishing 54 for eight. Shane Warne hit eight fours in a rumbustious 47 from 46 balls but when he sliced Caddick into Malcolm's mitts at third man, Australia were all out for 118. A disbelieving audience stood to applaud England from the field - but what would their batsmen, confronted by Glenn McGrath and Co, do in 56 overs before the close. Was this to be a 20-wickets-in-a-day scenario?

That looked possible when Michael Atherton and Butcher perished to fine deliveries and Alec Stewart top-edged a pull. At an uneasy 50 for three, Hussain and Thorpe came together with the day's play still finely balanced. To the crowd's rapture, the batsmen responded with authority and style. They added 64 in 19 overs before tea and then, as Australia's attack was depleted by the loss of Jason Gillespie with a hamstring injury, took control. England closed at 200 for three - 82 ahead - with Hussain 80 and Thorpe 83.

On Thursday night, throughout England in pubs and clubs, in bedrooms and lounges, over kitchen tables and garden fences, in parks, on trains, down mines and in cavernous, steam-filled industrial cleaning

plants, a historic day's cricket was discussed. Reality checks were taken. This being England, of course, they would, even now, mess it up. Both batsmen would perish early on Friday and the eventual lead would be about 150.

Not a bit of it. Hussain and Thorpe added another 138 runs in two hours on Friday morning. Ruthlessly punitive of the bad ball, they extended their partnership to 288 in 294 minutes, surpassing England's previous fourth-wicket record against Australia - Wally Hammond and Eddie Paynter's 222 at Lord's in 1938. Thorpe was finally caught at mid-on and John Crawley, padded up for almost five hours, fatally edged his 14th delivery but Hussain continued fluently. He spanked three fours in an over from Warne before the spinner finally got his man with a textbook leg-break. Hussain's 207, spanning 337 balls with 38 fours, was his highest score in all cricket. Thorpe's 138 (245 deliveries, 19 fours) was his best Test score. While they rested their weary plates in the evening session, Mark Ealham and Robert Croft eased England to 449 for six at the close.

Thorpe reaches his century

On Saturday came that injection of reality. Australia began their second innings at 11.45am with the Rea Bank Stand in full voice, demanding that England lay more heroics before them. Elliott and Taylor, however, were resolute. Taylor battled heroically through his confidence-crisis as both batsmen contributed 66 to an opening-stand of 133 before Elliott, facing Croft, played down the Northern Line when the ball was on the Bakerloo. Blewett was soon into his stride as his captain gradually reacquainted himself with long-lost fluency. The immensely popular Taylor reached the most gallant of centuries just before the close, at which Australia were 256 for one.

Taylor acknowledges his 100 as Australia fight to save the match

On the fourth morning, it appeared that England would not, after all, finish the job as the captain and Blewett extended their partnership to 194. A chink of light appeared when Croft caught and bowled Taylor to end the captain's vigil at four minutes under five hours. The Glamorgan spinner then ousted Blewett off bat and pad and Gough returned to strike two massive blows, dismissing Bevan with Hussain's assistance in the gully and Mark Waugh with a lifter off a length. Shortly before 3pm, Australia were into a wobble at 399 for five, only 39 ahead with five wickets down, when a thunderstorm broke over Birmingham. Just as England had broken through again, would their victory charge be washed away?

Atherton leaves the field at Edgbaston after England's triumph

The interruption lasted 50 minutes after which Steve Waugh dug in again until he was trapped by Gough. Healy and Warne also defied hard and it seemed that England would have to sweat for every wicket but Healy's departure to Ealham triggered the loss of the last four wickets for 12 runs in 16 balls. In 15 crazy minutes of collapse, Australia threw away almost 10 hours of resistance from their top order and England were presented with a target of 118 in more than a day.

They required less than 22 overs as, aware of a dodgy weather forecast, the top three attacked vigorously. Butcher crashed 14 off 10 balls, Atherton gathered 57 from 65 and Stewart 40 from 54 to compete one of Test cricket's most sensational victories. England were overjoyed. Warwickshire were delighted because the much-maligned pitch had played well and Australia, while well-beaten, were dignified and far from downhearted in defeat. They radiated inner-strength almost as if they knew they would come back to win the series - which, of course, they did.

Hussain had truly come of age for England

Chapter 34

1998

England v South Africa June 4 1998

On June 14, 1960, South African batsmen John Waite and Neil Adcock trudged off the Edgbaston turf, Adcock having just been bowled by Brian Statham to complete his country's 100-run defeat. It is not recorded whether either man said to the other, as they passed through the pavilion's gleaming picket gates; "Y'know, mate, I think it might be 38 long years before our boys play a Test match here again." If either did, their partner would probably have rubbished the notion but, in fact, it would have been spot-on. When South Africa, following their exile from Test cricket, next paid a Test visit to Birmingham, Waite and Adcock were aged 68 and 67 respectively. Neither made the team.

Allan Donald did, though, to provide emotional weight to what transpired to be one of Edgbaston's less inspiring Test occasions. Donald, as great a team man as fast-bowler, had become Warwickshire's favourite adopted son, having served the county brilliantly, on and off, since 1987. To him went the honour of delivering the opening ball of the match but there were to be no home-ground heroics from 'Big Al' in a match of low momentum, which concluded in total anti-climax.

On the first day England, put in, ground to 249 for one from 92 overs. Michael Atherton closed his mind to the devastating news that Ginger Spice had quit the Spice Girls and concentrated hard to prove that his appetite for runs remained unimpaired by

Warwickshire's South Africans Bob Woolmer, Shaun Pollock, Brian Macmillan and Allan Donald

The end of Atherton's 103, caught by Boucher off Donald

his recent resignation as captain. To the delight of new skipper Alec Stewart (and head groundsman Steve Rouse) Atherton and Mark Butcher piled up an opening stand of 179, England's best first-wicket offering in any Test since Atherton and Graham Gooch's 203 against Australia at Adelaide in 1990.

The pitch was no shirt-front. There was assistance for the seamers but much of the bowling, although brisk (Donald and Lance Klusener averaged 84mph and Shaun Pollock 82mph) was ill-directed. When Butcher (77 from 214 balls) swept to square-leg, Stewart strode in at number three because the wicket happened to fall just as intended number three Nasser Hussain was busy having a number two. Stewart quickly settled alongside Atherton who reached his 12th Test century just before the close.

An ideal foundation had been set.

While England built upon that base throughout Friday their work, against much-improved bowling, was too slow. Importantly, the tourists quickly removed Atherton, who edged a Donald lifter in the second over of the morning. Stewart and Hussain added 60 in 23 overs but, after Stewart edged to first slip and Hussain was, not for the first or last time in Test cricket, torpedoed by a shooter, the rest of the batting was torpid. Throughout the afternoon, slow left-arm Paul Adams bottled up the run-flow from the City End with a 17-over spell which cost 26 runs. Mark Ealham's five runs occupied 39 balls. Ramprakash and Cork added 55 at two an over. "Get on with it" yelled an occupant of the Rea Bank Stand. "Get your finger out," advised another. "It's

Adams delivers in unique style

Six for Rhodes off Fraser

Lance Klusener lets fly

better to think you're half dry than to know you're all wet," offered another, obscurely. England's slow progress reduced, rather than drove home, their advantage and their day received an unwelcome late twist when Darren Gough was struck on the glove by a rising ball from Donald. X-rays confirmed a broken index finger, ruling the Yorkshireman out of the rest of the match.

When South Africa's reply began at the start of Saturday, all attention was focused on the figure of

263 required to avoid the follow-on. The day began well for England as Gerhardus Liebenberg bat-padded to Derbyshire's Ben Spendlove (fielding as substitute for Gough) and Gary Kirsten sliced to Butcher at third slip. 38 for two. Jacques Kallis and Darryl Cullinan provided sterner obstacles and with every minute of their resistance came a strengthening of the suspicion that England would regret their dilatory progress on Friday. Hope stirred as Cork ousted Kallis and Hansie Cronje in the space of seven balls. When Angus Fraser bowled

Kallis departs, caught by Stewart

Daryll Cullinan just before the close, South Africa were 191 for five, still with work to do to avoid that follow-on.

They began on Sunday still needing another 71 with five wickets in hand. Fraser quickly removed Pollock and Mark Boucher but Jonty Rhodes found a robust partner in Lance Klusener. The latter's 57 included 11 fours in an eighth-wicket partnership of 104 which closed when Rhodes' stay was finally ended after 156 balls by the busy Fraser. England's lead was eventually pared down to 119.

The sense of adventure which had been so woefully lacking in England's first innings now manifested itself in their second. Thorpe (43 from 59 balls) and Stewart (28 from 34) led the quest for quick runs so that, by the close on Sunday, they had stretched their advantage to 289. Stewart immediately declared to leave his bowlers an entire day to dismiss the opposition. With the pitch expected to offer assistance to the spin of Robert Croft as well as the seamers, the South Africans would have their work cut out.

In fact, their survival was made straightforward by rain which was forecast for late morning but arrived early. As the English Midlands went through their diverse Monday motions, England's players could only prowl the dressing-room hoping for the clouds to clear. Amid scenes of great joy at West Midlands Safari Park, Zena the zebra was born. There was delight, too, for the children of Bromsgrove and Redditch who, a report revealed, possessed the healthiest teeth in the region (a remarkable 0.54 missing, filled or decayed teeth per child). Across Birmingham and beyond, factories screamed, buses rumbled, tills pinged, memos were circulated, music blared and birds sang and from the Robert Jones and Agnes Hunt Orthopaedic Hospital, near Oswestry, came an urgent plea for a mate for their sex-starved peacock Percy but, at Edgbaston, still it rained and another was added to the list of fascinating Test match finishes not to have unfolded.

Chapter 35

1999

England v New Zealand July 1 1999

The 1999 visit of New Zealand to Edgbaston was a Test match played in fast-forward mode. It was all over early on Saturday afternoon, 33 wickets having fallen in 216.1 overs and 21 having tumbled on the second day. Bowlers raced in and whooped with delight. Batsmen came and went like ducks on a shooting-range. It was hectic, helter-skelter cricket which, although the clatter of wickets owed much to bad batting, did nothing to quieten nagging arguments over the merits of the Edgbaston square. Still, it was entertaining stuff in a slapstick sort of way and several players will, for varying reasons, long remember the occasion. Into the madcap mish-mash of Nasser Hussain's first Test as England captain did Alex Tudor, Chris Read and Roger Twose, in particular, sprinkle their own pinch of pathos.

A disappointing return for Twose, out third ball to Mullally

Caddick celebrates

Doull's counter-attack is over, stumped off Tufnell

Twose's was first into the pot. Twelve months earlier, Warwickshire's members had welcomed one of their most cherished adopted sons – Allan Donald – back as a Test opponent. This time it was the turn of Twose, whose versatile and combative talents had featured so prominently in the Bears' glory years of the early-to-mid 90s. The left-hander had quit Warwickshire in 1995 to settle in New Zealand so here was a poignant return for the 31-year-old and proudly did he stride, across the turf he had trod so often before, to open the batting on the first morning. Ruefully did he retrace his steps two minutes later, having edged Alan Mullally's third delivery to Graham Thorpe in the slips. That set the tone for two days of batting mayhem, to which the only appropriate musical accompaniment would have been 'Yakety Sax'.

Thorpe was busied twice more in the cordon to send Stephen Fleming (Thorpe's 50th catch for England) and Craig McMillan on their way. A succession of batsmen hinted at longevity but were then guilty of poor strokes, most notably Nathan Astle who thrashed at a wide one from Mark Butcher to supply the bowler with his first Test

wicket and the catcher, wicket-keeper Read, with his first Test catch. Read's opposite number Adam Parore, reprieved by Stewart on seven, organised a fightback from 104 for six with a pugnacious 73 from 140 balls but when he nicked Mullally from the last ball of the day, England considered their job well done. All the seamers had taken wickets and Phil Tufnell did just what any captain likes his spinner to do – outwit the tail. New Zealand, all out for 226.

If Thursday had offered any watching youngsters – although there were not too many, with the ground barely half-full - some classic vignettes of feckless batting, Friday brought a masterclass in it. For only the fourth time in Test history, both sides lost 10 wickets in a day. By the 11th over England's batsmen had undone their bowlers' good work by folding to 33 for four. Alec Stewart, in his 87th Test, fell offering no stroke to his third ball. Butcher was run out by yards after his enthusiasm for a sharp single was not shared by Hussain, who then received a pearler from Simon Doull which pitched middle and hit off. Thorpe edged Geoff Allott.

Astle becomes the first Test victim of both Butcher and Read

Mark Ramprakash troubled the scorers only to inscribe 26 dots beside his name and then a 'W' when he edged Chris Cairns. Leicestershire's Aftab Habib, on his debut, managed 25 dots and a single before leaving the gate wide open at the expense of his wicket. After Read was caught in the gully, Andrew Caddick and Tudor, having come together at 45 for seven, roused the crowd with a partnership of 70 in 19 overs but England still faced a first-innings deficit of 100.

Out again to open went Twose. His first ball, from Caddick, thumped into pad and back trudged the former Warwickshire man with a pair to his name. Caddick and Mullally then tore through the papery batting as batsman after batsman showed a

Nash is caught by an acrobatic Hussain

disinclination to leave the ball outside off-stump. Read enjoyed a dream debut as New Zealanders kept nibbling and nicking. Hours earlier, the crowd had shaken their heads as England slumped to 45 for seven. Now they cheered their socks off as the tourists hurtled to 52 for eight.

Fleming watched in despair from the non-striker's end until joined by Doull whose positive approach helped to add 54 in 12 overs with his captain. It was the buoyant Read who, in alliance with Tufnell, ousted both men. When the young Nottinghamshire keeper terminated Doull's innings of 46 from 50

balls with an adroit stumping, England opened their second innings on the same day they had opened their first. In the first three innings of this bizarre match the only four scores greater than 30 had come from non-specialist batsmen; Parore, Caddick, Tudor and Doull. The specialists' nightmare continued when England were left with five overs to face before the close. Although only seven balls were possible before bad light stopped play, one of them, a yorker from Allott, did for Stewart.

England began on Saturday morning with two batsmen still to settle at the crease – Butcher on three and Tudor still to score – and requiring another 205 runs from a minimum of 278 overs. In the light of the batting ordeals so far in the game, a close call, many thought. Yet miraculously the fog in which batsmen had appeared to operate for two days lifted and Tudor could be seen despatching the ball to all parts. The cloud cover dissipated to assist the batsmen but New Zealand's bowlers were instruments of their own downfall by serving up four-balls galore. Tudor and Butcher added 73 in 17 overs for the second wicket and Tudor and Hussain 98 in 19 for the third. Hussain's 44 occupied only 57 balls yet he was outscored by the rampant Surrey fast-bowler. As the tourists wilted, the only question left to answer was whether 21-year-old Tudor would reach a remarkable century in only his third Test.

Tudor reaches his maiden Test half century

When Thorpe arrived at the crease with 34 required, he was quick to ask his Surrey team-mate if he wanted him to take it easy but Tudor said no; victory was all that mattered. Thorpe duly galloped to 21 in 21 balls and, as England closed in on their target, Tudor found himself on 95 with the scores level. Facing McMillan, he went for the requisite six but could only top-edge a four over the wicket-keeper's head. Tudor was left stranded on 99, from 119 balls with 21 fours, the highest innings by an England nightwatchman, superceding Harold Larwood's 98 against Australia in Sydney in 1933. It was an appropriately quirky conclusion to one of Edgbaston's strangest Tests.

Hussain's quick fire 44 is over

2000

England v West Indies June 15 2000

Courtney Walsh and Curtley Ambrose had already spent 12 years terrorising batsmen in Test cricket when they arrived at Edgbaston with West Indies in 2000. It was the opening contest of their valedictory series in England and, according to one or two sages in the English press, the pair were fading, if not spent, forces. As a team, those sages added, West Indies were a shadow of their former selves and arrived at Edgbaston vulnerable and ready to suffer their first series defeat to England since 1969. That was the theory.

Walsh and Ambrose had, however, spent their fast-bowling careers writing their own scripts and, at the ages of 37 and 36 respectively, had no intention of playing bit parts in somebody else's production. England were brushed aside in three days and this time the early finish had nothing to do with the pitch. It was simply a case of fallible batting torn apart by great fast-bowling.

After England were inserted by West Indies captain Jimmy Adams, all went well for 13 overs. As Walsh and Ambrose loosened up, Michael Atherton and

People will do anything to get a seat!

Knight of Warwickshire and England

Mark Ramprakash advanced the score to 26 - hardly comfortable but so far so good. Then Walsh delivered an in-ducker which Ramprakash inside-edged, via pad, into the hands of Wavell Hinds at short-leg. The bowler had his 450th Test wicket and England were 26 for one. Fifteen overs later they were 57 for four and there were familiar Caribbean high-fives and grins all over the place.

While Ambrose applied constant pressure, Walsh quickly harvested victims 451 and 452 as Atherton fished outside off-stump and Graeme Hick sliced into the slip cordon. Ambrose's reward arrived when Alec Stewart played on. Nasser Hussain and Nick Knight dug in courageously, if never convincingly. Hussain eked 15 runs from two hours before gloving Franklyn Rose to wicket-keeper Ridley Jacobs. Knight prised 26 runs, mostly to third man, from 85 minutes before edging Reon King to first slip. Former Warwickshire captain Brian Lara accepted that catch and another in the next over when Andrew Flintoff nibbled at Walsh. When another fine delivery ousted Robert Croft, Walsh had secured his 20th five-wicket haul in Tests - less than a month after harvesting his 18th and 19th, against Pakistan at Barbados and Antigua.

Andrew Caddick and Darren Gough toughed it out for a while but their partnership of 39 was terminated when the former called the latter for a quick single. "Good running," ventured a straw-hat wearer in the Press Box Stand only for that opinion to be exposed as crass and reckless as Jacobs whipped off a glove and threw Gough out by a yard. Ed Giddins, the 11th Warwickshire player to represent England in an Edgbaston Test, recorded the expected duck when he skied an attempted pull and those harbingers of West Indian doom were looking sheepishly at an England total of 179.

West Indies had 19 overs to face on Thursday night and England needed to strike quickly. They did so –

Gough's 11th ball earned a marginal lbw decision against Chris Gayle and when Hinds fell to Caddick, the tourists were wobbling at 24 for two. Lara, greeted by boos among the grudging applause from the home members, reined in his aggressive instincts to help Sherwin Campbell steer the tourists through to the close without further loss. At 50 for two, overnight, they had, courtesy of the old maestros, total control.

West Indies started briskly on Friday when 24 runs arrived from the first four overs. Campbell soon passed 50 from 88 balls and Lara smashed Giddins for 21 runs in 18 balls as England failed to match the collective pressure which the West Indies bowlers had imposed. Increasingly did they look to Gough for inspiration. The Yorkshireman responded first by bowling Campbell through the gate then softening up Lara with two short deliveries before luring him, with a ball of fuller length, into a fatal drive. With West Indies 136 for four – still 43 behind - the door was ajar for England. Shivnarine Chanderpaul and Adams slammed it shut, first with caution - only 27 runs arrived in an hour after lunch

West Indies celebrate Walsh's 450th Test Wicket

Two of the all-time greats Ambrose and Walsh embrace

– then aggression. Chanderpaul climbed with particular relish into the overpitching Caddick before Flintoff found his edge to end a perky contribution of 73 from 119 balls with 11 fours. Jacobs soon edged Caddick but Adams, like his predecessors Viv Richards and Richie Richardson in the Tests of 1991 and 1995, laid a true captain's innings before the Birmingham punters. His first three hours at the crease having yielded just one boundary, he now accelerated and a driven three off Giddins took him to 50 from 169 balls. Culpably, England failed to remove his less vaunted partners. Ambrose survived for 83 minutes, despite a short-pitched barrage from Gough, and Rose then settled in alongside his captain, hoisted Croft for a massive straight six and advanced to 33 by the close. Adams was 66 overnight with his team 336 for seven - 157 in front.

On Saturday morning West Indies added another 61 before Adams, having prolonged his resistance to 299 balls and 391 minutes, fell, two short of a century, to an acrobatic catch by Flintoff low at cover. The scene was set for a rearguard action by the home side and as the ale flowed in the Rea Bank Stand the Dambusters tune led a medley of raucous, patriotic songs. England's batsmen

responded with a nosedive to 14 for three.
All three wickets fell to Walsh - at an age when most fast-bowlers dwell only in nostalgia, the Jamaican was simply unstoppable. He pinned Ramprakash lbw, located Hussain's edge and then sentenced Hick to his first first-class pair, albeit with some assistance from umpire Srinny Venkat who adjudged caught-behind when the Worcestershire batsman appeared to evade a lifter. Walsh didn't care about that as he went off to graze with figures of three for 10 in 10 overs. He was enjoying one of the greatest matches of his great career. The bowling of his long-time comrade suffered nothing by comparison; Ambrose was destined to take just a single wicket in the match but played a significant part in another crushing victory for his team.

Even when Walsh rested, there was no respite for England. Stewart played on for the second time in the match and a union of 36 in 10 overs by Atherton and Knight constituted little more than the doomed squawking of a turkey on Christmas Eve. Atherton dragged an attempted cut onto his stumps and Flintoff was bowled neck and crop by King before Hinds, at short-leg, found himself central to the next three wickets. He swooped to catch Croft, Caddick and finally Knight who, having survived the pace barrage for exactly three hours, was caught off pad and glove off the rather less fearsome

Here we go again...thinks David Graveney

Ramprakash, at silly point

Rare joy for England as Lara goes

Chanderpaul and Adams during their vital stand

Adams. On his way back to the pavilion, Knight passed Warwickshire team-mate Giddins who survived 16 balls before a slow yorker from the West Indian captain completed his pair. England's meek surrender was complete. The Dambusters were grounded and silent.

Chapter 37

2001

England v Australia July 5 2001

Most 99-year-olds, bless 'em, are sedate old dears. Some are still quick-minded, articulate and thoroughly good company but incapable, in the main, of providing an explosive cavalcade of spectacular surprises and thrills. That is just not the average 99-year-old's cup of tea. It is, however, exactly what Edgbaston's Test history unveiled as it reached that ripe old age.

Australia's visit for the opening Test of 2001 began with one of the most amazing days of cricket ever to unfold in the history of this or, as far as we know, any other world. The Aussies knew all about opening-day extravagance at Edgbaston, of course - remember 1997 and 54 for eight before lunch. This time they hit back during six hours of rip-roaring, knockabout cricket of a momentum and intensity which one-day cricket, with its contrived nature, could never match. A staggering day brought 427 runs including 234 in boundaries, a breathtaking last-wicket stand and a post-tea onslaught of withering proportions.

The first session was plain. After Nasser Hussain lost England's 12th Ashes toss out of 13, Marcus Trescothick edged Jason Gillespie's first ball to first slip but Michael Atherton and Mark Butcher added 104 in 24 overs. The introduction of Shane Warne, at 106 for one, lit the touch-paper. To the leg-spinner's second ball, Butcher eased forward and gloved a catch to Ricky Ponting at short cover. 106 for two. Twenty-eight overs later England were 191 for nine.

That special Ashes atmosphere

Lee celebrates as Ward is dismissed

When the rock that was Atherton crumbled, after assembling 57 runs from 107 balls, to a catch at second slip, a familiar procession ensued. Hussain fatally offered no stroke to Glenn McGrath. Surrey's Ian Ward, in his third Test, managed 50 minutes at the crease before his defence was burst asunder by McGrath. Warne then wickedly confronted debutant Usman Afzaal with a superb leg-break and hurried through the lower middle order with four wickets in 22 balls. Ashley Giles' first Test innings on his home ground brought seven runs from 13 deliveries before he was caught, cutting, by wicket-keeper Adam Gilchrist.

At 191 for nine, with the innings in subsidence, the packed crowd were resigned to another English implosion as Andrew Caddick loped out to join Alec Stewart. A sensational hour followed as the last-wicket pair lashed 103 - only the fourth last-wicket century stand in Ashes history - from 13 overs. Caddick hammered 49 from 40 balls, including seven fours and a six, and was blazing away handsomely when Stewart perished, trapped by McGrath for 65 from 82 balls with nine fours. The last-wicket pair left the field to a tumultuous ovation.

Australia's response was simply glorious. The first hint that they were not fazed by that onslaught arrived from the first ball of their innings. Darren Gough dropped it short and Michael Slater thrashed it

Stewart reaches 50

to the point boundary. The next ball was pummelled to the fence in the same direction and, at the end of Gough's over, Australia were 18 for 0. Gough and Caddick, ring-rusty having been rested from early-season county games, continued to pitch short and Slater and Matthew Hayden took advantage to add 98 in 15 overs. Giles, hurried into the attack as the fast-bowlers were flayed, dismissed Hayden with the assistance of Craig White's wonderful diving catch at mid-wicket. Gough then trapped Ponting but, by the close, Australia had charged to 133 for two from 22 overs. Slater had compiled a scintillating 76 from 77 balls. What an innings. What a day.

On Friday morning there was immediate joy for the majority of another capacity 20,000 crowd as Gough's first ball bowled Slater through the gate. That brought in Steve Waugh to join his twin Mark, however, and between interruptions for rain and bad light, the brothers quietly tightened Australia's grip on the game. They added 133 in 40 overs and after Mark, never at his most fluent, edged Caddick, Steve smoothed on to his 26th Test century. At the close he was unbeaten on 101 out of 332 for four, his team 38 ahead.

Steve Waugh acknowledges his 100

Again on Saturday morning, Gough struck early, ousting Steve Waugh, to give the home supporters a crumb of hope and again that crumb was ruthlessly swept away by the tourists. Between further stoppages for rain - the covers took the form of groundsheets only following an early-season Brumbrella breakdown - Damien Martyn and Adam Gilchrist plundered 160 from 34 overs to expose the folly of England's selection of only four specialist bowlers. Martyn's 105, his maiden Test century, spanned 222 balls and included 15 fours before it was snuffed out by the unlikely device of Butcher's slow-mediums. Martyn lifted to cover to trigger the Surrey batsman's day in the Test limelight as a bowler as he winkled out four wickets for five runs. Warne and Brett Lee sliced to slip and Gillespie missed a straight one. McGrath, however, survived and Butcher was to be punished for his temerity.

Gilchrist, on 93 when McGrath arrived, helped a Caddick bouncer over the wicket-keeper's head to reach his century from 118 balls. He celebrated by inflicting upon Butcher the most expensive over by an English bowler in Ashes history – 22 runs

Head for cover - even this incredible match could not evade the rain

(606460). It was an enchanting display of uninhibited hitting - 152 from 143 balls, including 20 fours and five sixes – and when it ended with a catch at long-on, the last-wicket partnership had yielded 63 in eight overs. McGrath's share of that 63 was just a single. Gilchrist had lodged one of the great Test innings at Edgbaston and received a standing ovation. Caddick's analysis, 36-0-163-1,

Exit Steve Waugh but Australia were soon piling on more punishment

The vultures gather

Mark Waugh. Gough completed a pair and when Giles edged to slip, an innings-and-118 runs defeat was secured. All the English supporters could do was rise to applaud the Australian team who took a lap of honour to field the acclaim of the supporters of the country they had just thrashed.

remains the most expensive by an England bowler on the ground.

Australia, all out 576, led by 282 and McGrath struck a colossal psychological blow with his ninth delivery when Atherton edged to Mark Waugh at second slip. Trescothick and Butcher took England to 48 for one by the close and resisted brightly for a while on Sunday morning when they added another 51 in 11 overs. Butcher then nicked a brute of a delivery from Lee and when another lifter, from Gillespie, struck Hussain on the glove, the captain was forced to retire. He headed off to nurse a broken finger and watch his ship sink without trace as the last seven wickets tumbled in pitiful fashion for 22 runs in 63 balls. Lee beat Ward for pace. Gillespie, at full throttle, found Stewart's edge, rounded off an unhappy debut for Afzaal and was too quick for White. Only Trescothick defied, admirably for 208 minutes, before becoming the seventh man to perish when he edged Warne to

Gilchrist's gloves autographed by the man himself

Chapter 38

2002

England v Sri Lanka May 30 2002

Way back in 1902, England's cricket team arrived for the inaugural Test at Edgbaston with an XI which remains, in the view of many people who know their cricketing onions, the finest ever to participate in the dear, diverse, resilient old beast of an arena that is Test match cricket. On May 30, 2002, exactly 100 years and one day after that first match began, Nasser Hussain's England team stepped out of the Edgbaston pavilion to tackle Sri Lanka and begin to bring the first century of Test cricket on those six esteemed acres of Birmingham greensward to a close.

Edgbaston's century was supplied with a lavish send-off by Hussain's class of 2002. Nobody could argue that they constituted a candidate for finest XI ever to participate in the dear, diverse, resilient old beast of an arena that is Test match cricket but they were more than good enough for Sri Lanka. The tourists were hurried to defeat by an innings and 111 runs by mid-afternoon on the fourth day.

Sri Lanka became the seventh country to provide England with Test match opposition in Birmingham, following Australia (11 visits), West Indies (seven), Pakistan (six), India (five) and South Africa and New Zealand (four each). Edgbaston's creases have

Opening of the Eric Hollies Stand by Hollies' daughter Jackie Rawlinson

Man of the Match Matthew Hoggard

historically proved a daunting strip of terrain for countries paying their first Test visits to them. Remember 1902: Australia, dismantled by Wilfred Rhodes and George Hirst, all out for 36 in 23 overs. 1924: South Africa rattled out for 30 in 12.3 overs by Sussex pacemen Arthur Gilligan and Maurice Tate. 1958: New Zealand smothered for 94 in 69.3 overs by that swinging band, Fred Trueman and the Seammeisters. Then there was 1967: India skinned for 92 in 36.3 overs by David Brown, John Snow, Ray Illingworth and Robin Hobbs. Stage-fright has often appeared to strike opposing batsmen on their first treading of Edgbaston's Test match boards and, sure enough, it afflicted Sri Lanka. They managed to top 100 but, on a good pitch, their total of 162 was well below-par and sowed the seeds of heavy defeat.

For this second Test of a series of three, England needed to improve radically upon their performance in the first, at Lord's, in which the tourists had much the better of a draw. On an opening day truncated by rain, the requisite improvement took the form of a display of collective intelligent seam-bowling. After Hussain won the toss, the Sri Lankans were soon 23 for two after Matthew Hoggard and Andrew Caddick each struck early, ousting Marvin Atapattu and Sanath Jayasuriya with the assistance of wicket-keeper Alec Stewart. Kumar Sangakkara and Mahela Jayawardena added 53 for the third wicket but the former's departure, to another catch by Stewart after a rash back-foot force at Andrew Flintoff, triggered a steep clatter. As the English seamers maintained a nagging line, the last eight wickets fell for 86 runs. Jayawardene defied for 90 minutes for 47 with

Another victim for Hoggard as Jayasuria is bowled for 10

Muralitharan kept his side in the match by his immensely skilled fingertips. Carrying the Sri Lankan attack all but alone, the spinner bowled Butcher and Hussain with deliveries which turned a foot and a half. When Murali ousted Stewart, caught off pad and glove at short-leg, the 14,000 crowd had witnessed a minor master-class from the spinner.

Graham Thorpe (30) and Andrew Flintoff (14) steered their side to 401 for five (239 ahead) at the close but, on Saturday morning, England continued to falter. Murali trapped Flintoff, caught at short-leg, and left-arm seamer Nuwan Zoysa ran through the lower order, including Giles who bagged the ninth duck (Mike Smith three, Giles and Ed Giddins two each, Dick Lilley and David Brown one each) for

seven fours but then received a brute of a lifter from Caddick and Flintoff accepted the catch at second slip. Warwickshire's Ashley Giles, recalled to the XI after being bizarrely omitted at Lord's where England went in without a spinner, delivered only four overs as Caddick, Hoggard, Flintoff and Alex Tudor shared nine of the 10 wickets. The other - a slapstick run out when Buddika Fernando and Muthiah Muralitharan disagreed over the practicality of a sharp single - summed up the feckless nature of much of the tourists' work.

England had seven overs batting before the close and Sri Lanka soon turned to talisman Muralitharan, back in the team, although far from 100 per cent fit, after missing the Lord's Test with a shoulder injury. He failed to part Marcus Trescothick and Michael Vaughan, though, who eased England to 24 without loss at stumps and then Trescothick, nine not out overnight, dominated Friday with a brutal exhibition of clean hitting. The Somerset opener added 92 for the first wicket with Vaughan and then, after the Yorkshireman swept a catch to square leg, 202 for the second with Mark Butcher against some innocuous fare from the tourists. Just before tea, Trescothick, having hit 161 from 232 balls with three sixes and 23 fours, clipped Chaminda Vaas into the hands of Hashan Tillekeratne at mid-wicket and in the final session

Trescothick acknowledges his 100

England clinch victory as Vaas is stumped by Stewart off Warwickshire's Giles

England by a Warwickshire batsman in an Edgbaston Test. When Caddick edged Zoysa, England had lost four wickets for 28 runs and had slipped from 294 for one to 454 for nine. Still, though, there was Thorpe and he found a willing and unlikely partner in Hoggard. The number 11 stayed two hours and six minutes for an unbeaten 17 to escort Thorpe to his 11th Test century and the last wicket yielded 91 before the Surrey batsman top-edged Fernando to third man. His

123, from 229 balls with 12 fours, with assistance from the gallant Hoggard, had snuffed out the flicker of hope which Murali had conjured for Sri Lanka.

Trailing by 383, the tourists were soon 30 for two after Hoggard torpedoed Jayasuriya and Sangakkara with blistering yorkers. Atapattu and Jayawardene calmly steered their side to 132 for two at the close of the third day but on Sunday, England closed the game out with remorseless efficiency.

There was some morning resistance from Atapattu, Jayawardene, Aravinda De Silva and Tillekeratne but after the new ball was taken, two overs after lunch, Caddick and Hoggard briskly unzipped the Sri Lankan middle order and tail. Hoggard's five for 92 was his best haul for England in home Tests but the last wicket fell, fittingly, to a Warwickshire player. Giles lured Vaas out of his ground, Stewart completed the stumping and the first century of Test cricket at Edgbaston was at an end with England, handsomely victorious, propelled to their first duel of the second 100 years, against South Africa in 2003, with their record in Birmingham still formidable; played 38, won 19, drawn 12, lost seven.

The three scorers at the Test; Ray Burrows, David Wainwright and Colin Mackenzie

Chapter 39

Scorecards

Test match results at Edgbaston 1902-2002

The Ashes, 1902, 1st Test

England v Australia
Result: Match drawn
Toss: England

29,30,31 May 1902 (3-day match)
5-Test series level 0-0
Umpires: W Hearn and J Phillips (Aus)

Close of Play:
* Day 1: England 351/9 (Lockwood 41*, Rhodes 24*)
* Day 2: England 376/9d, Australia 36 and 8/0 (Trumper 8*, Duff 0*)

England 1st innings

			R	4	6
*AC MacLaren	run out		9		0
CB Fry	c Kelly	b Jones	0	0	0
KS Ranjitsinhji	b Armstrong		13		0
Hon.FS Jackson		b Jones	53		0
JT Tyldesley	lbw	b Howell	138		0
+AFA Lilley	c Jones	b Noble	2	0	0
GH Hirst	c Armstrong	b Trumper	48		0
GL Jessop	c Hopkins	b Trumper	6		0
LC Braund		b Jones	14		0
WH Lockwood	not out		52		0
W Rhodes	not out		38		0
Extras	(lb 3)		3		
Total	(9 wickets declared, 142 overs)		376		

FoW: 1-5, 2-13, 3-35, 4-112, 5-121, 6-212, 7-230, 8-264, 9-295.

Bowling

	O	M	R	W
Jones	28	9	76	3
Noble	44	15	112	1
Trumper	13	5	35	2
Armstrong	25	6	64	1
Howell	26	8	58	1
Hopkins	6	2	28	0

Australia 1st innings

			R	4	6
VT Trumper		b Hirst	18		0
RA Duff	c Jessop	b Rhodes	2	0	0
C Hill	c Braund	b Hirst	1	0	0
SE Gregory	lbw	b Hirst	0	0	0
*J Darling	c Jessop	b Rhodes	3	0	0
MA Noble	st Lilley	Rhodes	3	0	0
WW Armstrong	c Lilley	b Rhodes	0	0	0
AJY Hopkins	c Lilley	b Rhodes	5		0
+JJ Kelly	not out		1	0	0
E Jones	c Jackson	b Rhodes	0	0	0
WP Howell	c Fry	b Rhodes	0	0	0
Extras	(b 3)		3		
Total	(all out, 23 overs)		36		

FoW: 1-9, 2-10, 3-14, 4-17, 5-25, 6-25, 7-31, 8-35, 9-35, 10-36.

Bowling

	O	M	R	W
Hirst	11	4	15	3
Rhodes	11	3	17	7
Braund	1	0	1	0

Australia 2nd innings (following on)

			R	4	6
VT Trumper	c Braund	b Rhodes	14		0
RA Duff	c Fry	b Braund	15		0
C Hill	not out		10		0
SE Gregory	not out		1	0	0
Extras	(lb 4, w 1, nb 1)		6		
Total	(2 wickets, 28 overs)		46		

DNB: *J Darling, MA Noble, WW Armstrong, AJY Hopkins, +JJ Kelly, E Jones, WP Howell.

FoW: 1-16, 2-41.

Bowling

	O	M	R	W
Hirst	9	6	10	0
Rhodes	10	5	9	1
Braund	5	0	14	1
Jackson	4	2	7	0

The Ashes, 1909, 1st Test

England v Australia
Result: England won by 10 wickets
Toss: Australia
Test Debuts:

27,28,29 May 1909 (3-day match)
England leads the 5-Test series 1-0
Umpires: J Carlin and F Parris
GJ Thompson (Eng); W Bardsley, WJ Whitty (Aus).

Close of Play: * Day 1: Aus 22/2 (Armstrong 10*, Trumper 7*)
* Day 2: Aus 74, Eng 121, Aus 67/2 (Gregory 26*, Ransford 28*)

Australia 1st innings

			R	4	6
A Cotter	c Hirst	b Blythe	2	0	0
W Bardsley	c MacLaren	b Hirst	2	0	0
WW Armstrong		b Hirst	24		0
VT Trumper	c Hirst	b Blythe	10		0
*MA Noble	c Jessop	b Blythe	15		0
SE Gregory	c Rhodes	b Blythe	0	0	0
VS Ransford		b Hirst	1		0
CG Macartney	c MacLaren	b Blythe	10		0
+H Carter	lbw	b Hirst	0	0	0
JDA O'Connor	lbw	b Blythe	8		0
WJ Whitty	not out		0	0	0
Extras	(lb 1, nb 1)		2		
Total	(all out, 46 overs)		74		

FoW: 1-5, 2-7, 3-30, 4-46, 5-47, 6-52, 7-58, 8-59, 9-71, 10-74.

Bowling

	O	M	R	W
Hirst	23	8	28	4
Blythe	23	6	44	6

England 1st innings

			R	4	6
*AC MacLaren		b Macartney	5		0
JB Hobbs	lbw	b Macartney	0	0	0
JT Tyldesley		b O'Connor	24		0
CB Fry		b Macartney	0	0	0
AO Jones	c Carter	b Armstrong	28		0
GH Hirst	lbw	b Armstrong	15		0
GL Jessop		b Armstrong	22		0
W Rhodes	not out		15		0
+AFA Lilley	c Ransford	b Armstrong	0	0	0
GJ Thompson	run out		6		0
C Blythe	c Macartney	b Armstrong	1	0	0
Extras	(b 4, lb 1)		5		
Total	(all out, 55.3 overs)		121		

FoW: 1-0, 2-13, 3-13, 4-61, 5-61, 6-90, 7-103, 8-107, 9-116, 10-121.

Bowling

	O	M	R	W
Whitty	17	5	43	0
Macartney	17	6	21	3
Noble	1	0	2	0
O'Connor	5	2	23	1
Armstrong	15.3	7	27	5

Australia 2nd innings

			R	4	6
*MA Noble	c Jones	b Hirst	11		0
CG Macartney	lbw	b Blythe	1	0	0
SE Gregory	c Thompson	b Blythe	43		0
VS Ransford		b Blythe	43		0
VT Trumper	c Rhodes	b Hirst	1	0	0
W Bardsley	c Thompson	b Blythe	6		0
WW Armstrong	c Jessop	b Blythe	0	0	0
+H Carter	c Hobbs	b Hirst	1	0	0
A Cotter	c Tyldesley	b Hirst	15		1
JDA O'Connor	c Lilley	b Hirst	13		0
WJ Whitty	not out		9		0
Extras	(b 7, lb 1)		8		
Total	(all out, 52.5 overs)		151		

FoW: 1-4, 2-16, 3-97, 4-99, 5-103, 6-103, 7-106, 8-123, 9-125, 10-151.

Bowling

	O	M	R	W
Hirst	23.5	4	58	5
Blythe	24	3	58	5
Thompson	4	0	19	0
Rhodes	1	0	8	0

England 2nd innings (target: 105 runs)

		R	4	6
JB Hobbs	not out	62		0
CB Fry	not out	35		0
Extras	(b 5, lb 3)	8		
Total	(0 wickets, 32.2 overs)	105		

DNB: *AC MacLaren, JT Tyldesley, AO Jones, GH Hirst, GL Jessop, W Rhodes, +AFA Lilley, GJ Thompson, C Blythe.

Bowling

	O	M	R	W
Whitty	5	11	8	0
Macartney	11	2	35	0
O'Connor	3.2	1	17	0
Armstrong	13	5	27	0

England v South Africa, 1924, 1st Test
Edgbaston, Birmingham   14,16,17 June 1924 (3-day match)
Result: England won by an innings and 18 runs   England leads the 5-Test series 1-0
Toss: South Africa   Umpires: HR Butt and W Reeves
Test Debuts: APF Chapman, R Kilner, H Sutcliffe, MW Tate, GEC Wood (Eng);
                         HG Deane, GM Parker, MJ Susskind (SA).

Close of Play:
* Day 1: England 398/7 (Kilner 40*, Gilligan 4*)
* Day 2: England 438, South Africa 30 and 274/4 (Catterall 52*, Blanckenberg 56*)

England 1st innings			R	4	6
JB Hobbs	lbw	b Blanckenberg	76		0
H Sutcliffe		b Parker	64		1
FE Woolley	c Ward	b Parker	64		1
EH Hendren	c Nourse	b Parker	4		0
APF Chapman		b Parker	8		0
PGH Fender	c Taylor	b Blanckenberg	36		0
R Kilner		c & b Pegler	59		0
MW Tate	c Taylor	b Parker	19		0
*AER Gilligan		b Pegler	13		0
+GEC Wood		b Parker	1	0	0
CH Parkin	not out		8		0
Extras	(b 4, lb 11, nb 1)		16		
Total	(all out, 124 overs)		438		

FoW: 1-136, 2-164, 3-247, 4-255, 5-315, 6-356, 7-386, 8-407, 9-410, 10-438.

Bowling	O	M	R	W
Parker	37	2	152	6
Pegler	36	8	106	2
Blanckenberg	32	5	95	2
Nupen	18	2	66	0
Nourse	1	0	3	0

South Africa 1st innings			R	4	6
*HW Taylor		b Tate	7		0
RH Catterall		b Gilligan	0	0	0
MJ Susskind	c Kilner	b Tate	3	0	0
AW Nourse	lbw	b Gilligan	1	0	0
JMM Commaille	not out		1	0	0
JM Blanckenberg		b Tate	4	0	0
HG Deane		b Gilligan	2	0	0
EP Nupen		b Gilligan	0	0	0
SJ Pegler		b Tate	0	0	0
+TA Ward		b Gilligan	1	0	0
GM Parker	lbw	b Gilligan	0	0	0
Extras	(b 1, lb 7, nb 3)		11		
Total	(all out, 12.3 overs)		30		

FoW: 1-1, 2-4, 3-6, 4-14, 5-20, 6-23, 7-23, 8-24, 9-30, 10-30.

Bowling	O	M	R	W
Gilligan	6.3	4	7	6
Tate	6	1	12	4

South Africa 2nd innings (following on)			R	4	6
*HW Taylor		c & b Tate	34		0
JMM Commaille	c Hendren	b Tate	29		0
MJ Susskind		b Gilligan	51		0
AW Nourse	c Wood	b Gilligan	34		0
RH Catterall	c Hobbs	b Tate	120		2
JM Blanckenberg	c Chapman	b Gilligan	56		0
HG Deane	run out		5		0
EP Nupen	lbw	b Tate	5		0
+TA Ward		b Gilligan	19		0
SJ Pegler	c Hobbs	b Gilligan	6		0
GM Parker	not out		2	0	0
Extras	(b 4, lb 18, w 1, nb 6)		29		
Total	(all out, 143.4 overs)		390		

FoW: 1-54, 2-101, 3-152, 4-161, 5-275, 6-284, 7-295, 8-350, 9-372, 10-390.

Bowling	O	M	R	W
Gilligan	28	6	83	5
Tate	50.4	19	103	4
Parkin	16	5	38	0
Kilner	22	10	40	0
Fender	17	5	56	0
Woolley	10	2	41	0

England v South Africa, 1929, 1st Test
Edgbaston, Birmingham   15,17,18 June 1929 (3-day match)
Result: Match drawn   5-Test series level 0-0
Toss: England   Umpires: J Hardstaff snr and TW Oates
Test Debuts: KS Duleepsinhji, ET Killick (Eng); JAJ Christy, B Mitchell,
                         HGO Owen-Smith, NA Quinn (SA).

Close of Play:
* Day 1: England 245, South Africa 59/0 (Catterall 33*, Mitchell 25*)
* Day 2: South Africa 250, England 34/0 (Sutcliffe 10*, Killick 23*)

England 1st innings			R	4	6
H Sutcliffe	c Cameron	b Ochse	26		0
ET Killick	c Morke	b Ochse	31		0
WR Hammond		b Quinn	18		0
KS Duleepsinhji	c Vincent	b Morkel	12		0
EH Hendren		b Morkel	70		0
M Leyland	c Taylor	b Ochse	3	0	0
PGH Fender	c Cameron	b Quinn	6		0
MW Tate	c Mitchell	b Morkel	40		1
H Larwood	lbw	b Ochse	6		0
*JC White	run out		5		0
+G Duckworth	not out		11		0
Extras	(b 9, lb 3, w 4, nb 1)		17		
Total	all out, 81.1 overs		245		

FoW: 1-59, 2-66, 3-92, 4-96, 5-111, 6-128, 7-215, 8-215, 9-222, 10-245.

Bowling	O	M	R	W
Morkel	20	4	40	3
Quinn	27	8	62	2
Ochse	25.1	2	79	4
Vincent	7	0	37	0
Mitchell	2	0	10	0

South Africa 1st innings			R	4	6
RH Catterall	lbw	b Fender	67		0
B Mitchell		b Tate	88		0
JAJ Christy		b Larwood	1	0	0
HW Taylor		b Larwood	2	0	0
DPB Morkel		b Tate	5		0
*HG Deane		c & b Fender	29		0
+HB Cameron		b Larwood	5		0
HGO Owen-Smith		b Tate	25		0
CL Vincent	not out		14		0
NA Quinn		b Larwood	1	0	0
AL Ochse		b Larwood	2	0	0
Extras	(b 6, lb 2, w 1, nb 2)		11		
Total	(all out, 172.4 overs)		250		

FoW: 1-119, 2-120, 3-122, 4-130, 5-174, 6-182, 7-224, 8-239, 9-248, 10-250.

Bowling	O	M	R	W
Larwood	42.4	17	57	5
Tate	44	14	65	3
Fender	32	10	64	2
Hammond	22	12	25	0
White	32	19	28	0

England 2nd innings			R	4	6
H Sutcliffe		b Morkel	114		0
ET Killick		b Quinn	23		0
WR Hammond	not out		138		0
PGH Fender	c Vincent	b Ochse	12		0
KS Duleepsinhji	lbw	b Ochse	1	0	0
EH Hendren	not out		8		0
Extras	(lb 10, w 2)		12		
Total	(4 wickets declared, 100 overs)		308		

DNB: M Leyland, MW Tate, H Larwood, *JC White, +G Duckworth.
FoW: 1-34, 2-255, 3-278, 4-280.

Bowling	O	M	R	W
Morkel	22	6	54	1
Quinn	20	2	55	1
Ochse	28	2	88	2
Vincent	19	3	55	0
Owen-Smith	6	0	29	0
Christy	5	1	15	0

South Africa 2nd innings (target: 304 runs)			R	4	6
RH Catterall	c White	b Fender	98		0
B Mitchell	not out		61	0	
Extras	(b 9, nb 3)		12		
Total	(1 wicket, 59.4 overs)		171		

DNB: JAJ Christy, HW Taylor, DPB Morkel, *HG Deane, +HB Cameron,
     HGO Owen-Smith, CL Vincent, NA Quinn, AL Ochse.
FoW: 1-171.

Bowling	O	M	R	W
Larwood	11	6	12	0
Tate	16	4	43	0
Fender	15.4	3	55	1
Hammond	3	1	19	0
White	13	5	23	0
Duleepsinhji	1	0	7	0

England v West Indies, 1957, 1st Test

Edgbaston, Birmingham   30,31 May, 1,3,4 June 1957 (5-day match)
Result: Match drawn   5-Test series level 0-0
Toss: England   Umpires: DE Davies and CS Elliott
Test Debuts: R Gilchrist, RB Kanhai (WI).

Close of Play:
* Day 1: England 186, West Indies 83/1 (Kanhai 42*, Walcott 40*)
* Day 2: West Indies 316/5 (Smith 70*, Worrell 48*)
* Day 3: West Indies 474, England 102/2 (Close 34*, May 21*)
* Day 4: England 378/3 (May 193*, Cowdrey 78*)

England 1st innings

			R	4	6
PE Richardson	c Walcott	b Ramadhin	47		0
DB Close	c Kanhai	b Gilchrist	15		0
DJ Insole		b Ramadhin	20		0
*PBH May	c Weekes	b Ramadhin	30		0
MC Cowdrey	c Gilchrist	b Ramadhin	4		0
TE Bailey		b Ramadhin	1	0	0
GAR Lock		b Ramadhin	0	0	0
+TG Evans		b Gilchrist	14		0
JC Laker		b Ramadhin	7		0
FS Trueman	not out		29		1
JB Statham		b Atkinson	13		0
Extras	(b 3, lb 3)		6		
Total	(all out, 79.4 overs)		186		

FoW: 1-32, 2-61, 3-104, 4-115, 5-116, 6-118, 7-121, 8-130, 9-150, 10-186.

Bowling	O	M	R	W
Worrell	9	1	27	0
Gilchrist	27	4	74	2
Ramadhin	31	16	49	7
Atkinson	12.4	3	30	1

West Indies 1st innings

			R	4	6
BH Pairaudeau		b Trueman	1	0	0
+RB Kanhai	lbw	b Statham	42		0
CL Walcott	c Evans	b Laker	90		0
ED Weekes		b Trueman	9		0
GS Sobers	c Bailey	b Statham	53		0
OG Smith	lbw	b Laker	161		1
FMM Worrell		b Statham	81		0
*JDC Goddard	c Lock	b Laker	24		0
DS Atkinson	c Statham	b Laker	1	0	0
S Ramadhin	not out		5		0
R Gilchrist	run out		0	0	0
Extras	(b 1, lb 6)		7		
Total	(all out, 191.4 overs)		474		

FoW: 1-4, 2-83, 3-120, 4-183, 5-197, 6-387, 7-466, 8-469, 9-474, 10-474.

Bowling	O	M	R	W
Statham	39	4	114	3
Trueman	30	4	99	2
Bailey	34	11	80	0
Laker	54	17	119	4
Lock	34.4	15	55	0

England 2nd innings

			R	4	6
PE Richardson	c sub	b Ramadhin	34		0
DB Close	c Weekes	b Gilchrist	42		0
DJ Insole	b Ramadhin		0	0	0
*PBH May	not out		285		2
MC Cowdrey	c sub	b Smith	154		0
+TG Evans	not out		29		0
Extras	(b 23, lb 16)		39		
Total	(4 wickets declared, 258 overs)		583		

DNB: TE Bailey, GAR Lock, JC Laker, FS Trueman, JB Statham.
FoW: 1-63, 2-65, 3-113, 4-524.

Bowling	O	M	R	W
Gilchrist	26	2	67	1
Ramadhin	98	35	179	2
Atkinson	72	29	137	0
Sobers	30	4	77	0
Smith	26	4	72	1
Goddard	6	2	12	0

West Indies 2nd innings (target: 296 runs)

			R	4	6
BH Pairaudeau		b Trueman	7		0
+RB Kanhai	c Close	b Trueman	1	0	0
GS Sobers	c Cowdrey	b Lock	14		0
ED Weekes	c Trueman	b Lock	33		0
FMM Worrell	c May	b Lock	0	0	0
CL Walcott	c Lock	b Laker	1	0	0
OG Smith	lbw	b Laker	5		0
*JDC Goddard	not out		0	0	0
DS Atkinson	not out		4		0
Extras	(b 7		7		
Total	(7 wickets, 60 overs)		72		

DNB: S Ramadhin, R Gilchrist.
FoW: 1-1, 2-9, 3-25, 4-27, 5-43, 6-66, 7-68.

Bowling	O	M	R	W
Statham	2	0	6	0
Trueman	5	3	7	2
Laker	24	20	13	2
Lock	27	19	31	3
Close	2	1	8	0

England v New Zealand, 1958, 1st Test

Edgbaston, Birmingham   5,6,7,9 June 1958 (5-day match)
Result: England won by 205 runs   England leads the 5-Test series 1-0
Toss: England   Umpires: JS Buller and CS Elliott
Test Debuts: MJK Smith (Eng); JW D'Arcy, T Meale, WR Playle (NZ).

Close of Play:
* Day 1: England 221, New Zealand 41/3 (D'Arcy 18*, Playle 0*)
* Day 2: New Zealand 94, England 131/3 (Richardson 71*, Cowdrey 21*)
* Day 3: England 215/6d, New Zealand 69/4 (Harford 15*, Reid 1*)

England 1st innings

			R	4	6
PE Richardson	lbw	b MacGibbon	4		0
MJK Smith	lbw	b MacGibbon	0	0	0
TW Graveney	c Alabaster	b Hayes	7		0
*PBH May	c Petrie	b MacGibbon	84		0
MC Cowdrey		b MacGibbon	81		0
TE Bailey	c Petrie	b Alabaster	2	0	0
+TG Evans	c Petrie	b MacGibbon	2	0	0
GAR Lock	lbw	b Alabaster	4		0
FS Trueman		b Alabaster	0	0	0
JC Laker	not out		11		1
PJ Loader		b Alabaster	17		0
Extras	(lb 3, w 4, nb 2)		9		
Total	(all out, 75.5 overs)		221		

FoW: 1-4, 2-11, 3-29, 4-150, 5-153, 6-172, 7-185, 8-191, 9-191, 10-221.

Bowling	O	M	R	W
Hayes	15	2	57	1
MacGibbon	27	11	64	5
Cave	12	2	29	0
Reid	6	3	16	0
Alabaster	15.5	4	46	4

New Zealand 1st innings

			R	4	6
LSM Miller	lbw	b Trueman	7		0
JW D'Arcy	c Evans	b Trueman	19		0
NS Harford		b Bailey	9		0
*JR Reid		b Bailey	7		0
WR Playle		b Trueman	4		0
T Meale	lbw	b Trueman	7		0
AR MacGibbon	c Evans	b Laker	5		0
+EC Petrie	lbw	b Loader	1	0	0
JC Alabaster		b Trueman	9		0
HB Cave	not out		12		0
JA Hayes	run out		14		0
Extras			0		
Total	(all out, 69.3 overs)		94		

FoW: 1-12, 2-21, 3-39, 4-43, 5-46, 6-54, 7-59, 8-67, 9-68, 10-94.

Bowling	O	M	R	W
Trueman	21	8	31	5
Loader	21.3	6	37	1
Bailey	20	9	17	2
Lock	2	2	0	0
Laker	5	2	9	1

England 2nd innings

			R	4	6
PE Richardson	c Cave	b MacGibbon	100		0
MJK Smith	c Petrie	b MacGibbon	7		0
TW Graveney	c Petrie	b Cave	19		0
*PBH May	c Petrie	b MacGibbon	11		0
MC Cowdrey	c Reid	b Hayes	70		1
TE Bailey	not out		6		0
+TG Evans	c Reid	b Cave	0	0	0
Extras	(b 1, lb 1)		2		
Total	(6 wickets declared, 96.2 overs)		215		

DNB: GAR Lock, FS Trueman, JC Laker, PJ Loader.
FoW: 1-24, 2-71, 3-94, 4-198, 5-214, 6-215.

Bowling	O	M	R	W
Hayes	20	3	51	1
MacGibbon	24	8	41	3
Cave	28.2	9	70	2
Reid	9	2	18	0
Alabaster	15	7	33	0

New Zealand 2nd innings (target: 343 runs)

			R	4	6
LSM Miller		b Trueman	8		0
JW D'Arcy	c Trueman	b Loader	25		0
WR Playle	c Bailey	b Loader	8		0
NS Harford	c Graveney	b Loader	23		0
T Meale	c Smith	b Lock	10		1
*JR Reid		b Bailey	13		0
HB Cave		b Bailey	1	0	0
AR MacGibbon	c Cowdrey	b Laker	26		0
JC Alabaster	c Laker	b Lock	11		0
+EC Petrie	not out		5		0
JA Hayes	c Bailey	b Lock	5		0
Extras	(lb 1, w 1)		2		
Total	(all out, 77.3 overs)		137		

FoW: 1-19, 2-42, 3-49, 4-64, 5-93, 6-94, 7-95, 8-123, 9-131, 10-137.

Bowling	O	M	R	W
Trueman	17	5	33	1
Loader	23	11	40	3
Bailey	20	9	23	2
Lock	8.3	3	25	3
Laker	9	4	14	1

England v South Africa, 1960, 1st Test

Edgbaston, Birmingham
Result: England won by 100 runs
Toss: England
Test Debuts:

9,10,11,13,14 June 1960 (5-day match)
England leads the 5-Test series 1-0
Umpires: JG Langridge and WE Phillipson
RW Barber, PM Walker (Eng); JP Fellows-Smith, GM Griffin, S O'Linn (SA).

Close of Play:
* Day 1: England 175/3 (Subba Row 32*, Smith 42*)
* Day 2: England 292, South Africa 114/5 (Waite 42*, O'Linn 18*)
* Day 3: South Africa 186, England 89/4 (Smith 18*, Illingworth 6*)
* Day 4: England 203, South Africa 120/3 (McLean 68*, Waite 21*)

England 1st innings

			R	4	6
G Pullar	c McLean	b Goddard	37		0
*MC Cowdrey	c Waite	b Adcock	3	0	0
ER Dexter		b Tayfield	52		0
R Subba Row	c Waite	b Griffin	56		0
MJK Smith	c Waite	b Adcock	54		0
+JM Parks	c Waite	b Adcock	35		0
R Illingworth		b Tayfield	1	0	0
RW Barber	lbw	b Adcock	5		0
PM Walker	c Goddard	b Adcock	9		0
FS Trueman		b Tayfield	11		0
JB Statham	not out		14		0
Extras	(b 4, lb 9, nb 2)		15		
Total	(all out, 150.5 overs)		292		

FoW: 1-19, 2-80, 3-100, 4-196, 5-225, 6-234, 7-255, 8-262, 9-275, 10-292.

Bowling	O	M	R	W
Adcock	41.5	14	62	5
Griffin	21	3	61	1
Goddard	33	17	47	1
Tayfield	50	19	93	3
Fellows-Smith	5	1	14	0

South Africa 1st innings

			R	4	6
*DJ McGlew	c Parks	b Trueman	11		0
TL Goddard	c Smith	b Statham	10		0
AJ Pithey	lbw	b Statham	6		0
RA McLean	c Statham	b Trueman	21		0
+JHB Waite	b Illingworth		58		0
PR Carlstein	lbw	b Trueman	4		0
S O'Linn	c Cowdrey	b Illingworth	42		0
JP Fellows-Smith	lbw	b Illingworth	18		0
GM Griffin		b Trueman	6		0
HJ Tayfield	run out		6		0
NAT Adcock	not out		1	0	0
Extras	(b 2, nb 1)		3		
Total	(all out, 82.5 overs)		186		

FoW: 1-11, 2-21, 3-40, 4-52, 5-61, 6-146, 7-168, 8-179, 9-179, 10-186.

Bowling	O	M	R	W
Statham	28	8	67	2
Trueman	24.5	4	58	4
Dexter	1	0	4	0
Barber	6	0	26	0
Illingworth	17	11	15	3
Walker	6	1	13	0

England 2nd innings

			R	4	6
*MC Cowdrey		b Adcock	0	0	0
R Subba Row	c Waite	b Tayfield	32		0
ER Dexter		b Adcock	26		0
MJK Smith	c O'Linn	b Tayfield	28		0
+JM Parks		b Griffin	4		0
R Illingworth	c Waite	b Adcock	16		0
RW Barber	c McLean	b Tayfield	4		0
PM Walker	c Goddard	b Griffin	37		0
FS Trueman		b Tayfield	25		1
JB Statham	c McLean	b Griffin	22		0
G Pullar	not out		1	0	0
Extras	(b 2, lb 4, nb 2)		8		
Total	(all out, 86 overs)		203		

FoW: 1-0, 2-42, 3-69, 4-74, 5-112, 6-112, 7-118, 8-163, 9-202, 10-203.

Bowling	O	M	R	W
Adcock	28	8	57	3
Griffin	21	4	44	3
Goddard	10	5	32	0
Tayfield	27	12	62	4

South Africa 2nd innings (target: 310 runs)

			R	4	6
*DJ McGlew	c Parks	b Statham	5		0
TL Goddard	c Walker	b Statham	0	0	0
AJ Pithey		b Illingworth	17		0
RA McLean	lbw	b Trueman	68		0
+JHB Waite	not out		56		0
PR Carlstein		b Trueman	10		0
S O'Linn	lbw	b Barber	12		0
JP Fellows-Smith	lbw	b Illingworth	5		0
HJ Tayfield		b Illingworth	3	0	0
GM Griffin	c Walker	b Trueman	14		1
NAT Adcock		b Statham	7		0
Extras	(b 7, lb 5)		12		
Tota	(all out, 84 overs)		209		

FoW: 1-4, 2-5, 3-58, 4-120, 5-132, 6-156, 7-161, 8-167, 9-200, 10-209.

Bowling	O	M	R	W
Statham	18	5	41	3
Trueman	22	4	58	3
Dexter	6	4	4	0
Barber	10	2	29	1
Illingworth	24	6	57	3
Walker	4	2	8	0

The Ashes, 1961, 1st Test England v Australia

Edgbaston, Birmingham
Result: Match drawn
Toss: England
Test Debuts:

8,9,10,12,13 June 1961 (5-day match)
5-Test series level 0-0
Umpires: JS Buller and FS Lee
JT Murray (Eng); WM Lawry (Aus).

Close of Play:
* Day 1: England 180/8 (Allen 11*, Trueman 14*)
* Day 2: England 195, Australia 359/5 (Simpson 36*, Davidson 16*)
* Day 3: Australia 516/9d, England 5/0 (Pullar 0*, Subba Row 5*)
* Day 4: England 106/1 (Subba Row 68*, Dexter 5*)

England 1st innings

			R	4	6
G Pullar		b Davidson	17		0
R Subba Row	c Simpson	b Mackay	59		0
ER Dexter	c Davidson	b Mackay	10		0
*MC Cowdrey		b Misson	13		0
KF Barrington	c Misson	b Mackay	21		0
MJK Smith	c Lawry	b Mackay	0	0	0
R Illingworth	c Grout	b Benaud	15		0
+JT Murray	c Davidson	b Benaud	16		0
DA Allen	run out		11		0
FS Trueman	c Burge	b Benaud	20		1
JB Statham	not out		7		0
Extras	(b 3, lb 3)		6		
Total	(all out, 84.3 overs)		195		

FoW: 1-36, 2-53, 3-88, 4-121, 5-121, 6-122, 7-153, 8-156, 9-181, 10-195.

Bowling	O	M	R	W
Davidson	26	6	70	1
Misson	15	6	47	1
Mackay	29	10	57	4
Benaud	14.3	8	15	3

Australia 1st innings

			R	4	6
WM Lawry	c Murray	b Illingworth	57		0
CC McDonald	c Illingworth	b Statham	22		0
RN Harvey	lbw	b Allen	114		0
NC O'Neill		b Statham	82		0
PJP Burge	lbw	b Allen	25		0
RB Simpson	c & b Trueman		76		0
AK Davidson	c & b Illingworth		22		0
KD Mackay	c Barrington	b Statham	64		0
*R Benaud	not out		36		0
+ATW Grout	c Dexter	b Trueman	5		0
Extras	(b 8, lb 4, nb 1)		13		
Total	(9 wickets declared, 152.5 overs)	516			

DNB: FM Misson.

FoW: 1-47, 2-106, 3-252, 4-299, 5-322, 6-381, 7-469, 8-501, 9-516.

Bowling	O	M	R	W
Trueman	36.5	1	136	2
Statham	43	6	147	3
Illingworth	44	12	110	2
Allen	24	4	88	2
Dexter	5	1	22	0

England 2nd innings

			R	4	6
G Pullar	c Grout	b Misson	28		0
R Subba Row		b Misson	112		0
ER Dexter	st Grout	b Simpson	180		0
*MC Cowdrey		b Mackay	14		0
KF Barrington	not out		48		0
MJK Smith	not out		1	0	0
Extras	(lb 18)		18		
Total	(4 wickets, 154 overs)		401		

DNB: R Illingworth, +JT Murray, DA Allen, FS Trueman, JB Statham.

FoW: 1-93, 2-202, 3-239, 4-400.

Bowling	O	M	R	W
Davidson	31	10	60	0
Misson	28	6	82	2
Simpson	34	12	87	1
Mackay	41	13	87	1
Benaud	20	4	67	0

England v Pakistan, 1962, 1st Test

Edgbaston, Birmingham
Result: England won by an innings and 24 runs
Toss: England

31 May, 1,2,4 June 1962 (5-day match)
England leads the 5-Test series 1-0
Umpires: JS Buller and CS Elliott

Close of Play:
* Day 1: England 386/4 (Graveney 96*, Parfitt 23*)
* Day 2: England 544/5d, Pakistan 149/5 (Imtiaz Ahmed 1*, Mathias 2*)
* Day 3: Pakistan 246 and 158/4 (Saeed Ahmed 30*, Javed Burki 9*)

England 1st innings

			R	4	6
G Pullar	b D'Souza		22		0
MC Cowdrey	c Imtiaz Ahmed	b Intikhab Alam	159		0
*ER Dexter	c Javed Burki	b Intikhab Alam	72		2
TW Graveney	c Ijaz Butt	b Mahmood Hussain	97		0
KF Barrington	lbw	b Mahmood Hussain	9		0
PH Parfitt	not out		101		2
DA Allen	not out		79		0
Extras	(lb 5)		5		
Total	(5 wickets declared, 146 overs)		544		

DNB: +G Millman, GAR Lock, FS Trueman, JB Statham.

FoW: 1-31, 2-197, 3-304, 4-330, 5-391.

Bowling

	O	M	R	W
Mahmood Hussain	43	14	130	2
D'Souza	46	9	161	1
Intikhab Alam	25	2	117	2
Nasim-ul-Ghani	30	7	109	0
Saeed Ahmed	2	0	22	0

Pakistan 1st innings

			R	4	6
Hanif Mohammad	c Millman	b Allen	47		0
Ijaz Butt	c Lock	b Statham	10		0
Saeed Ahmed	c Graveney	b Trueman	5		0
Mushtaq Mohammad	c Cowdrey	b Lock	63		0
*Javed Burki	c Barrington	b Allen	13		0
+Imtiaz Ahmed	b Trueman		39		0
W Mathias	b Statham		21		0
Nasim-ul-Ghani	b Statham		0	0	0
Intikhab Alam	b Lock		16		0
Mahmood Hussain	b Statham		0	0	0
A D'Souza	not out		23		0
Extras	(b 8, lb 1)		9		
Total	(all out, 101 overs		246		

FoW: 1-11, 2-30, 3-108, 4-144, 5-146, 6-202, 7-206, 8-206, 9-206, 10-246.

Bowling

	O	M	R	W
Statham	21	9	54	4
Trueman	13	3	59	2
Dexter	12	6	23	0
Allen	32	16	62	2
Lock	19	8	37	2
Parfitt	2	1	2	0
Barrington	2	2	0	0

Pakistan 2nd innings (following on)

			R	4	6
Hanif Mohammad	c Cowdrey	b Allen	31		0
Ijaz Butt	c Trueman	b Allen	33		0
+Imtiaz Ahmed	c Graveney	b Lock	46		1
Mushtaq Mohammad	c Millman	b Allen	8		0
Saeed Ahmed	c Parfitt	b Lock	65		0
*Javed Burki	b Statham		19		0
W Mathias	b Statham		4		0
Nasim-ul-Ghani	c Parfitt	b Trueman	35		0
Intikhab Alam	c Cowdrey	b Lock	0	0	0
Mahmood Hussain	c Graveney	b Trueman	22		0
A D'Souza	not out		9		0
Extras	(b 1, lb 1)		2		
Total	(all out, 123 overs		274		

FoW: 1-60, 2-77, 3-119, 4-127, 5-187, 6-199, 7-207, 8-207, 9-257, 10-274.

Bowling

	O	M	R	W
Trueman	24	5	70	2
Statham	19	6	32	2
Dexter	7	2	16	0
Lock	36	14	80	3
Allen	36	16	73	3
Cowdrey	1	0	1	0

The Wisden Trophy, 1963, 3rd Test England v West Indies

Edgbaston, Birmingham
Result: England won by 217 runs
Toss: England
Test Debuts:

4,5,6,8,9 July 1963 (5-day match)
5-Test series level 1-1
Umpires: CS Elliott and LH Gray
PJ Sharpe (Eng).

Close of Play:
* Day 1: England 157/5 (Close 41*, Parks 7*)
* Day 2: England 216
* Day 3: West Indies 110/4 (Butcher 14*, Sobers 1*)
* Day 4: West Indies 186, England 226/8 (Sharpe 69*, Lock 23*)

England 1st innings

			R	4	6
PE Richardson	b Hall		2	0	0
MJ Stewart	lbw	b Sobers	39	1	
*ER Dexter	b Sobers		29		0
KF Barrington	b Sobers		9		0
DB Close	lbw	b Sobers	55		0
PJ Sharpe	c Kanhai	b Gibbs	23		0
+JM Parks	c Murray	b Sobers	12		0
FJ Titmus	c Griffith	b Hall	27		0
FS Trueman	b Griffith		4		0
GAR Lock	b Griffith		1	0	0
D Shackleton	not out		6		0
Extras	(lb 6, nb 3)		9		
Total	(all out, 98.4 overs)		216		

FoW: 1-2, 2-50, 3-72, 4-89, 5-129, 6-172, 7-187, 8-194, 9-200, 10-216.

Bowling

	O	M	R	W
Hall	16.4	2	56	2
Griffith	21	5	48	2
Sobers	31	10	60	5
Worrell	14	5	15	0
Gibbs	16	7	28	1

West Indies 1st innings

			R	4	6
CC Hunte	b Trueman		18		0
MC Carew	c & b Trueman		40		1
RB Kanhai	c Lock	b Shackleton	32		0
BF Butcher	lbw	b Dexter	15		0
JS Solomon	lbw	b Dexter	0	0	0
GS Sobers	b Trueman		19		0
*FMM Worrell	b Dexter		1	0	0
+DL Murray	not out		20		0
WW Hall	c Sharpe	b Dexter	28		0
CC Griffith	lbw	b Trueman	5		0
LR Gibbs	b Trueman		0	0	0
Extras	(lb 7, w 1)		8		
Total	(all out, 69 overs)		186		

FoW: 1-42, 2-79, 3-108, 4-109, 5-128, 6-130, 7-130, 8-178, 9-186, 10-186.

Bowling

	O	M	R	W
Trueman	26	5	75	5
Shackleton	21	9	60	1
Lock	2	1	5	0
Dexter	20	5	38	4

England 2nd innings

			R	4	6
PE Richardson	c Murray	b Griffith	14		0
MJ Stewart	c Murray	b Griffith	27		0
KF Barrington	b Sobers		1	0	0
DB Close	c Sobers	b Griffith	13		0
*ER Dexter	st Murray	b Gibbs	57		0
PJ Sharpe	not out		85		0
+JM Parks	c Sobers	b Gibbs	5		0
FJ Titmus	b Gibbs		0	0	0
FS Trueman	c Gibbs	b Sobers	1	0	0
GAR Lock	b Gibbs		56		0
Extras	(b 9, lb 9, nb 1)		19		
Total	(9 wickets declared, 105.2 overs		278		

DNB: D Shackleton.
FoW: 1-30, 2-31, 3-60, 4-69, 5-170, 6-184, 7-184, 8-189, 9-278.

Bowling

	O	M	R	W
Hall	16	1	47	0
Griffith	28	7	55	3
Sobers	27	4	80	2
Worrell	8	3	28	0
Gibbs	26.2	4	49	4

West Indies 2nd innings (target: 309 runs)

			R	4	6
CC Hunte	c Barrington	b Trueman	5		0
MC Carew	lbw	b Shackleton	1	0	0
RB Kanhai	c Lock	b Trueman	38		0
BF Butcher	b Dexter		14		0
GS Sobers	c Sharpe	b Shackleton	9		0
JS Solomon	c Parks	b Trueman	14		0
*FMM Worrell	c Parks	b Trueman	0	0	0
+DL Murray	c Parks	b Trueman	3	0	0
WW Hall	b Trueman		0		0
CC Griffith	lbw	b Trueman	0	0	0
LR Gibbs	not out		4		0
Extras	(lb 2, w 1)		3		
Total	(all out, 34.3 overs)		91		

FoW: 1-2, 2-10, 3-38, 4-64, 5-78, 6-80, 7-86, 8-86, 9-86, 10-91.

Bowling

	O	M	R	W
Trueman	14.3	2	44	7
Shackleton	17	4	37	2
Dexter	3	1	7	1

England v New Zealand, 1965, 1st Test

Edgbaston, Birmingham   27-31 May 1 June 1965 (5-day match)
Result: England won by 9 wickets   England leads the 3-Test series 1-0
Toss: England   Umpires: CS Elliott and WFF Price

Close of Play:
* Day 1: England 232/3 (Barrington 61*, Cowdrey 44*)
* Day 2: England 435, New Zealand 59/1 (Dowling 30*, Sinclair 4*)
* Day 3: New Zealand 116 and 215/4 (Morgan 33*, Dick 41*)
* Day 4: New Zealand 413, England 8/0 (Boycott 5*, Barber 3*)

England 1st innings

			R	M	4	6
G Boycott	c Dick	b Motz	23			0
RW Barber		b Motz	31			0
ER Dexter	c Dick	b Motz	57	134	8	0
KF Barrington	c Dick	b Collinge	137	437	11	1
MC Cowdrey		b Collinge	85	10		0
*MJK Smith	lbw	b Collinge	0		0	0
+JM Parks	c Cameron	b Reid	34			0
FJ Titmus	c Congdon	b Motz	13			0
TW Cartwright		b Motz	4			0
FS Trueman	c Pollard	b Cameron	3		0	0
FE Rumsey	not out		21			0
Extras	(b 10, lb 6, nb 11)		27			
Total	(all out, 156.4 overs)		435			

FoW: 1-54, 2-76, 3-164, 4-300, 5-300, 6-335, 7-368, 8-391, 9-394, 10-435.

Bowling	O	M	R	W
Collinge	29.4	8	63	3
Cameron	43	10	117	1
Motz	43	14	108	5
Pollard	18	4	60	0
Congdon	7	2	17	0
Reid	16	5	43	1

New Zealand 1st innings

			R	M	4	6
GT Dowling		b Titmus	32			0
BE Congdon	c Smith	b Titmus	24	76		0
BW Sinclair		b Titmus	14			0
*JR Reid		b Trueman	2		0	0
B Sutcliffe	retired hurt		4			0
RW Morgan	c Parks	b Barber	22			0
+AE Dick	c Titmus	b Cartwright	0		0	0
V Pollard	lbw	b Titmus	4			0
RC Motz	c Trueman	b Cartwright	0		0	0
RO Collinge	c Dexter	b Barber	4			0
FJ Cameron	not out		4			0
Extras	(b 1, lb 1, nb 4)		6			
Total	(all out, 63 overs)		116			

FoW: 1-54 (Congdon), 2-63 (Dowling), 3-67 (Reid), 4-86 (Sinclair), 5-97 (Dick), 6-104 (Pollard), 7-105 (Motz), 8-108 (Morgan), 9-115 (Collinge).

Bowling	O	M	R	W
Rumsey	9	2	22	0
Trueman	18	3	49	1
Titmus	26	17	18	4
Cartwright	7	3	14	2
Barber	3	2	7	2

New Zealand 2nd innings (following on)

			R	M	4	6
GT Dowling		b Titmus	41	136		0
BE Congdon		b Titmus	47			1
BW Sinclair	st Parks	b Barber	2		0	0
*JR Reid	c Barrington	b Titmus	44	51	7	1
RW Morgan	lbw	b Trueman	43		6	0
+AE Dick		b Barber	42	69	7	0
B Sutcliffe	c Titmus	b Dexter	53		4	0
V Pollard	not out		81	240	12	0
RC Motz		c & b Barber	21	33	4	0
RO Collinge	c Parks	b Trueman	9			0
FJ Cameron		b Trueman	0		0	0
Extras	(b 17, lb 11, nb 2)		30			
Total	(all out, 175.4 overs)		413			

FoW: 1-72, 2-105, 3-131, 4-145, 5-220, 6-249, 7-353, 8-386, 9-413, 10-413.

Bowling	O	M	R	W
Rumsey	17	5	32	0
Trueman	32.4	8	79	3
Titmus	59	30	85	2
Cartwright	12	6	12	0
Barber	45	15	132	4
Barrington	5	0	25	0
Dexter	5	1	18	1

England 2nd innings (target: 95 runs)

			R	M	4	6
G Boycott	not out		44	103		0
RW Barber	c sub	b Morgan	51			0
ER Dexter	not out		0		0	0
Extras	(nb 1)		1			
Total	(1 wicket, 30.5 overs)		96			

DNB: KF Barrington, MC Cowdrey, *MJK Smith, +JM Parks, FJ Titmus, TW Cartwright, FS Trueman, FE Rumsey.

FoW: 1-92.

Bowling	O	M	R	W
Collinge	5	1	14	0
Cameron	3	0	11	0
Motz	13	3	34	0
Pollard	1	0	5	0
Congdon	2	1	6	0
Reid	5	2	7	0
Morgan	1.5	0	18	1

England v India, 1967, 3rd Test

Edgbaston, Birmingham   13,14,15 July 1967 (5-day match)
Result: England won by 132 runs   England wins the 3-Test series 3-0
Toss: England   Umpires: AE Fagg and WFF Price
Batsman of the match: JT Murray and AL Wadekar
Bowler of the match: R Illingworth, RNS Hobbs and EAS Prasanna
Fielder of the match: AL Wadekar

Close of Play:
* Day 1: England 298, India 9/0 (Engineer 6*, Kunderan 2*)
* Day 2: India 92, England 203

England 1st innings

			R	M	B	4	6
G Boycott	st Engineer	b Bedi	25	61	59	3	0
C Milburn	c Wadekar	b Chandrasekhar	40	73	65	6	0
KF Barrington	c Wadekar	b Prasanna	75	140	162	9	2
TW Graveney	c Venkataraghavan	b Chandrasekhar	10	17	15	2	0
DL Amiss	c Wadekar	b Venkataraghavan	5	27	20	1	0
*DB Close	c Subramanya	b Prasanna	26	90	80	3	0
+JT Murray	c Subramanya	b Chandrasekhar	77	126	145	8	0
R Illingworth	c Wadekar	b Prasanna	2	7	4	0	0
DJ Brown	run out		3	5	4	0	0
JA Snow	c Engineer	b Bedi	10	47	42	0	0
RNS Hobbs	not out		15	55	41	2	0
Extras	(b 5, lb 5)		10				
Total	(all out, 106 overs)		298				

FoW: 1-63, 2-67, 3-89, 4-112, 5-182, 6-183, 7-186, 8-191, 9-241, 10-298.

Bowling	O	M	R	W
Subramanya	10	2	28	0
Kunderan	4	0	13	0
Bedi	27	6	76	2
Chandrasekhar	32	8	94	3
Venkataraghavan	13	3	26	1
Prasanna	20	5	51	3

India 1st innings

			R	M	B	4	6
+FM Engineer	c Graveney	b Brown	23	64	45	1	0
BK Kunderan		b Brown	2	20	17	0	0
AL Wadekar	c Amiss	b Snow	5	13	16	0	0
CG Borde		b Snow	8	35	23	1	0
*Nawab of Pataudi jnr		b Brown	0	1	2	0	0
Hanumant Singh	c Amiss	b Illingworth	15	40	36	3	0
V Subramanya		b Hobbs	10	44	34	2	0
S Venkataraghavan	not out		19	27	34	4	0
EAS Prasanna		b Illingworth	1	2	3	0	0
BS Bedi		c & b Hobbs	1	3	5	0	0
BS Chandrasekhar	st Murray	b Hobbs	0	9	7	0	0
Extras	(b 4, lb 2, nb 2)		8				
Total	(all out, 36.3 overs)		92				

FoW: 1-9, 2-18, 3-35, 4-35, 5-41, 6-66, 7-72, 8-73, 9-82, 10-92.

Bowling	O	M	R	W
Snow	12	3	28	2
Brown	11	6	17	3
Illingworth	7	4	14	2
Hobbs	6.3	1	25	3

England 2nd innings

			R	M	B	4	6
G Boycott		b Subramanya	6	2	5	1	0
C Milburn		b Bedi	15	28	26	2	0
KF Barrington	c Kunderan	b Chandrasekhar	13	34	26	2	0
TW Graveney	c Subramanya	b Prasanna	17	54	72	2	0
DL Amiss	c Wadekar	b Prasanna	45	139	136	8	0
*DB Close	c Chandrasekhar	b Prasanna	47	85	85	4	1
+JT Murray		b Bedi	4	11	13	1	0
R Illingworth	c Pataudi	b Prasanna	10	35	33	1	0
DJ Brown	not out		29	48	46	6	0
JA Snow	c Borde	b Chandrasekhar	9	10	15	1	0
RNS Hobbs	c Prasanna	b Chandrasekhar	2	6	5	0	0
Extras	(b 4, lb 2)		6				
Total	(all out, 76.5 overs)		203				

FoW: 1-6, 2-32, 3-34, 4-66, 5-144, 6-149, 7-149, 8-179, 9-193, 10-203.

Bowling	O	M	R	W
Subramanya	4	0	22	1
Bedi	24	9	60	2
Chandrasekhar	20.5	6	43	3
Venkataraghavan	2	1	4	0
Prasanna	24	9	60	4
Pataudi	2	0	8	0

India 2nd innings (target: 410 runs)

			R	M	B	4	6
+FM Engineer	c Barrington	b Hobbs	28	59	31	3	0
BK Kunderan	c Murray	b Close	33	128	117	4	0
AL Wadekar	c Boycott	b Illingworth	70	195	214	9	0
CG Borde		b Illingworth	10	16	18	2	0
*Nawab of Pataudi jnr	c Hobbs	b Close	47	131	145	8	0
Hanumant Singh	c Milburn	b Illingworth	6	11	11	1	0
V Subramanya	c Milburn	b Illingworth	4	17	19	0	0
S Venkataraghavan	c Hobbs	b Close	17	38	50	1	0
EAS Prasanna		b Hobbs	15	14	15	2	0
BS Bedi	not out		15	39	30	2	0
BS Chandrasekhar	c Boycott	b Close	22	23	30	4	0
Extras	(b 5, lb 5)		10				
Total	(all out, 112.4 overs)		277				

FoW: 1-48, 2-91, 3-102, 4-185, 5-201, 6-203, 7-207, 8-226, 9-240, 10-277.

Bowling	O	M	R	W
Snow	14	0	33	0
Brown	2	1	1	0
Illingworth	43	13	92	4
Hobbs	32	10	73	2
Close	21.4	7	68	4

The Ashes, 1968, 3rd Test England v Australia

Edgbaston, Birmingham   11,12,13,15,16 July 1968 (5-day match)
Result: Match drawn   Australia leads the 5-Test series 1-0
Toss: England   Umpires: CS Elliott and H Yarnold
Batsman of the match: MC Cowdrey and IM Chappell
Bowler of the match: R Illingworth, DL Underwood and EW Freeman

Close of Play:
* Day 1: No play
* Day 2: England 258/3 (Cowdrey 95*, Graveney 32*)
* Day 3: England 409, Australia 109/1 (Cowper 54*, Chappell 40*)
* Day 4: Australia 222, England 142/3d, Australia 9/0 (Redpath 6*, Cowper 3*)

England 1st innings

			R	M	B	4	6
JH Edrich	c Taber	b Freeman	88	280	245	10	0
G Boycott	lbw	b Gleeson	36	155	148	3	0
*MC Cowdrey		b Freeman	104	244	247	15	0
KF Barrington	lbw	b Freeman	0	6	4	0	0
TW Graveney		b Connolly	96	243	220	10	0
BR Knight	c Chappell	b Connolly	6	12	12	0	0
+APE Knott		b McKenzie	4	37	23	0	0
R Illingworth	lbw	b Gleeson	27	89	84	2	0
DJ Brown		b Connolly	0	1	3	0	0
JA Snow	c Connolly	b Freeman	19	36	31	2	0
DL Underwood	not out		14	27	24	1	0
Extras	(b 4, lb 6, w 1, nb 4)		15				
Total	(all out, 172.5 overs)		409				

FoW: 1-80, 2-188, 3-189, 4-282, 5-293, 6-323, 7-374, 8-374, 9-376, 10-409.

Bowling	O	M	R	W
McKenzie	47	14	115	1
Freeman	30.5	8	78	4
Connolly	35	8	84	3
Gleeson	46	19	84	2
Cowper	7	1	25	0
Walters	7	3	8	0

Australia 1st innings

			R	M	B	4	6
*WM Lawry	retired hurt		6	6	6	1	0
IR Redpath		b Brown	0	16	8	0	0
RM Cowper		b Snow	57	149	128	8	0
IM Chappell		b Knight	71	197	180	9	0
KD Walters		c & b Underwood	46	126	101	5	0
AP Sheahan		b Underwood	4	15	16	1	0
+HB Taber	c Barrington	b Illingworth	16	50	53	2	0
EW Freeman		b Illingworth	6	15	15	1	0
GD McKenzie	not out		0	26	22	0	0
JW Gleeson	c Illingworth	b Underwood	3	8	14	0	0
AN Connolly		b Illingworth	0	2	6	0	0
Extras	(b 1, lb 10, nb 2)		13				
Total	(all out, 91 overs)		222				

FoW: 1-10, 2-121, 3-165, 4-176, 5-213, 6-213, 7-219, 8-222, 9-222.

Bowling	O	M	R	W
Snow	17	3	46	1
Brown	13	2	44	1
Knight	14	2	34	1
Underwood	25	9	48	3
Illingworth	22	10	37	3

England 2nd innings

			R	M	B	4	6
JH Edrich	c Cowper	b Freeman	64	137	104	6	0
G Boycott	c Taber	b Connolly	31	83	87	3	0
TW Graveney	not out		39	67	50	4	0
BR Knight		b Connolly	1	3	2	0	0
+APE Knott	not out		4	8	10	1	0
Extras	(lb 2, nb 1)		3				
Total	(3 wickets declared, 42 overs)		142				

DNB: *MC Cowdrey, KF Barrington, R Illingworth, DJ Brown, JA Snow, DL Underwood.

FoW: 1-57, 2-131, 3-134.

Bowling	O	M	R	W
McKenzie	18	1	57	0
Freeman	9	2	23	1
Connolly	15	3	59	2

Australia 2nd innings (target: 330 runs)

			R	M	B	4	6
IR Redpath	lbw	b Snow	22	57	45	2	0
RM Cowper	not out		25	101	86	4	0
IM Chappell	not out		18	42	41	2	0
Extras	(lb 1, nb 2)		3				
Total	(1 wicket, 28.2 overs)		68				

DNB: *WM Lawry, KD Walters, AP Sheahan, +HB Taber, EW Freeman, GD McKenzie, JW Gleeson, AN Connolly.

FoW: 1-44.

Bowling	O	M	R	W
Snow	9	1	32	1
Brown	6	1	15	0
Underwood	8	4	14	0
Illingworth	5.2	2	4	0

England v Pakistan, 1971, 1st Test

Edgbaston, Birmingham   3,4,5,7,8 June 1971 (5-day match)
Result: Match drawn   3-Test series level 0-0
Toss: Pakistan   Umpires: CS Elliott and TW Spencer
Test Debuts: Imran Khan (Pak).

Close of Play:
* Day 1: Pakistan 270/1 (Zaheer Abbas 159*, Mushtaq Mohammad 72*)
* Day 2: Pakistan 602/7 (Asif Iqbal 98*, Wasim Bari 4*)
* Day 3: Pakistan 608/7d, England 320/7 (Knott 114*, Shuttleworth 7*)
* Day 4: England 353 and 184/3 (Luckhurst 87*, D'Oliveira 6*)

Pakistan 1st innings

			R	M	B	4	6
Aftab Gul		b D'Oliveira	28	115	85	3	0
Sadiq Mohammad		c & b Lever	17	84	59	0	0
Zaheer Abbas	c Luckhurst	b Illingworth	274	544	467	38	0
Mushtaq Mohammad	c Cowdrey	b Illingworth	100	347	283	13	0
Majid Khan	c Lever	b Illingworth	35	92	84	3	0
Asif Iqbal	not out		104	192	169	16	0
*Intikhab Alam	c Underwood	b D'Oliveira	9	16	23	2	0
Imran Khan	run out		5	12	5	0	0
+Wasim Bari	not out		4	16	12	0	0
Extras	(b 6, lb 14, nb 12)		32				
Total	(7 wickets declared, 195 overs)		608				

DNB: Asif Masood, Pervez Sajjad.

FoW: 1-68, 2-359, 3-441, 4-456, 5-469, 6-567, 7-581.

Bowling	O	M	R	W
Ward	29	3	115	0
Lever	38	7	126	1
Shuttleworth	23	2	83	0
D'Oliveira	38	17	78	2
Underwood	41	13	102	0
Illingworth	26	5	72	3

England 1st innings

			R	M	B	4	6
JH Edrich	c Zaheer Abbas	b Asif Masood	0	1	2	0	0
BW Luckhurst	c Sadiq Mohammad	b Pervez Sajjad	35	151	106	5	0
MC Cowdrey		b Asif Masood	16	41	36	3	0
DL Amiss		b Asif Masood	4	23	13	1	0
BL D'Oliveira	c Mushtaq Mohammad	b Intikhab Alam	73	132	136	14	0
*R Illingworth		b Intikhab Alam	1	19	22	0	0
+APE Knott		b Asif Masood	116	185	175	22	0
P Lever	c Pervez Sajjad	b Asif Masood	47	116	94	3	1
K Shuttleworth	c Imran Khan	b Pervez Sajjad	21	103	84	1	0
DL Underwood	not out		9	72	57	0	0
A Ward	c Mushtaq Mohammad	b Pervez Sajjad	0	6	10	0	0
Extras	(b 16, lb 6, w 3, nb 6)		31				
Total	(all out, 120.5 overs)		353				

FoW: 1-0, 2-29, 3-46, 4-112, 5-127, 6-148, 7-307, 8-324, 9-351, 10-353.

Bowling	O	M	R	W
Asif Masood	34	6	111	5
Imran Khan	23	9	36	0
Majid Khan	4	1	8	0
Intikhab Alam	31	13	82	2
Pervez Sajjad	15.5	6	46	3
Mushtaq Mohammad	13	3	39	0

England 2nd innings (following on)

			R	M	B	4	6
JH Edrich	c Wasim Bari	b Asif Masood	15	62	51	2	0
BW Luckhurst	not out		108	327	279	14	0
MC Cowdrey		b Asif Masood	34	93	105	5	0
DL Amiss	c Pervez Sajjad	b Asif Masood	22	70	54	2	0
BL D'Oliveira	c Mushtaq Mohammad	b Asif Iqbal	22	66	54	3	0
*R Illingworth	c Wasim Bari	b Asif Masood	1	13	9	0	0
+APE Knott	not out		4	11	4	1	0
Extras	(b 4, lb 5, w 6, nb 8)		23				
Total	(5 wickets, 90.5 overs)		229				

DNB: P Lever, K Shuttleworth, DL Underwood, A Ward.

FoW: 1-34, 2-114, 3-169, 4-218, 5-221.

Bowling	O	M	R	W
Asif Masood	23.5	7	49	4
Imran Khan	5	0	19	0
Intikhab Alam	20	8	52	0
Pervez Sajjad	14	4	27	0
Mushtaq Mohammad	8	2	23	0
Asif Iqbal	20	6	36	1

The Wisden Trophy, 1973, 2nd Test England v West Indies
Edgbaston, Birmingham
Result: Match drawn
Toss: West Indies

9,10,11,13,14 August 1973 (5-day match)
West Indies leads the 3-Test series 1-0
Umpires: HD Bird and AE Fagg

Close of Play:
* Day 1: West Indies 190/5 (Fredericks 98*, Murray 15*)
* Day 2: West Indies 327, England 96/0 (Boycott 52*, Amiss 42*)
* Day 3: England 265/7 (Fletcher 37*, Arnold 3*)
* Day 4: England 305, West Indies 205/5 (Sobers 21*, Murray 0*)

West Indies 1st innings

			R	M	B	4	6
RC Fredericks	c Amiss	b Underwood	150	510	443	17	0
RGA Headley		b Old	1	31	27	0	0
*RB Kanhai	c Greig	b Arnold	2	8	7	0	0
CH Lloyd	lbw	b Old	15	34	29	2	0
AI Kallicharran	c Hayes	b Arnold	34	82	65	3	0
GS Sobers		b Old	21	72	58	2	0
+DL Murray		b Underwood	25	205	139	0	0
BD Julien	c Greig	b Arnold	54	110	83	9	0
KD Boyce	lbw	b Illingworth	12	16	16	2	0
VA Holder	c Boycott	b Underwood	6	31	30	0	0
LR Gibbs	not out		1	4	3	0	0
Extras	(lb 2, w 1, nb 3)		6				
Total	(all out, 149.3 overs		327				

FoW: 1-14, 2-17, 3-39, 4-93, 5-128, 6-242, 7-280, 8-302, 9-325, 10-327.

Bowling

	O	M	R	W
Arnold	37	13	74	3
Old	30	3	86	3
Greig	26	3	84	0
Illingworth	32	19	37	1
Underwood	24.3	10	40	3

England 1st innings

			R	M	B	4	6
G Boycott	not out		56	202	155	4	0
DL Amiss	c Murray	b Julien	56	223	165	2	0
BW Luckhurst	lbw	b Sobers	12	87	57	1	0
FC Hayes	c Kallicharran	b Holder	29	148	149	2	0
AW Greig	c Fredericks	b Julien	27	82	84	1	1
+APE Knott		b Holder	0	22	12	0	0
KWR Fletcher	c Holder	b Sobers	52	214	151	6	0
*R Illingworth	lbw	b Holder	27	95	77	2	0
CM Old	run out		0	3	1	0	0
GG Arnold	c Kallicharran	b Sobers	24	108	96	1	0
DL Underwood	c Murray	b Gibbs	2	8	12	0	0
Extras	(b 4, lb 1, nb 15)		20				
Total	(all out, 156.4 overs)		305				

FoW: 1-119 (Amiss), 2-139 (Luckhurst), 3-191 (Greig), 4-191 (Hayes), 5-197 (Knott), 6-249 (Illingworth), 7-249 (Old), 8-299 (Arnold), 9-302 (Fletcher), 10-305 (Underwood).

Bowling

	O	M	R	W
Holder	44	16	83	3
Sobers	30	6	62	3
Boyce	19	2	48	0
Julien	26	8	55	2
Gibbs	35.4	21	32	1
Lloyd	2	0	5	0

West Indies 2nd innings

			R	M	B	4	6
RC Fredericks	c Knott	b Arnold	12	47	33	1	0
RGA Headley	c Knott	b Old	11	63	40	2	0
*RB Kanhai	c Arnold	b Illingworth	54	123	107	5	0
CH Lloyd	c Knott	b Underwood	94	172	139	8	1
AI Kallicharran		b Underwood	4	19	22	1	0
GS Sobers		b Arnold	74	160	147	12	0
+DL Murray	hit wicket	b Arnold	15	69	79	0	0
BD Julien		b Greig	11	58	31	0	0
KD Boyce	c Knott	b Arnold	0	1	1	0	0
VA Holder	c Luckhurst	b Greig	10	22	19	1	0
LR Gibbs	not out		3	10	8	0	0
Extras	(lb 10, nb 4)		14				
Total	(all out, 103.4 overs)		302				

FoW: 1-24, 2-42, 3-136, 4-153, 5-197, 6-247, 7-283, 8-283, 9-293, 10-302.

Bowling

	O	M	R	W
Arnold	20	1	43	4
Old	14	0	65	1
Greig	7.4	0	35	2
Illingworth	26	6	67	1
Underwood	32	9	66	2
Luckhurst	4	2	12	0

England 2nd innings (target: 325 runs)

			R	M	B	4	6
BW Luckhurst	c Murray	b Lloyd	42	125	122	3	0
DL Amiss	not out		86	197	186	9	0
FC Hayes	lbw	b Lloyd	0	6	10	0	0
KWR Fletcher	not out		44	62	89	5	0
Extras	(b 8, nb 2)		10				
Total	(2 wickets, 67 overs)		182				

DNB: G Boycott, AW Greig, +APE Knott, *R Illingworth, CM Old, GG Arnold, DL Underwood.
FoW: 1-96, 2-100.

Bowling

	O	M	R	W
Holder	7	1	17	0
Sobers	7	1	21	0
Julien	18	3	32	0
Gibbs	12	2	32	0
Lloyd	12	3	26	2
Fredericks	4	0	23	0
Kanhai	7	1	21	0

England v India, 1974, 3rd Test
Edgbaston, Birmingham
Result: England won by an innings and 78 runs
Toss: India
Test Debuts:

4,5,6,8 July 1974 (5-day match)
England wins the 3-Test series 3-0
Umpires: WE Alley and CS Elliott
SS Naik (Ind).

Close of Play:
* Day 1: No play
* Day 2: India 165, England 117/0 (Amiss 57*, Lloyd 53*)
* Day 3: England 459/2d, India 12/2 (Naik 3*)

India 1st innings

			R	M	B	4	6
SM Gavaskar	c Knott	b Arnold	0	1	1	0	0
SS Naik		b Arnold	4	28	19	0	0
*AL Wadekar	c Knott	b Hendrick	36	72	62	3	0
GR Viswanath		b Hendrick	28	68	55	1	0
AV Mankad	c Knott	b Arnold	14	73	56	0	0
+FM Engineer	not out		64	137	111	6	0
ED Solkar	lbw	b Old	3	21	14	0	0
S Abid Ali	run out		6	29	25	1	0
S Venkataraghavan	b Underwood		0	13	14	0	0
EAS Prasanna	c Greig	b Hendrick	0	15	9	0	0
BS Bedi	c Old	b Hendrick	0	1	1	0	0
Extras	(b 1, lb 1, nb 8)		10				
Total	(all out, 59.2 overs)		165				

FoW: 1-0, 2-17, 3-62, 4-81, 5-115, 6-129, 7-153, 8-156, 9-165, 10-165.

Bowling

	O	M	R	W
Arnold	14	3	43	3
Old	13	0	43	1
Hendrick	14.2	1	28	4
Greig	3	0	11	0
Underwood	15	3	30	1

England 1st innings

			R	M	B	4	6
DL Amiss	c Mankad	b Prasanna	79	165	180	6	0
D Lloyd	not out		214	448	396	17	0
*MH Denness	c & b Bedi		100	213	189	10	0
KWR Fletcher	not out		51	68	80	5	0
Extras	(b 4, lb 5, w 1, nb 5)		15				
Total	(2 wickets declared, 140 overs)		459				

DNB: JH Edrich, AW Greig, +APE Knott, CM Old, GG Arnold, DL Underwood, M Hendrick.
FoW: 1-157, 2-368.

Bowling

	O	M	R	W
Abid Ali	18	2	63	0
Solkar	18	5	52	0
Bedi	45	4	152	1
Venkataraghavan	23	1	71	0
Prasanna	35	4	101	1
Gavaskar	1	0	5	0

India 2nd innings

			R	M	B	4	6
SM Gavaskar	c Knott	b Old	4	7	8	0	0
SS Naik	lbw	b Greig	77	207	165	9	0
S Abid Ali		b Arnold	3	11	6	0	0
*AL Wadekar	lbw	b Old	5	10	9	1	0
GR Viswanath	c Greig	b Hendrick	25	58	51	2	0
AV Mankad	hit wicket	b Old	43	97	83	4	0
+FM Engineer	lbw	b Hendrick	33	70	46	6	0
ED Solkar	c Edrich	b Arnold	8	19	18	1	0
S Venkataraghavan	c Lloyd	b Greig	5	16	20	0	0
EAS Prasanna		b Hendrick	4	8	5	1	0
BS Bedi	not out		1	1	1	0	0
Extras	(lb 3, nb 5)		8				
Total	(all out, 67.4 overs)		216				

FoW: 1-6, 2-12, 3-21, 4-59, 5-146, 6-172, 7-183, 8-196, 9-211, 10-216.

Bowling

	O	M	R	W
Arnold	19	3	61	2
Hendrick	14.4	4	43	3
Underwood	3	1	3	0
Old	15	3	52	3
Greig	16	3	49	2

The Ashes, 1975, 1st Test England v Australia

Edgbaston, Birmingham   10,11,12,14 July 1975 (5-day match)
Result: Australia won by an innings & 85 runs Australia leads the 4-Test series 1-0
Toss: England   Umpires: HD Bird and AE Fagg
Test Debuts: GA Gooch (Eng); A Turner (Aus).

Close of Play:
* Day 1: Australia 243/5 (Edwards 22*, Marsh 47*)
* Day 2: Australia 359, England 83/7 (Underwood 8*, Old 0*)
* Day 3: England 101 and 93/5 (Knott 10*, Old 2*)

Australia 1st innings			R	M	B	4	6
RB McCosker		b Arnold	59	180	135	3	0
A Turner	c Denness	b Snow	37	125	96	4	0
*IM Chappell	c Fletcher	b Snow	52	109	95	7	0
GS Chappell	lbw	b Old	0	11	8	0	0
R Edwards	c Gooch	b Old	56	256	163	5	0
KD Walters	c Old	b Greig	14	32	26	2	0
+RW Marsh	c Fletcher	b Arnold	61	110	97	8	1
MHN Walker	c Knott	b Snow	7	28	22	0	0
JR Thomson	c Arnold	b Underwood	49	76	67	5	0
DK Lillee	c Knott	b Arnold	3	12	8	0	0
AA Mallett	not out		3	25	19	0	0
Extras	(b 1, lb 8, nb 9)		18				
Total	(all out, 121 overs)		359				

FoW: 1-80, 2-126, 3-135, 4-161, 5-186, 6-265, 7-286, 8-332, 9-343, 10-359.

Bowling	O	M	R	W
Arnold	33	3	91	3
Snow	33	6	86	3
Old	33	7	111	2
Greig	15	2	43	1
Underwood	7	3	10	1

England 1st innings			R	M	B	4	6
JH Edrich	lbw	b Lillee	34	164	123	2	0
DL Amiss	c Thomson	b Lillee	4	36	25	0	0
KWR Fletcher	c Mallett	b Walker	6	14	13	1	0
*MH Denness	c GS Chappell	b Walker	3	46	26	0	0
GA Gooch	c Marsh	b Walker	0	1	3	0	0
AW Greig	c Marsh	b Walker	8	15	12	2	0
+APE Knott		b Lillee	14	33	21	2	0
DL Underwood		b Lillee	10	25	22	1	0
CM Old	c GS Chappell	b Walker	13	30	26	2	0
JA Snow	lbw	b Lillee	0	8	3	0	0
GG Arnold	not out		0	2	1	0	0
Extras	(lb 3, w 5, nb 1)		9				
Total	(all out, 45.3 overs)		101				

FoW: 1-9, 2-24, 3-46, 4-46, 5-54, 6-75, 7-78, 8-87, 9-97, 10-101.

Bowling	O	M	R	W
Lillee	15	8	15	5
Thomson	10	3	21	0
Walker	17.3	5	48	5
Mallett	3	1	8	0

England 2nd innings (following on)			R	M	B	4	6
JH Edrich	c Marsh	b Walker	5	26	17	1	0
DL Amiss	c sub (GJ Gilmour)	b Thomson	5	85	78	0	0
KWR Fletcher	c Walters	b Lillee	51	129	99	6	0
*MH Denness		b Thomson	8	25	23	0	0
GA Gooch	c Marsh	b Thomson	0	7	7	0	0
AW Greig	c Marsh	b Walker	7	32	26	1	0
+APE Knott	c McCosker	b Thomson	38	176	125	4	0
CM Old	c Walters	b Lillee	7	22	22	0	0
JA Snow	c Marsh	b Thomson	34	46	40	4	1
DL Underwood		b Mallett	3	17	14	0	0
GG Arnold	not out		6	3	4	1	0
Extras	(lb 5, w 2, nb 2)		9				
Total	(all out, 75.2 overs)		173				

FoW: 1-7, 2-18, 3-20, 4-52, 5-90, 6-100, 7-122, 8-151, 9-167, 10-173.

Bowling	O	M	R	W
Lillee	20	8	45	2
Thomson	18	8	38	5
Walker	24	9	47	2
Mallett	13.2	6	34	1

England v Pakistan, 1978, 1st Test

Edgbaston, Birmingham   1,2,3,5 June 1978 (5-day match)
Result: England won by an innings and 57 runs   England leads the 3-Test series 1-0
Toss: Pakistan   Umpires: HD Bird and KE Palmer
Test Debuts: DI Gower (Eng).   Man of the Match: CM Old

Close of Play:
* Day 1: Pakistan 162/9 (Sarfraz Nawaz 32*, Liaqat Ali 9*)
* Day 2: Pakistan 164, England 256/3 (Radley 97*, Roope 22*)
* Day 3: England 452/8d, Pakistan 95/1 (Sadiq Mohammad 62*, Iqbal Qasim 0*)

Pakistan 1st innings			R	M	B	4	6
Mudassar Nazar		c & b Botham	14	34	30	0	0
Sadiq Mohammad	c Radley	b Old	23	75	49	3	0
Mohsin Khan		b Willis	35	125	100	4	0
Javed Miandad	c Taylor	b Old	15	69	58	2	0
Haroon Rashid	c Roope	b Willis	3	3	5	0	0
Wasim Raja	c Taylor	b Old	17	42	22	2	0
Sarfraz Nawaz	not out		32	87	55	5	0
*+Wasim Bari		b Old	0	1	1	0	0
Iqbal Qasim	c Taylor	b Old	0	1	2	0	0
Sikander Bakht	c Roope	b Old	0	1	1	0	0
Liaqat Ali	c Brearley	b Old	9	49	56	1	0
Extras	(lb 3, nb 13)		16				
Total	(all out, 60.4 overs)		164				

FoW: 1-20, 2-56, 3-91, 4-94, 5-103, 6-125, 7-125, 8-126, 9-126, 10-164.

Bowling	O	M	R	W
Willis	16	2	42	2
Old	22.4	6	50	7
Botham	15	4	52	1
Wood	3	2	2	0
Edmonds	4	2	2	0

England 1st innings			R	M	B	4	6
*JM Brearley	run out		38	164	121	2	0
B Wood	lbw	b Sikander Bakht	14	64	52	1	0
CT Radley	lbw	b Sikander Bakht	106	310	234	11	0
DI Gower	c Javed Miandad	b Sikander Bakht	58	103	102	9	0
GRJ Roope		b Sikander Bakht	32	120	83	3	0
G Miller	c Wasim Bari	b Mudassar Nazar	48	160	124	5	0
IT Botham	c Iqbal Qasim	b Liaqat Ali	100	195	140	11	0
CM Old	c Mudassar Nazar	b Iqbal Qasim	5	40	22	0	0
PH Edmonds	not out	4	5	4	0	0	
Extras	(lb 26, w 5, nb 16)		47				
Total	(8 wickets declared, 144 overs)		452				

DNB: +RW Taylor, RGD Willis.

FoW: 1-36, 2-101, 3-190, 4-275, 5-276, 6-399, 7-448, 8-452.

Bowling	O	M	R	W
Sarfraz Nawaz	6	1	12	0
Liaqat Ali	42	9	114	1
Mudassar Nazar	27	7	59	1
Iqbal Qasim	14	2	56	1
Sikander Bakht	45	13	132	4
Wasim Raja	10	1	32	0

Pakistan 2nd innings			R	M	B	4	6
Mudassar Nazar		b Edmonds	30	110	112	3	0
Sadiq Mohammad		b Old	79	164	123	9	0
Iqbal Qasim	retired hurt		5	49	32	0	0
Mohsin Khan	c Old	b Miller	38	157	115	3	0
Javed Miandad	c Brearley	b Edmonds	39	64	65	4	0
Haroon Rashid		b Willis	4	41	35	0	0
Wasim Raja		b Edmonds	9	25	23	1	0
Sarfraz Nawaz	not out		6	66	62	0	0
*+Wasim Bari	c Miller	b Edmonds	3	10	17	0	0
Sikander Bakht	c Roope	b Miller	2	15	25	0	0
Liaqat Ali		b Willis	3	17	19	0	0
Extras	(b 4, lb 4, w 1, nb 4)		13				
Total	(all out, 103.4 overs)		231				

FoW: 1-94, 2-123, 3-176, 4-193, 5-214, 6-220, 7-224, 8-227, 9-231.

Bowling	O	M	R	W
Willis	23.4	3	70	2
Old	25	12	38	1
Botham	17	3	47	0
Edmonds	26	10	44	4
Miller	12	4	19	2

England v India, 1979, 1st Test

Edgbaston, Birmingham
Result: England won by an innings and 83 runs
Toss: England
Test Debuts:
Man of the Match:

12,13,14,16 July 1979 (5-day match)
England leads the 4-Test series 1-0
Umpires: DJ Constant and BJ Meyer
B Reddy (Ind).
DI Gower

Close of Play:
Day 1: England 318/3 (Boycott 113, Gower 43*)
Day 2: England 633/5d, India 59/2 (Gavaskar 25)
Day 3: India 297 and 7/0 (Gavaskar 3, Chauhan 2*)

England 1st innings			R	M	B	4	6
*JM Brearley	c Reddy	b Kapil De	24	116	95	2	0
G Boycott	lbw	b Kapil Dev	155	458	341	12	0
DW Randall	c Reddy	b Kapil Dev	15	31	31	3	0
GA Gooch	c Reddy	b Kapil Dev	83	122	109	13	1
DI Gower	not out		200	365	279	24	0
IT Botham		b Kapil Dev	33	33	39	4	1
G Miller	not out		63	144	116	5	0
Extras	(b 4, lb 27, w 11, nb 18)		60				
Total	(5 wickets declared, 165.2 overs)		633				

DNB: PH Edmonds, +RW Taylor, RGD Willis, M Hendrick.

FoW: 1-66, 2-90, 3-235, 4-426, 5-468.

Bowling	O	M	R	W
Kapil Dev	48	15	146	5
Ghavri	38	5	129	0
Amarnath	13.2	2	47	0
Chandrasekhar	29	1	113	0
Venkataraghavan	31	4	107	0
Gaekwad	3	0	12	0
Chauhan	3	0	19	0

India 1st innings			R	M	B	4	6
SM Gavaskar	run out		61	178	160	3	0
CPS Chauhan	c Gooch	b Botham	4	16	8	1	0
DB Vengsarkar	c Gooch	b Edmonds	22	58	57	4	0
GR Viswanath	c Botham	b Edmonds	78	213	181	9	0
AD Gaekwad	c Botham	b Willis	25	126	124	3	0
M Amarnath		b Willis	31	67	47	6	0
N Kapil Dev	lbw	b Botham	1	4	6	0	0
KD Ghavri	c Brearley	b Willis	6	29	25	1	0
+B Reddy		b Hendrick	21	75	57	3	0
*S Venkataraghavan	c Botham	b Hendrick	28	52	46	3	2
BS Chandrasekhar	not out		0	4	0	0	0
Extras	(b 1, lb 4, w 3, nb 12)		20				
Total	(all out, 116.1 overs)		297				

FoW: 1-15, 2-59, 3-129, 4-205, 5-209, 6-210, 7-229, 8-251, 9-294, 10-297.

Bowling	O	M	R	W
Willis	24	9	69	3
Botham	26	4	86	2
Hendrick	24.1	9	36	2
Edmonds	26	11	60	2
Boycott	5	1	8	0
Mille	11	3	18	0

India 2nd innings (following on)			R	M	B	4	6
SM Gavaskar	c Gooch	b Hendrick	68	137	117	10	0
CPS Chauhan	c Randall	b Willis	56	167	142	8	0
DB Vengsarkar	c Edmonds	b Hendrick	7	32	24	0	0
GR Viswanath	c Taylor	b Botham	51	133	119	6	0
AD Gaekwad	c Gooch	b Botham	15	60	54	3	0
M Amarnath	lbw	b Botham	10	77	69	1	0
N Kapil Dev	c Hendrick	b Botham	21	18	17	4	0
KD Ghavri	c Randall	b Hendrick	4	30	25	0	0
+B Reddy	lbw	b Hendrick	0	7	1	0	0
*S Venkataraghavan	lbw	b Botham	0	4	6	0	0
BS Chandrasekhar	not out		0	4	3	0	0
Extras	(b 7, lb 12, nb 2)		21				
Tota	(all out, 95.4 overs)		253				

FoW: 1-124, 2-136, 3-136, 4-182, 5-227, 6-240, 7-249, 8-250, 9-251, 10-253.

Bowling	O	M	R	W
Willis	14	3	45	1
Botham	29	8	70	5
Hendrick	20.4	8	45	4
Edmonds	17	6	37	0
Miller	9	1	27	0
Gooch	6	3	8	0

The Ashes, 1981, 4th Test England v Australia

Edgbaston, Birmingham
Result: England won by 29 runs
Toss: England
Test Debuts:
Man of the Match:

30,31 July, 1,2 August 1981 (5-day match)
England leads the 6-Test series 2-1
Umpires: HD Bird and DO Oslear
MF Kent (Aus).
IT Botham

Close of Play:
Day 1: England 189, Australia 19/2 (Wood 6, Bright 0*)
Day 2: Australia 258, England 49/1 (Boycott 9, Gower 20*)
Day 3: England 219, Australia 9/1 (Dyson 5, Border 2*)

England 1st innings			R	M	B	4	6
G Boycott	c Marsh	b Alderman	13	44	42	1	0
*JM Brearley	c Border	b Lillee	48	166	109	6	0
DI Gower	c Hogg	b Alderman	0	10	10	0	0
GA Gooch	c Marsh	b Bright	21	50	43	3	0
MW Gatting	c Alderman	b Lillee	21	89	46	2	0
P Willey		b Bright	16	66	59	2	0
IT Botham		b Alderman	26	58	43	3	0
JE Emburey		b Hogg	3	39	33	0	0
+RW Taylor		b Alderman	0	1	3	0	0
CM Old	not out		11	35	23	0	0
RGD Willis	c Marsh	b Alderman	13	11	15	2	0
Extras	(b 1, lb 5, nb 10)		17				
Tota	(all out, 69.1 overs)		189				

FoW: 1-29 (Boycott), 2-29 (Gower), 3-60 (Gooch), 4-101 (Brearley), 5-126 (Gatting), 6-145 (Willey), 7-161 (Botham), 8-161 (Taylor), 9-165 (Emburey), 10-189 (Willis).

Bowling	O	M	R	W
Lillee	18	4	6	2
Alderman	23.1	8	42	5
Hogg	16	3	49	1
Bright	12	4	20	2

Australia 1st innings			R	M	B	4	6
GM Wood	run out (Old)		38	174	139	2	0
J Dyson		b Old	1	14	11	0	0
AR Border	c Taylor	b Old	2	25	24	0	0
RJ Bright	lbw	b Botham	27	63	51	4	0
*KJ Hughes	lbw	b Old	47	112	101	7	0
GN Yallop		b Emburey	30	98	70	3	0
MF Kent	c Willis	b Emburey	46	109	81	6	0
+RW Marsh		b Emburey	2	25	24	0	0
DK Lillee		b Emburey	18	40	43	3	0
RM Hogg	run out		0	1	0	0	0
TM Alderman	not out		3	6	3	0	0
Extras	(b 4, lb 19, nb 21)		44				
Total	(all out, 86.5 overs)		258				

FoW: 1-5 (Dyson), 2-14 (Border), 3-62 (Bright), 4-115 (Wood), 5-166 (Hughes), 6-203 (Yallop), 7-220 (Marsh), 8-253 (Kent), 9-253 (Hogg), 10-258 (Lillee).

Bowling	O	M	R	W
Willis	19	3	63	0
Old	21	8	44	3
Emburey	26.5	12	43	4
Botham	20	1	64	1

England 2nd innings			R	M	B	4	6
G Boycott	c Marsh	b Bright	29	190	136	3	0
*JM Brearley	lbw	b Lillee	13	17	17	2	0
DI Gower	c Border	b Bright	23	70	59	2	0
GA Gooch		b Bright	21	116	93	3	0
MW Gatting		b Bright	39	103	71	3	0
P Willey		b Bright	5	23	22	1	0
IT Botham	c Marsh	b Lillee	3	15	11	0	0
CM Old	c Marsh	b Alderman	23	27	24	3	0
JE Emburey	not out		37	92	79	5	0
+RW Taylor	lbw	b Alderman	8	70	47	0	0
RGD Willis	c Marsh	b Alderman	2	3	5	0	0
Extras	(lb 6, w 1, nb 9)		16				
Total	(all out, 92 overs)		219				

FoW: 1-18 (Brearley), 2-52 (Gower), 3-89 (Boycott), 4-98 (Gooch), 5-110 (Willey), 6-115 (Botham), 7-154 (Old), 8-167 (Gatting), 9-217 (Taylor), 10-219 (Willis).

Bowling	O	M	R	W
Lillee	26	9	5	2
Alderman	22	5	65	3
Hogg	10	3	19	0
Bright	34	17	68	5

Australia 2nd innings (target: 151 runs)			R	M	B	4	6
GM Wood	lbw	b Old	2	7	5	0	0
J Dyson	lbw	b Willis	13	62	46	1	0
AR Border	c Gatting	b Emburey	40	213	175	4	0
*KJ Hughes	c Emburey	b Willis	5	16	11	0	0
GN Yallop	c Botham	b Emburey	30	114	96	5	0
MF Kent		b Botham	10	68	45	1	0
+RW Marsh		b Botham	4	9	8	1	0
RJ Bright	lbw	b Botham	0	1	1	0	0
DK Lillee	c Taylor	b Botham	3	19	19	0	0
RM Hogg	not out		0	11	6	0	0
TM Alderman		b Botham	0	2	3	0	0
Extras	(b 1, lb 2, nb 11)		14				
Total	(all out, 67 overs)		121				

FoW: 1-2 (Wood), 2-19 (Dyson), 3-29 (Hughes), 4-87 (Yallop), 5-105 (Border), 6-114 (Marsh), 7-114 (Bright), 8-120 (Lillee), 9-121 (Kent), 10-121 (Alderman).

Bowling	O	M	R	W
Willis	20	6	37	2
Old	11	4	19	1
Emburey	22	10	40	2
Botham	14	9	11	5

England v Pakistan, 1982, 1st Test

Edgbaston, Birmingham
29,30,31 July, 1 August 1982 (5-day match)
Result: England won by 113 runs — England leads the 3-Test series 1-0
Toss: England
Umpires: DGL Evans and KE Palmer
Test Debuts: IA Greig, EE Hemmings (Eng).
Man of the Match: Imran Khan

Close of Play:
Day 1: England 272, Pakistan 4/1 (Mohsin Khan 0, Tahir Naqqash 0*)
Day 2: Pakistan 251, England 51/0 (Randall 30, Tavare 15*)
*Day 3: England 291

England 1st innings

			R	M	B	4	6
DW Randall		b Imran Khan	17	35	23	3	0
CJ Tavare	c Javed Miandad	b Abdul Qadir	54	252	180	8	0
AJ Lamb	c Wasim Bari	b Sikander Bakht	6	12	10	1	0
DI Gower	c Wasim Bari	b Imran Khan	74	164	144	12	0
IT Botham		b Imran Khan	2	14	6	0	0
MW Gatting		b Tahir Naqqash	17	67	54	2	0
G Miller		b Imran Khan	47	98	92	6	0
IA Greig	c sub	b Imran Khan	14	76	55	2	0
EE Hemmings	lbw	b Imran Khan	2	2	5	0	0
+RW Taylor	lbw	b Imran Khan	1	10	4	0	0
*RGD Willis	not out		0	8	8	0	0
Extras	(b 4, lb 10, w 6, nb 18)		38				
Total	(all out, 92.3 overs)		272				

FoW: 1-29, 2-37, 3-164, 4-172, 5-179, 6-228, 7-263, 8-265, 9-271, 10-272.

Bowling

	O	M	R	W
Imran Khan	25.3	11	52	7
Tahir Naqqash	15	4	46	1
Sikander Bakht	18	5	58	1
Mudassar Nazar	5	2	8	0
Abdul Qadir	29	7	70	1

Pakistan 1st innings

			R	M	B	4	6
Mudassar Nazar	lbw	b Botham	0	1	2	0	0
Mohsin Khan	c Willis	b Botham	26	48	35	5	0
Tahir Naqqash	c Taylor	b Greig	12	17	17	2	0
Mansoor Akhtar	c Miller	b Hemmings	58	176	151	7	0
Javed Miandad	c Willis	b Hemmings	30	59	40	3	0
Zaheer Abbas	lbw	b Greig	40	124	93	4	0
Wasim Raja	c Tavare	b Willis	26	62	55	3	0
*Imran Khan	c Taylor	b Willis	22	42	35	2	1
+Wasim Bari	not out		16	49	25	2	0
Abdul Qadir	lbw	b Greig	7	22	20	0	0
Sikander Bakht	c Hemmings	b Greig	1	8	8	0	0
Extras	(b 5, lb 2, w 1, nb 5)		13				
Total	(all out, 79.2 overs)		251				

FoW: 1-0, 2-29, 3-53, 4-110, 5-164, 6-198, 7-217, 8-227, 9-248, 10-251.

Bowling

	O	M	R	W
Botham	24	1	86	2
Greig	14.2	3	53	4
Willis	15	3	42	2
Hemmings	24	5	56	2
Miller	2	1	1	0

England 2nd innings

			R	M	B	4	6
DW Randall		b Imran Khan	105	249	156	11	0
CJ Tavare	c Mohsin Khan	b Imran Khan	17	88	70	2	0
AJ Lamb	lbw	b Tahir Naqqash	5	45	27	1	0
DI Gower	c Mudassar Nazar	b Tahir Naqqash	13	21	19	2	0
MW Gatting	c Wasim Bari	b Tahir Naqqash	5	12	14	1	0
IT Botham	lbw	b Tahir Naqqash	0	1	1	0	0
G Miller		b Tahir Naqqash	5	19	21	0	0
IA Greig		b Abdul Qadir	7	28	27	0	0
EE Hemmings	c Mansoor Akhtar	b Abdul Qadir	19	64	52	2	0
+RW Taylor	c Abdul Qadir	b Wasim Raja	54	172	149	4	0
*RGD Willis	not out		28	129	103	3	0
Extras	(b 10, lb 11, w 7, nb 5)		33				
Total	(all out, 105.3 overs)		291				

FoW: 1-62, 2-98, 3-127, 4-137, 5-137, 6-146, 7-170, 8-188, 9-212, 10-291.

Bowling

	O	M	R	W
Imran Khan	32	5	84	2
Tahir Naqqash	18	7	40	5
Sikander Bakht	13	5	34	0
Abdul Qadir	40	10	100	2
Wasim Raja	2.3	2	0	1

Pakistan 2nd innings (target: 313 runs)

			R	M	B	4	6
Mudassar Nazar	lbw	b Botham	0	1	2	0	0
Mohsin Khan	lbw	b Botham	35	79	55	5	0
Mansoor Akhtar	c Taylor	b Botham	0	2	4	0	0
Javed Miandad	run out		10	49	29	1	0
Zaheer Abbas	c Taylor	b Willis	4	36	25	0	0
Wasim Raja	c Gower	b Willis	16	21	13	1	0
*Imran Khan		b Miller	65	138	103	6	2
+Wasim Bari	c Taylor	b Botham	12	46	35	2	0
Tahir Naqqash		c & b Hemmings	39	42	44	6	0
Abdul Qadir	c Randall	b Miller	9	29	34	2	0
Sikander Bakht	not out		1	7	2	0	0
Extras	(lb 3, nb 5)		8				
Total	(all out, 56.4 overs)		199				

FoW: 1-0, 2-0, 3-38, 4-54, 5-66, 6-77, 7-98, 8-151, 9-178, 10-199.

Bowling

	O	M	R	W
Botham	21	7	70	4
Greig	4	1	19	0
Willis	14	2	49	2
Hemmings	10	4	27	1
Miller	7.4	1	26	2

The Wisden Trophy, 1984, 1st Test England v West Indies

Edgbaston, Birmingham
14,15,16,18 June 1984 (5-day match)
Result: West Indies won by an innings and 180 runs — West Indies leads the 5-Test series 1-0
Toss: England
Umpires: HD Bird and BJ Meyer
Test Debuts: TA Lloyd (Eng).
Man of the Match: HA Gomes

Close of Play:
Day 1: England 191, West Indies 53/2 (Gomes 4, Richards 14*)
Day 2: West Indies 421/7 (Harper 0)
Day 3: West Indies 606, England 112/4 (Downton 34, Botham 30*)

England 1st innings

			R	M	B	4	6
G Fowler	c Dujon	b Garner	0	8	9	0	0
TA Lloyd	retired hurt		10	30	17	1	0
DW Randall		b Garner	0	6	3	0	0
*DI Gower	c Harper	b Holding	10	67	49	1	0
AJ Lamb	c Lloyd	b Baptiste	15	41	32	2	0
IT Botham	c Garner	b Harper	64	144	82	10	0
G Mille	c Dujon	b Garner	22	43	42	4	0
DR Pringle	c Dujon	b Holding	4	11	7	1	0
+PR Downton	lbw	b Garner	33	112	101	3	0
NGB Cook	c Lloyd	b Marshall	2	16	15	0	0
RGD Willis	not out		10	22	12	1	0
Extras	(b 8, lb 5, nb 8)		21				
Total	(all out, 59.3 overs)		191				

FoW: 1-1, 2-5, 3-45, 4-49, 5-89, 6-103, 7-168, 8-173, 9-191.

Bowling

	O	M	R	W
Marshall	14	4	37	1
Garner	14.3	2	53	4
Holding	16	4	44	2
Baptiste	11	3	28	1
Harper	4	1	8	1

West Indies 1st innings

			R	M	B	4	6
CG Greenidge	lbw	b Willis	19	52	47	3	0
DL Haynes	lbw	b Willis	8	38	24	1	0
HA Gomes	c Miller	b Pringle	143	381	279	16	0
IVA Richards	c Randall	b Cook	117	208	154	17	1
+PJL Dujon	c Gower	b Miller	23	62	51	2	0
*CH Lloyd	c Pringle	b Botham	71	110	89	8	0
MD Marshall	lbw	b Pringle	2	8	5	0	0
RA Harper		b Pringle	14	45	31	3	0
EAE Baptiste	not out		87	160	131	11	0
MA Holding	c Willis	b Pringle	69	114	80	8	4
J Garner	c Lamb	b Pringle	0	3	6	0	0
Extras	(b 6, lb 17, w 2, nb 28)		53				
Total	(all out, 143 overs)		606				

FoW: 1-34, 2-35, 3-241, 4-294, 5-418, 6-418, 7-421, 8-455, 9-605, 10-606.

Bowling

	O	M	R	W
Willis	25	3	108	2
Botham	34	7	127	1
Pringle	31	5	108	5
Cook	38	6	127	1
Miller	15	1	83	1

England 2nd innings

			R	M	B	4	6
G Fowler	lbw	b Garner	7	45	40	0	0
+PR Downton	c Greenidge	b Harper	56	275	187	3	0
DW Randall	c Lloyd	b Garner	1	9	9	0	0
*DI Gower	c Dujon	b Garner	12	15	17	1	0
AJ Lamb	c Richards	b Marshall	13	50	32	1	0
IT Botham	lbw	b Garner	38	80	66	4	1
G Miller	c Harper	b Marshall	11	12	10	1	0
DR Pringle	not out	46	99	88	5	0
NGB Cook	run out	9	17	12	1	0
RGD Willis	c Dujon	b Garner	22	26	13	3	0
TA Lloyd	absent hurt	-				
Extras	(b 1, lb 5, w 4, nb 10)		20				
Tota	(all out, 76.5 overs)		235				

FoW: 1-17, 2-21, 3-37, 4-65, 5-127, 6-138, 7-181, 8-193, 9-235.

Bowling

	O	M	R	W
Marshall	23	7	65	2
Garner	23.5	7	55	5
Holding	12	3	29	0
Baptiste	5	1	18	0
Harper	13	3	48	1

The Ashes, 1985, 5th Test England v Australia

Edgbaston, Birmingham | 15,16,17,19,20 August 1985 (5-day match)
Result: England won by an innings and 118 runs | England leads the 6-Test series 2-1
Toss: England | Umpires: DJ Constant and DR Shepherd
Test Debuts: | LB Taylor (Eng).
Man of the Match: | RM Ellison

Close of Play:
Day 1: Australia 181/2 (Wessels 76, Border 43*)
Day 2: Australia 335/8 (Lawson 53, Thomson 28*)
Day 3: Australia 335, England 355/1 (Robinson 140, Gower 169*)
Day 4: England 595/5d, Australia 37/5 (Ritchie 0, Phillips 1*)

Australia 1st innings

			R	M	B	4	6
GM Wood	c Edmonds	b Botham	19	53	45	3	0
AMJ Hilditch	c Downton	b Edmonds	39	112	71	5	0
KC Wessels	c Downton	b Ellison	83	226	205	8	0
*AR Border	c Edmonds	b Ellison	45	157	111	5	0
GM Ritchie	c Botham	b Ellison	8	38	22	1	0
+WB Phillips	c Robinson	b Ellison	15	55	42	3	0
SP O'Donnell	c Downton	b Taylor	1	9	3	0	0
GF Lawson	run out		53	140	93	7	0
CJ McDermott	c Gower	b Ellison	35	69	51	4	0
JR Thomson	not out		28	55	43	2	1
RG Holland	c Edmonds	b Ellison	0	1	4	0	0
Extras	(lb 4, w 1, nb 4)		9				
Total	(all out, 113.5 overs)		335				

FoW: 1-44, 2-92, 3-189, 4-191, 5-207, 6-208, 7-218, 8-276, 9-335, 10-335.

Bowling

	O	M	R	W
Botham	27	1	108	1
Taylor	26	5	78	1
Ellison	31.5	9	77	6
Edmonds	20	4	47	1
Emburey	9	2	21	0

England 1st innings

			R	M	B	4	6
GA Gooch	c Phillips	b Thomson	19	48	28	4	0
RT Robinson		b Lawson	148	393	294	18	0
*DI Gower	c Border	b Lawson	215	452	314	25	1
MW Gatting	not out		100	214	127	12	0
AJ Lamb	c Wood	b McDermott	46	86	62	5	0
IT Botham	c Thomson	b McDermott	18	11	7	1	2
+PR Downton	not out		0	3	0	0	0
Extras	(b 7, lb 20, nb 22)		49				
Total	(5 wickets declared, 134 overs)		595				

DNB: JE Emburey, RM Ellison, PH Edmonds, LB Taylor.

FoW: 1-38, 2-369, 3-463, 4-572, 5-592.

Bowling

	O	M	R	W
Lawson	37	1	135	2
McDermott	31	2	155	2
Thomson	19	1	101	1
Holland	25	4	95	0
O'Donnell	16	3	69	0
Border	6	1	13	0

Australia 2nd innings

			R	M	B	4	6
GM Wood	c Robinson	b Ellison	10	12	14	1	0
AMJ Hilditch	c Ellison	b Botham	10	82	51	1	0
KC Wessels	c Downton	b Ellison	10	52	36	1	0
RG Holland	lbw	b Ellison	0	1	1	0	0
*AR Border		b Ellison	2	18	17	0	0
GM Ritchie	c Lamb	b Emburey	20	125	102	0	0
+WB Phillips	c Gower	b Edmonds	59	102	90	11	0
SP O'Donnell		b Botham	11	40	39	1	0
GF Lawson	c Gower	b Edmonds	3	7	8	0	0
CJ McDermott	c Edmonds	b Botham	8	23	22	1	0
JR Thomson	not out		4	3	5	1	0
Extras	(b 1, lb 3, nb 1)		5				
Total	(all out, 64.1 overs)		142				

FoW: 1-10, 2-32, 3-32, 4-35, 5-36, 6-113, 7-117, 8-120, 9-137, 10-142.

Bowling

	O	M	R	W
Botham	14.1	2	52	3
Taylor	13	4	27	0
Ellison	9	3	27	4
Edmonds	15	9	13	2
Emburey	13	5	19	1

England v India, 1986, 3rd Test

Edgbaston, Birmingham | 3,4,5,7,8 July 1986 (5-day match)
Result: Match drawn | India wins the 3-Test series 2-0
Toss: England | Umpires: HD Bird and BJ Meyer
Test Debuts: | MR Benson, NV Radford (Eng).
Man of the Match: | MW Gatting
Men of the Series: | MW Gatting and DB Vengsarkar

Close of Play:
Day 1: England 315/6 (Gatting 141, Foster 13*)
Day 2: England 390, India 182/3 (Amarnath 59, Azharuddin 20*)
*Day 3: India 390
Day 4: England 231/9 (Emburey 24, Radford 1*)

England 1st innings

			R	M	B	4	6
GA Gooch	c More	b Kapil Dev	0	2	4	0	0
MR Benson		b Maninder Singh	21	98	66	2	0
CWJ Athey	c More	b Kapil Dev	0	6	3	0	0
DI Gower	lbw	b Sharma	49	53	81	6	0
*MW Gatting	not out		183	383	294	20	2
DR Pringle	c Amarnath	b Shastri	44	106	95	5	1
JE Emburey	c Shastri	b Maninder Singh	38	92	69	6	0
NA Foster		b Binny	17	52	52	3	0
PH Edmonds		b Sharma	18	50	30	2	0
+BN French		b Sharma	8	34	23	1	0
NV Radford	c Gavaskar	b Sharma	0	15	10	0	0
Extras	(lb 7, nb 5)		12				
Total	(all out, 116.3 overs)		390				

FoW: 1-0, 2-0, 3-61, 4-88, 5-184, 6-278, 7-327, 8-367, 9-384, 10-390.

Bowling

	O	M	R	W
Kapil Dev	31	6	89	2
Binny	17	1	53	1
Sharma	29.3	2	130	4
Maninder Singh	25	3	66	2
Shastri	14	1	45	1

India 1st innings

			R	M	B	4	6
SM Gavaskar		b Pringle	29	57	36	4	0
K Srikkanth	c Pringle	b Radford	23	40	34	3	0
M Amarnath		b Edmonds	79	260	237	9	0
DB Vengsarkar	c Gooch	b Radford	38	104	101	4	0
M Azharuddin	c French	b Foster	64	209	134	6	0
RJ Shastri	c Gooch	b Foster	18	79	54	2	0
*N Kapil Dev	c French	b Foster	26	40	21	5	0
+KS More	c French	b Emburey	48	157	119	4	0
RMH Binny	c Gower	b Emburey	40	106	87	4	0
C Sharma	c Gower	b Pringle	9	14	10	2	0
Maninder Singh	not out		0	12	9	0	0
Extras	(b 3, lb 7, w 1, nb 5)		16				
Total	(all out, 139.5 overs)		390				

FoW: 1-53, 2-58, 3-139, 4-228, 5-266, 6-275, 7-302, 8-370, 9-385, 10-390.

Bowling

	O	M	R	W
Radford	35	3	131	2
Foster	41	9	93	3
Pringle	21	2	61	2
Edmonds	24	7	55	1
Emburey	18.5	7	40	2

England 2nd innings

			R	M	B	4	6
GA Gooch	lbw	b Sharma	40	50	43	5	0
MR Benson		b Shastri	30	139	96	2	0
CWJ Athey	c More	b Sharma	38	171	114	2	0
DI Gower	c Gavaskar	b Sharma	26	68	52	1	1
*MW Gatting	lbw	b Sharma	26	51	44	3	0
DR Pringle	c More	b Maninder Singh	7	35	31	1	0
JE Emburey	not out		27	119	110	2	0
NA Foster	run out		0	4	4	0	0
PH Edmonds	c Binny	b Maninder Singh	10	54	40	1	0
+BN French	c More	b Sharma	1	32	31	0	0
NV Radford	c Azharuddin	b Sharma	1	16	14	0	0
Extras	(b 10, lb 6, w 2, nb 11)		29				
Total	(all out, 94 overs)		235				

FoW: 1-49, 2-102, 3-152, 4-163, 5-190, 6-190, 7-190, 8-217, 9-229, 10-235.

Bowling

	O	M	R	W
Kapil Dev	7	1	38	0
Binny	16	1	41	0
Sharma	24	4	58	6
Maninder Singh	22	5	41	2
Shastri	23	8	39	1
Amarnath	2	1	2	0

India 2nd innings (target: 236 runs)

			R	M	B	4	6
SM Gavaskar	c French	b Foster	54	159	135	6	0
K Srikkanth	c Pringle	b Edmonds	23	81	50	4	0
M Amarnath	c French	b Edmonds	16	55	47	2	0
DB Vengsarkar	c French	b Edmonds	0	5	3	0	0
M Azharuddin	not out		29	146	106	2	0
RJ Shastri	c Emburey	b Edmonds	0	5	6	0	0
+KS More	not out		31	124	125	2	0
Extras	(b 1, lb 15, w 1, nb 4)		21				
Total	(5 wickets, 78 overs)		174				

DNB: *N Kapil Dev, RMH Binny, C Sharma, Maninder Singh.
FoW: 1-58, 2-101, 3-101, 4-104, 5-105.

Bowling

	O	M	R	W
Radford	3	0	17	0
Foster	22	9	48	1
Pringle	16	5	33	0
Edmonds	28	11	31	4
Emburey	7	1	19	0
Gatting	2	0	10	0

England v Pakistan, 1987, 4th Test

Edgbaston, Birmingham
Result: Match drawn
Toss: England
Man of the Match:

23,24,25,27,28 July 1987 (5-day match)
Pakistan leads the 5-Test series 1-0
Umpires: BJ Meyer and AGT Whitehead
MW Gatting

Close of Play:
Day 1: Pakistan 250/3 (Mudassar Nazar 102, Saleem Malik 13*)
Day 2: Pakistan 439, England 18/0 (Broad 14, Robinson 2*)
Day 3: England 273/5 (Gatting 35, Botham 16*)
Day 4: England 521, Pakistan 38/0 (Mudassar Nazar 6, Shoaib Mohammad 32*)

Pakistan 1st innings

			R	M	B	4	6
Mudassar Nazar	lbw	b Dilley	124	416	362	16	0
Shoaib Mohammad	c Foster	b Edmonds	18	65	49	2	0
Mansoor Akhtar		b Foster	26	86	87	4	0
Javed Miandad	lbw	b Dilley	75	156	145	8	1
Saleem Malik	c French	b Dilley	24	127	95	3	0
Ijaz Ahmed	lbw	b Botham	20	49	35	4	0
*Imran Khan	c Emburey	b Dilley	0	1	1	0	0
+Saleem Yousuf	not out		91	182	152	14	0
Wasim Akram	c Botham	b Foster	26	52	44	4	1
Abdul Qadir	c Edmonds	b Dilley	6	36	30	0	0
Mohsin Kamal	run out		10	61	47	1	0
Extras	(b 4, lb 11, w 1, nb 3)		19				
Total	(all out, 173.3 overs)		439				

FoW: 1-44, 2-83, 3-218, 4-284, 5-289, 6-289, 7-317, 8-360, 9-384, 10-439.

Bowling	O	M	R	W
Dilley	35	6	92	5
Foster	37	8	107	2
Emburey	26	7	48	0
Edmonds	24.3	12	50	1
Botham	48	13	121	1
Gatting	3	0	6	0

England 1st innings

			R	M	B	4	6
BC Broad	c Saleem Yousuf	b Imran Khan	54	206	148	5	0
RT Robinson	c Saleem Yousuf	b Wasim Akram	80	270	208	11	0
CWJ Athey		b Imran Khan	0	27	17	0	0
DI Gower	c Saleem Yousuf	b Imran Khan	61	141	105	10	0
*MW Gatting	c Wasim Akram	b Imran Khan	124	399	280	16	0
+BN French		b Imran Khan	0	2	2	0	0
IT Botham		c & b Wasim Akram	37	58	39	6	0
JE Emburey	bw	b Wasim Akram	58	179	141	8	1
NA Foster	run out		29	78	63	3	0
PH Edmonds	not out		24	36	26	3	0
GR Dilley		b Imran Khan	2	9	9	0	0
Extras	(b 1, lb 24, w 11, nb 16)		52				
Total	(all out, 169.5 overs)		521				

FoW: 1-119, 2-132, 3-157, 4-251, 5-251, 6-300, 7-443, 8-484, 9-512, 10-521.

Bowling	O	M	R	W
Imran Khan	41.5	8	129	6
Wasim Akram	43	12	83	3
Abdul Qadir	21	4	65	0
Mudassar Nazar	35	7	97	0
Mohsin Kamal	29	2	122	0

Pakistan 2nd innings

			R	M	B	4	6
Mudassar Nazar		b Dilley	10	67	47	1	0
Shoaib Mohammad	lbw	b Foster	50	152	136	7	0
Mansoor Akhtar	lbw	b Foster	17	58	34	2	0
Javed Miandad	c Emburey	b Foster	4	8	8	1	0
Saleem Malik		c & b Botham	17	12	14	4	0
Ijaz Ahmed		b Botham	11	24	18	1	0
*Imran Khan	lbw	b Foster	37	129	94	5	0
+Saleem Yousuf	c Gatting	b Edmonds	17	53	44	1	0
Wasim Akram	c Edmonds	b Dilley	6	15	18	1	0
Abdul Qadir	run out		20	46	26	2	0
Mohsin Kamal	not out		0	6	4	0	0
Extras	(lb 13, w 1, nb 2)		16				
Total	(all out, 73.3 overs)		205				

FoW: 1-47, 2-80, 3-85, 4-104, 5-104, 6-116, 7-156, 8-165, 9-204, 10-205.

Bowling	O	M	R	W
Foster	27	7	59	4
Dilley	18	3	53	2
Emburey	4	1	3	0
Botham	20.3	3	66	2
Edmonds	4	1	11	1

England 2nd innings (target: 124 runs)

			R	M	B	4	6
BC Broad	c Mudassar Nazar	b Imran Khan	30	23	23	5	0
RT Robinson	c Imran Khan	b Wasim Akram	4	27	10	0	0
DI Gower		b Imran Khan	18	28	15	2	0
IT Botham	c Mohsin Kamal	b Wasim Akram	6	8	7	1	0
*MW Gatting	run out		8	19	10	1	0
CWJ Athey	not out		14	35	20	1	0
JE Emburey	run out		20	29	18	1	1
PH Edmonds	run out		0	2	2	0	0
+BN French	not out		1	1	1	0	0
Extras	(lb 7, w 1)		8				
Total	(7 wickets, 17.4 overs)		109				

DNB: NA Foster, GR Dilley.
FoW: 1-37, 2-39, 3-53, 4-72, 5-73, 6-108, 7-108.

Bowling	O	M	R	W
Imran Khan	9	0	61	2
Wasim Akram	8.4	0	41	2

The Ashes, 1989, 3rd Test England v Australia

Edgbaston, Birmingham
Result: Match drawn
Toss: Australia
Test Debuts:
Man of the Match:

6,7,8,10,11 July 1989 (5-day match)
Australia leads the 6-Test series 2-0
Umpires: HD Bird and JW Holder
ARC Fraser (Eng).
DM Jones

Close of Play:
Day 1: Australia 232/4 (Jones 71, Waugh 17*)
Day 2: Australia 294/6 (Jones 101, Hughes 1*)
Day 3: Australia 391/7 (Jones 141, Hohns 40*)
Day 4: Australia 424, England 185/7 (Emburey 2, Fraser 12*)

Australia 1st innings

			R	M	B	4	6
GR Marsh	lbw	b Botham	42	147	134	2	0
MA Taylor	st Russell	b Emburey	43	138	99	5	0
DC Boon	run out		38	136	111	5	0
*AR Border		b Emburey	8	18	21	1	0
DM Jones	c sub (I Folley)	b Fraser	157	400	294	17	0
SR Waugh		b Fraser	43	80	54	6	0
+IA Healy		b Fraser	2	16	12	0	0
MG Hughes	c Botham	b Dilley	2	22	16	0	0
TV Hohns	c Gooch	b Dilley	40	122	98	4	0
GF Lawson		b Fraser	12	35	28	2	0
TM Alderman	not out		0	11	8	0	0
Extras	(lb 20, nb 17)		37				
Total	(all out, 142 overs)		424				

FoW: 1-88, 2-94, 3-105, 4-201, 5-272, 6-289, 7-299, 8-391, 9-421, 10-424.

Bowling	O	M	R	W
Dilley	31	3	123	2
Jarvis	23	4	82	0
Fraser	33	8	63	4
Botham	26	5	75	1
Emburey	29	5	61	2

England 1st innings

			R	M	B	4	6
GA Gooch	lbw	b Lawson	8	40	33	1	0
TS Curtis	lbw	b Hughes	41	121	81	7	0
*DI Gower	lbw	b Alderman	8	39	26	1	0
CJ Tavare	c Taylor	b Alderman	2	11	9	0	0
KJ Barnett	c Healy	b Waugh	10	31	21	2	0
IT Botham		b Hughes	46	157	110	6	0
+RC Russell	c Taylor	b Hohns	42	158	131	3	0
JE Emburey	c Boon	b Lawson	26	78	58	5	0
ARC Fraser	run out		12	25	29	1	0
GR Dilley	not out		11	87	63	1	0
PW Jarvis	lbw	b Alderman	22	40	31	2	0
Extras	(b 1, lb 2, nb 11)		14				
Total	(all out, 96.3 overs)		242				

FoW: 1-17, 2-42, 3-47, 4-75, 5-75, 6-171, 7-171, 8-185, 9-215, 10-242.

Bowling	O	M	R	W
Alderman	26.3	6	61	3
Lawson	21	4	54	2
Hughes	22	4	68	2
Waugh	11	3	38	1
Hohns	16	8	18	1

Australia 2nd innings

			R	M	B	4	6
GR Marsh		b Jarvis	42	110	86	4	0
MA Taylor	c Botham	b Gooch	51	172	148	4	0
DC Boon	not out		22	119	112	1	0
+IA Healy	not out		33	57	46	3	0
Extras	(b 4, lb 4, nb 2)		10				
Total	(2 wickets, 65 overs)		158				

DNB: *AR Border, DM Jones, SR Waugh, MG Hughes, TV Hohns, GF Lawson, TM Alderman.

FoW: 1-81, 2-109.

Bowling	O	M	R	W
Dilley	10	4	27	0
Fraser	12	0	29	0
Emburey	20	8	37	0
Jarvis	6	1	20	1
Gooch	14	5	30	1
Curtis	3	0	7	0

England v New Zealand, 1990, 3rd Test

Edgbaston, Birmingham   5,6,7,9,10 July 1990 (5-day match)
Result: England won by 114 runs   England wins the 3-Test series 1-0
Toss: New Zealand   Umpires: JW Holder and BJ Meyer
Test Debuts: CC Lewis (Eng); AC Parore (NZ).   Man of the Match: DE Malcolm
Men of the Series: MA Atherton and Sir RJ Hadlee

Close of Play:
Day 1: England 191/1 (Gooch 95, Stewart 8*)
Day 2: England 435, New Zealand 9/0 (Franklin 8, Wright 1*)
*Day 3: New Zealand 249
Day 4: England 158, New Zealand 101/2 (Jones 37, Crowe 10*)

England 1st innings

			R	M	B	4	6
*GA Gooch	c Hadlee	b Morrison	154	396	281	19	1
MA Atherton	lbw	b Snedden	82	205	176	12	0
AJ Stewart	c Parore	b Morrison	9	48	39	1	0
AJ Lamb	c Parore	b Hadlee	2	26	17	0	0
RA Smith	c Jones	b Bracewell	19	39	34	3	0
NH Fairbrother	lbw	b Snedden	2	11	8	0	0
+RC Russell		b Snedden	43	116	99	7	0
CC Lewis	c Rutherford	b Bracewell	32	97	76	4	0
GC Small	not out		44	107	89	7	0
EE Hemmings	c Parore	b Hadlee	20	64	4	2	1
DE Malcolm		b Hadlee	0	2	3	0	0
Extras	(b 4, lb 15, nb 9)		28				
Total	(all out, 141.5 overs)		435				

FoW: 1-170, 2-193, 3-198, 4-245, 5-254, 6-316, 7-351, 8-381, 9-435, 10-435.

Bowling	O	M	R	W
Hadlee	37.5	8	97	3
Morrison	26	7	81	2
Snedden	35	9	106	3
Bracewell	42	12	130	2
Jones	1	0	2	0

New Zealand 1st innings

			R	M	B	4	6
TJ Franklin	c Smith	b Hemmings	66	278	207	8	0
*JG Wright	c Russell	b Malcolm	24	96	74	4	0
AH Jones	c Russell	b Malcolm	2	31	14	0	0
MD Crowe	lbw	b Lewis	11	47	35	1	0
MJ Greatbatch		b Malcolm	45	94	82	8	0
KR Rutherford	c Stewart	b Hemmings	29	77	59	4	0
Sir RJ Hadlee	c Atherton	b Hemmings	8	28	19	0	0
JG Bracewell		b Hemmings	25	28	22	4	0
+AC Parore	not out		12	53	38	2	0
MC Snedden	lbw	b Hemmings	2	27	33	0	0
DK Morrison		b Hemmings	1	11	10	0	0
Extras	(b 9, lb 11, w 2, nb 2)		24				
Total	(all out, 98.3 overs)		249				

FoW: 1-45, 2-67, 3-90, 4-161, 5-163, 6-185, 7-223, 8-230, 9-243, 10-249.

Bowling	O	M	R	W
Small	18	7	44	0
Malcolm	25	7	59	3
Lewis	19	5	51	1
Hemmings	27.3	10	58	6
Atherton	9	5	17	0

England 2nd innings

			R	M	B	4	6
*GA Gooch		b Snedden	30	48	32	4	0
MA Atherton	c Rutherford	b Bracewell	70	192	132	5	0
AJ Stewart	lbw	b Bracewell	15	40	30	2	0
AJ Lamb	st Parore	b Bracewell	4	11	9	1	0
RA Smith		c & b Hadlee	14	32	25	2	0
NH Fairbrother	lbw	b Bracewell	3	6	8	0	0
+RC Russell	c sub (JJ Crowe)	b Hadlee	0	11	8	0	0
CC Lewis	c Parore	b Hadlee	1	16	23	0	0
GC Small	not out		11	32	22	2	0
EE Hemmings		b Hadlee	0	6	6	0	0
DE Malcolm	lbw	b Hadlee	0	3	3	0	0
Extras	(lb 6, nb 4)		10				
Total	(all out, 49 overs)		158				

FoW: 1-50, 2-87, 3-99, 4-129, 5-136, 6-141, 7-146, 8-157, 9-158, 10-158.

Bowling	O	M	R	W
Hadlee	21	3	53	5
Morrison	3	1	29	0
Snedden	9	0	32	1
Bracewell	16	5	38	4

New Zealand 2nd innings (target: 345 runs)

			R	M	B	4	6
TJ Franklin	lbw	b Malcolm	5	34	21	1	0
*JG Wright	c Smith	b Lewis	46	124	93	7	0
AH Jones	c Gooch	b Small	40	135	99	1	1
MD Crowe	lbw	b Malcolm	25	78	70	3	0
MJ Greatbatch	c Atherton	b Hemmings	22	64	45	4	0
KR Rutherford	c Lamb	b Lewis	18	51	29	2	0
Sir RJ Hadlee		b Malcolm	13	52	51	1	0
+AC Parore	c Lamb	b Lewis	20	82	72	2	0
JG Bracewell	c Atherton	b Malcolm	0	3	3	0	0
MC Snedden	not out		21	72	51	3	0
DK Morrison		b Malcolm	6	26	20	1	0
Extras	(lb 9, w 1, nb 4)		14				
Total	(all out, 91.4 overs)		230				

FoW: 1-25, 2-85, 3-111, 4-125, 5-155, 6-163, 7-180, 8-180, 9-203, 10-230.

Bowling	O	M	R	W
Small	16	5	56	1
Malcolm	24.4	8	46	5
Lewis	22	3	76	3
Hemmings	29	13	43	1

The Wisden Trophy, 1991, 4th Test England v West Indies

Edgbaston, Birmingham   25,26,27,28 July 1991 (5-day match)
Result: West Indies won by 7 wickets   West Indies leads the 5-Test series 2-1
Toss: West Indies   Umpires: B Dudleston and DR Shepherd
Test Debuts: H Morris (Eng).   Man of the Match: RB Richardson

Close of Play:
Day 1: England 184/9 (DeFreitas 7, Illingworth 0*)
Day 2: England 188, West Indies 253/4 (Richardson 103, Logie 24*)
Day 3: West Indies 292, England 156/8 (Pringle 26, Lewis 7*)

England 1st innings

			R	M	B	4	6
*GA Gooch		b Marshall	45	132	79	4	0
H Morris	c Dujon	b Patterson	3	9	9	0	0
MA Atherton	lbw	b Walsh	16	60	48	2	0
GA Hick	c Richards	b Ambrose	19	147	104	3	0
AJ Lamb	lbw	b Marshall	9	40	29	1	0
MR Ramprakash	c Logie	b Walsh	29	108	84	3	0
+RC Russell	c Richardson	b Ambrose	12	42	28	0	0
DR Pringle		b Ambrose	2	15	12	0	0
PAJ DeFreitas	c Richardson	b Marshall	10	47	32	1	0
CC Lewis	lbw	b Marshall	13	32	24	1	0
RK Illingworth	not out		0	10	2	0	0
Extras	(b 4, lb 3, nb 23)		30				
Total	(all out, 70.4 overs)		188				

FoW: 1-6, 2-53, 3-88, 4-108, 5-129, 6-159, 7-163, 8-163, 9-184, 10-188.

Bowling	O	M	R	W
Ambrose	23	6	64	3
Patterson	11	2	39	1
Walsh	21	6	43	2
Marshall	12.4	1	33	4
Hooper	3	2	2	0

West Indies 1st innings

			R	M	B	4	6
PV Simmons	c Hick	b Lewis	28	86	62	5	0
DL Haynes	c Russell	b DeFreitas	32	151	109	5	0
RB Richardson	lbw	b Lewis	104	273	229	13	0
CL Hooper		b Illingworth	31	72	64	5	0
*IVA Richards	c Lewis	b Pringle	22	43	26	4	0
AL Logie	c Atherton	b DeFreitas	28	77	54	5	0
+PJL Dujon	lbw	b DeFreitas	6	29	17	1	0
MD Marshall	not out		6	80	43	0	0
CEL Ambrose	c Hick	b Lewis	1	4	2	0	0
CA Walsh		c & b Lewis	18	37	32	2	0
BP Patterson		b Lewis	3	16	16	0	0
Extras	(lb 7, nb 6)		13				
Total	(all out, 107.3 overs)		292				

FoW: 1-52, 2-93, 3-148, 4-194, 5-257, 6-258, 7-266, 8-267, 9-285, 10-292.

Bowling	O	M	R	W
DeFreitas	25.3	9	40	2
Lewis	35	10	111	6
Pringle	23	9	48	1
Illingworth	17	2	75	1
Gooch	6	1	11	0
Hick	1	1	0	0

England 2nd innings

			R	M	B	4	6
*GA Gooch		b Patterson	40	150	91	4	0
H Morris	lbw	b Patterson	1	7	6	0	0
MA Atherton	c Hooper	b Patterson	1	2	2	0	0
GA Hick		b Ambrose	1	9	8	0	0
AJ Lamb	c Dujon	b Walsh	25	105	74	3	0
MR Ramprakash	c Dujon	b Marshall	25	104	74	3	0
+RC Russell	c Dujon	b Patterson	0	12	9	0	0
DR Pringle	c Logie	b Marshall	45	304	237	4	0
PAJ DeFreitas		b Patterson	7	26	20	1	0
CC Lewis	c sub	b Ambrose	65	145	94	10	0
RK Illingworth	not out		5	58	40	0	0
Extras	(b 5, lb 21, nb 14)		40				
Total	(all out, 105.4 overs)		255				

FoW: 1-2, 2-4, 3-5, 4-71, 5-94, 6-96, 7-127, 8-144, 9-236, 10-255.

Bowling	O	M	R	W
Ambrose	33	16	42	2
Patterson	31	6	81	5
Marshall	19.4	3	53	2
Walsh	7	1	20	1
Hooper	12	3	26	0
Simmons	3	0	7	0

West Indies 2nd innings (target: 152 runs)

			R	M	B	4	6
PV Simmons	lbw	b DeFreitas	16	37	23	3	0
DL Haynes	c Hick	b DeFreitas	8	26	22	1	0
RB Richardson	c Hick	b DeFreitas	0	2	0	0	0
CL Hooper	not out		55	142	101	8	0
*IVA Richards	not out		73	134	97	9	1
Extras	(lb 4, nb 1)		5				
Total	(3 wickets, 40.4 overs)		157				

DNB: AL Logie, +PJL Dujon, MD Marshall, CEL Ambrose, CA Walsh, BP Patterson.

FoW: 1-23, 2-23, 3-24.

Bowling	O	M	R	W
DeFreitas	13	2	54	3
Lewis	16	7	45	0
Pringle	7	1	31	0
Illingworth	4.4	0	23	0

England v Pakistan, 1992, 1st Test

Edgbaston, Birmingham   4,5,6,7,8 June 1992 (5-day match)
Result: Match drawn   5-Test series level 0-0
Toss: England   Umpires: MJ Kitchen and BJ Meyer
Match Referee: RM Cowper (Aus)
Test Debuts: Aamer Sohail, Ata-ur-Rehman, Inzamam-ul-Haq (Pak).
Man of the Match: AJ Stewart

Close of Play:
*Day 1: No play
Day 2: Pakistan 3/0 (Aamer Sohail 3, Rameez Raja 0*)
Day 3: Pakistan 290/3 (Javed Miandad 99, Saleem Malik 80*)
Day 4: Pakistan 446/4d, England 170/2 (Stewart 94, Smith 10*)

Pakistan 1st innings			R	M	B	4	6
Aamer Sohail	c Stewart	b DeFreitas	18	35	22	1	0
Rameez Raja	lbw	b DeFreitas	47	143	108	5	0
Asif Mujtaba	c Russell	b DeFreitas	29	87	73	5	0
*Javed Miandad	not out		153	415	337	19	0
Saleem Malik	lbw	b DeFreitas	165	370	297	19	1
Inzamam-ul-Haq	not out		8	24	14	1	0
Extras	(b 2, lb 5, nb 19)		26				
Total	(4 wickets declared, 137 overs)		446				

DNB: +Moin Khan, Mushtaq Ahmed, Waqar Younis, Aaqib Javed, Ata-ur-Rehman.

FoW: 1-33, 2-96, 3-110, 4-432.

Bowling	O	M	R	W
DeFreitas	33	6	121	4
Lewis	33	3	116	0
Pringle	28	2	92	0
Botham	19	6	52	0
Hick	13	1	46	0
Gooch	10	5	9	0
Ramprakash	1	0	3	0

England 1st innings			R	M	B	4	6
*GA Gooch	c Asif Mujtaba	b Aaqib Javed	8	38	23	0	0
AJ Stewart	c Saleem Malik	b Ata-ur-Rehman	190	351	261	31	0
GA Hick	c Javed Miandad	b Waqar Younis	51	94	102	7	0
RA Smith	lbw	b Mushtaq Ahmed	127	326	231	18	0
MR Ramprakash	c Moin Khan	b Ata-ur-Rehman	0	2	2	0	0
AJ Lamb	c Javed Miandad	b Ata-ur-Rehman	12	28	22	2	0
CC Lewis		b Mushtaq Ahmed	24	44	31	5	0
+RC Russell	not out		29	43	45	5	0
DR Pringle	not out		0	12	7	0	0
Extras	(b 5, lb 5, w 1, nb 7)		18				
Total	(7 wickets declared, 119 overs)		459				

DNB: IT Botham, PAJ DeFreitas.

FoW: 1-28, 2-121, 3-348, 4-348, 5-378, 6-415, 7-446.

Bowling	O	M	R	W
Waqar Younis	24	2	96	1
Aaqib Javed	16	3	86	1
Mushtaq Ahmed	50	8	156	2
Ata-ur-Rehman	18	5	69	3
Asif Mujtaba	8	1	29	0
Aamer Sohail	2	0	8	0
Saleem Malik	1	0	5	0

The Ashes, 1993, 5th Test England v Australia

Edgbaston, Birmingham   5,6,7,8,9 August 1993 (5-day match)
Result: Australia won by 8 wickets   Australia leads the 6-Test series 4-0
Toss: England   Umpires: JH Hampshire and DR Shepherd
TV Umpire: AGT Whitehead   Match Referee: CH Lloyd (WI)
Man of the Match: ME Waugh

Close of Play:
Day 1: England 276/9 (Emburey 55, Ilott 3*)
Day 2: England 276, Australia 258/5 (SR Waugh 57, Healy 12*)
Day 3: Australia 408, England 89/1 (Gooch 44, Smith 7*)
Day 4: England 251, Australia 9/0 (Slater 7, Taylor 2*)

England 1st innings			R	M	B	4	6
GA Gooch	c Taylor	b Reiffel	8	24	20	1	0
*MA Atherton		b Reiffel	72	192	157	9	0
RA Smith		b ME Waugh	21	66	59	2	0
MP Maynard	c SR Waugh	b May	0	12	9	0	0
+AJ Stewart		c & b Warne	45	83	92	6	1
GP Thorpe	c Healy	b May	37	75	53	6	0
N Hussain		b Reiffel	3	8	10	0	0
JE Emburey	not out		55	161	152	5	1
MP Bicknell	c ME Waugh	b Reiffel	14	66	59	1	0
PM Such		b Reiffel	1	2	3	0	0
MC Ilott	c Healy	b Reiffel	3	23	16	0	0
Extras	(b 4, lb 6, nb 7)		17				
Total	(all out, 101.5 overs, 364 min)		276				

FoW: 1-17 (Gooch), 2-71 (Smith), 3-76 (Maynard), 4-156 (Stewart), 5-156 (Atherton), 6-160 (Hussain), 7-215 (Thorpe), 8-262 (Bicknell), 9-264 (Such), 10-276 (Ilott).

Bowling	O	M	R	W	
Hughes	19	4	53	0	(1nb)
Reiffel	22.5	3	71	6	(4nb)
ME Waugh	15	5	43	1	(2nb)
SR Waugh	5	2	4	0	
May	19	9	32	2	
Warne	21	7	63	1	

Australia 1st innings			R	M	B	4	6
MA Taylor	run out		19	122	80	2	0
MJ Slater	c Smith	b Such	22	73	60	4	0
DC Boon	lbw	b Emburey	0	10	13	0	0
ME Waugh	c Thorpe	b Ilott	137	240	219	18	0
*AR Border	c Hussain	b Such	3	9	9	0	0
SR Waugh	c Stewart	b Bicknell	59	230	175	6	0
+IA Healy	c Stewart	b Bicknell	80	141	107	11	0
MG Hughes		b Bicknell	38	162	102	2	1
PR Reiffel		b Such	20	108	89	4	0
SK Warne	c Stewart	b Emburey	10	43	30	1	0
TBA May	not out		3	23	17	0	0
Extras	(b 7, lb 8, nb 2)		17				
Total	(all out, 149.5 overs, 579 min)		408				

FoW: 1-34 (Slater), 2-39 (Boon), 3-69 (Taylor), 4-80 (Border), 5-233 (ME Waugh), 6-263 (SR Waugh), 7-370 (Healy), 8-379 (Hughes), 9-398 (Warne), 10-408 (Reiffel).

Bowling	O	M	R	W	
Bicknell	34	9	99	3	(2nb)
Ilott	24	4	85	1	
Such	52.5	18	90	3	
Emburey	39	9	119	2	

England 2nd innings			R	M	B	4	6
GA Gooch		b Warne	48	178	150	6	0
*MA Atherton	c Border	b Warne	28	89	66	3	0
RA Smith	lbw	b Warne	19	69	70	2	0
MP Maynard	c Healy	b May	10	13	15	2	0
+AJ Stewart	lbw	b Warne	5	21	26	1	0
GP Thorpe	st Healy	b Warne	60	235	192	3	0
N Hussain	c SR Waugh	b May	0	4	7	0	0
JE Emburey	c Healy	b May	37	200	191	3	0
MP Bicknell	c SR Waugh	b May	0	1	2	0	0
PM Such	not out		7	50	42	1	0
MC Ilott		b May	15	44	41	3	0
Extras	(b 11, lb 9, nb 2)		22				
Total	(all out, 133.2 overs, 461 min)		251				

FoW: 1-60 (Atherton), 2-104 (Smith), 3-115 (Maynard), 4-115 (Gooch), 5-124 (Stewart), 6-125 (Hussain), 7-229 (Emburey), 8-229 (Bicknell), 9-229 (Thorpe), 10-251 (Ilott).

Bowling	O	M	R	W	
Hughes	18	7	24	0	
Reiffel	11	2	30	0	(2nb)
May	48.2	15	89	5	
Warne	49	23	82	5	
Border	2	1	1	0	
ME Waugh	5	2	5	0	

Australia 2nd innings (target: 120 runs)			R	M	B	4	6
MJ Slater	c Thorpe	b Emburey	8	43	41	0	0
MA Taylor	c Thorpe	b Such	4	35	24	0	0
DC Boon	not out		38	112	109	7	0
ME Waugh	not out		62	104	87	6	1
Extras	(b 3, lb 5)		8				
Total	(2 wickets, 43.3 overs)		120				

DNB: *AR Border, SR Waugh, +IA Healy, MG Hughes, PR Reiffel, SK Warne, TBA May.

FoW: 1-12 (Taylor), 2-12 (Slater).

Bowling	O	M	R	W
Bicknell	3	0	9	0
Ilott	2	0	14	0
Such	20.3	4	58	1
Emburey	18	4	31	1

The Wisden Trophy, 1995, 3rd Test England v West Indies

Edgbaston, Birmingham   6,7,8 July 1995 (5-day match)
Result: West Indies won by an innings and 64 runs West Indies leads the 3-Test series 2-1
Toss: England   Umpires: MJ Kitchen and ID Robinson (Zim)
TV Umpire: JW Holder   Match Referee: JR Reid (NZ)
Test Debuts: JER Gallian (Eng).   Man of the Match: SL Campbell

Close of Play:
Day 1: England 147, West Indies 104/1 (Campbell 38, Lara 21*)
Day 2: West Indies 300, England 59/3 (Smith 33, Cork 15*)

England 1st innings

			R	M	B	4	6
*MA Atherton	c Murray	b Ambrose	0	2	3	0	0
+AJ Stewart	lbw	b Benjamin	37	114	70	5	0
GA Hick	c Richardson	b Walsh	3	12	5	0	0
GP Thorpe	c Campbell	b Ambrose	30	46	33	5	0
RA Smith	c Arthurton	b Bishop	46	144	92	8	0
JER Gallian		b Benjamin	7	27	20	0	0
DG Cork	lbw	b Walsh	4	16	18	0	0
D Gough	c Arthurton	b Bishop	1	28	17	0	0
PJ Martin	c sub	b Walsh	1	25	12	0	0
RK Illingworth		b Bishop	0	11	7	0	0
ARC Fraser	not out		0	2	2	0	0
Extras	(lb 4, w 4, nb 10)		18				
Total	(all out, 44.2 overs)		147				

FoW: 1-4, 2-9, 3-53, 4-84, 5-100, 6-109, 7-124, 8-141, 9-147, 10-147.

Bowling

	O	M	R	W
Ambrose	7.5	1	26	2
Walsh	17.1	4	54	3
Bishop	6.2	0	18	3
Benjamin	13	4	45	2

West Indies 1st innings

			R	M	B	4	6
CL Hooper	c Stewart	b Cork	40	94	71	5	0
SL Campbell		b Cork	79	203	140	16	0
BC Lara	lbw	b Cork	21	52	42	4	0
JC Adams	lbw	b Cork	10	36	25	2	0
*RB Richardson		b Fraser	69	242	174	10	0
KLT Arthurton	lbw	b Fraser	8	35	21	2	0
+JR Murray	c Stewart	b Martin	26	33	24	5	0
IR Bishop	c Martin	b Illingworth	16	79	59	1	0
KCG Benjamin	run out		11	53	34	1	0
CA Walsh	run out		0	1	0	0	0
CEL Ambrose	not out		4	10	6	1	0
Extras	(b 5, lb 5, nb 6)		16				
Total	(all out, 98 overs)		300				

FoW: 1-73, 2-105, 3-141, 4-156, 5-171, 6-198, 7-260, 8-292, 9-292, 10-300.

Bowling

	O	M	R	W
Fraser	31	7	93	2
Gough	18	3	68	0
Cork	22	5	69	4
Martin	19	5	49	1
Illingworth	8	4	11	1

England 2nd innings

			R	M	B	4	6
*MA Atherton		b Walsh	4	32	21	0	0
RA Smith		b Bishop	41	156	84	8	0
GA Hick	c Hooper	b Bishop	3	2	2	0	0
GP Thorpe	c Murray	b Bishop	0	9	6	0	0
DG Cork	c sub	b Walsh	16	43	33	1	0
PJ Martin	lbw	b Walsh	0	9	5	0	0
JER Gallian	c Murray	b Walsh	0	1	2	0	0
D Gough	c Campbell	b Walsh	12	42	30	0	1
RK Illingworth	c Hooper	b Bishop	0	12	8	0	0
ARC Fraser	not out		1	4	1	0	0
+AJ Stewart	absent hurt		-				
Extras	(nb 12)		12				
Total	(all out, 30 overs)		89				

FoW: 1-17, 2-20, 3-26, 4-61, 5-62, 6-63, 7-88, 8-88, 9-89.

Bowling

	O	M	R	W
Walsh	15	2	45	5
Bishop	13	3	29	4
Benjamin	2	0	15	0

England v India, 1996, 1st Test

Edgbaston, Birmingham   6,7,8,9 June 1996 (5-day match)
Result: England won by 8 wickets   England leads the 3-Test series 1-0
Toss: India   Umpires: DB Hair (Aus) and DR Shepherd
TV Umpire: AA Jones   Match Referee: CW Smith (WI)
Test Debuts: RC Irani, AD Mullally, MM Patel (Eng); SB Joshi, PL Mhambrey, BKV Prasad, V Rathour (Ind).
Man of the Match: N Hussain

Close of Play:
Day 1: India 214, England 60/0 (Knight 27, Atherton 31*)
Day 2: England 313, India 5/0 (Rathour 5, Jadeja 0*)
Day 3: India 219, England 73/1 (Atherton 29, Hussain 18*)

India 1st innings

			R	M	B	4	6
V Rathour	c Knight	b Cork	20	66	52	1	0
A Jadeja	c Atherton	b Lewis	0	16	9	0	0
SV Manjrekar	c Atherton	b Lewis	23	68	47	4	0
SR Tendulkar		b Cork	24	71	41	4	0
*M Azharuddin	c Knight	b Irani	13	30	27	3	0
+NR Mongia		b Mullally	20	48	39	4	0
SB Joshi	c Thorpe	b Mullally	12	93	64	1	0
A Kumble	c Knight	b Cork	5	13	8	1	0
J Srinath	c Russell	b Mullally	52	94	65	9	0
PL Mhambrey	c Thorpe	b Cork	28	76	49	4	0
BKV Prasad	not out		0	24	18	0	0
Extras	(b 3, lb 10, nb 4)		17				
Total	(all out, 69.1 overs)		214				

FoW: 1-8 (Jadeja), 2-41 (Rathour), 3-64 (Azharuddin), 4-93 (Tendulkar), 5-103 (Mongia), 6-118 (Manjrekar), 7-127 (Kumble), 8-150 (Joshi), 9-203 (Srinath), 10-214 (Mhambrey).

Bowling

	O	M	R	W	
Lewis	18	2	44	2	
Cork	20.1	5	61	4	(3nb)
Mullally	22	7	60	3	(1nb)
Irani	7	4	22	1	
Patel	2	0	14	0	

England 1st innings

			R	M	B	4	6
NV Knight	c Mongia	b Srinath	27	78	48	4	0
*MA Atherton	c Rathour	b Mhambrey	33	122	98	5	0
N Hussain	c sub (R Dravid)	b Srinath	128	313	227	18	1
GP Thorpe		b Srinath	21	45	30	2	1
GA Hick	c Mhambrey	b Prasad	8	40	29	2	0
RC Irani	c Mongia	b Srinath	34	41	34	7	0
+RC Russell		b Prasad	0	22	14	0	0
CC Lewis	c Rathour	b Prasad	0	1	1	0	0
DG Cork	c Jadeja	b Prasad	4	8	9	0	0
MM Patel	lbw	b Kumble	18	52	35	2	0
AD Mullally	not out		14	47	25	3	0
Extras	(b 16, lb 3, nb 7)		26				
Total	(all out, 90.2 overs)		313				

FoW: 1-60 (Knight), 2-72 (Atherton), 3-109 (Thorpe), 4-149 (Hick), 5-195 (Irani), 6-205 (Russell), 7-205 (Lewis), 8-215 (Cork), 9-264 (Patel), 10-313 (Hussain).

Bowling

	O	M	R	W	
Srinath	28.2	5	103	4	(5nb)
Prasad	28	9	71	4	
Kumble	24	4	77	1	
Mhambrey	10	0	43	1	(3nb)

India 2nd innings

			R	M	B	4	6
V Rathour	c Hick	b Cork	7	12	11	1	0
A Jadeja	c Russell	b Lewis	6	37	27	1	0
+NR Mongia	c Hussain	b Cork	9	20	36	1	0
SR Tendulkar	c Thorpe	b Lewis	122	263	177	19	1
*M Azharuddin		b Mullally	0	3	3	0	0
SB Joshi	c Russell	b Mullally	12	99	15	1	0
SV Manjrekar	c Knight	b Lewis	18	48	64	2	0
A Kumble	run out (Knight/Hick)		15	70	54	2	0
J Srinath	lbw	b Lewis	1	18	14	0	0
PL Mhambrey		b Lewis	15	28	20	2	0
BKV Prasad	not out		0	16	6	0	0
Extras	(b 4, lb 9, nb 1)		14				
Total	(all out, 70.4 overs)		219				

FoW: 1-15 (Rathour), 2-17 (Jadeja), 3-35 (Mongia), 4-36 (Azharuddin), 5-68 (Joshi), 6-127 (Manjrekar), 7-185 (Kumble), 8-193 (Srinath), 9-208 (Tendulkar), 10-219 (Mhambrey).

Bowling

	O	M	R	W	
Lewis	22.4	6	72	5	
Cork	19	5	40	2	
Mullally	15	4	43	2	(1nb)
Irani	2	0	21	0	
Patel	8	3	18	0	
Hick	4	1	12	0	

England 2nd innings (target: 121 runs)

			R	M	B	4	6
NV Knight	lbw	b Prasad	14	152	29	1	0
*MA Atherton	not out		53	34	100	3	0
N Hussain	c Srinath	b Prasad	19	54	43	2	0
GP Thorpe	not out		17	57	36	2	0
Extras	(b 8, lb 7, w 1, nb 2)		18				
Total	(2 wickets, 33.5 overs)		121				

DNB: GA Hick, RC Irani, +RC Russell, CC Lewis, DG Cork, MM Patel, AD Mullally.
FoW: 1-37 (Knight), 2-77 (Hussain).

Bowling

	O	M	R	W	
Srinath	14.5	3	47	0	(5nb, 1w)
Prasad	14	0	50	2	
Kumble	5	3	9	0	

The Ashes, 1997, 1st Test England v Australia

Edgbaston, Birmingham
Result: England won by 9 wickets
Toss: Australia
TV Umpire: JW Holder
Test Debuts: MA Butcher (Eng).

5,6,7,8 June 1997 (5-day match)
England leads the 6-Test series 1-0
Umpires: SA Bucknor (WI) and P Willey
Match Referee: RS Madugalle (SL)
Man of the Match: N Hussain

Close of Play:
Day 1: Australia 118, England 200/3 (Hussain 80, Thorpe 83*)
Day 2: England 449/6 (Ealham 32, Croft 18*)
Day 3: England 478/9d, Australia 256/1 (Taylor 108, Blewett 61*)

Australia 1st innings			R	M	B	4	6
*MA Taylor	c Butcher	b Malcolm	7	23	16	1	0
MTG Elliott		b Gough	6	18	13	1	0
GS Blewett	c Hussain	b Gough	7	35	15	0	0
ME Waugh		b Gough	5	23	25	1	0
SR Waugh	c Stewart	b Caddick	12	31	20	3	0
MG Bevan	c Ealham	b Malcolm	8	31	21	1	0
+IA Healy	c Stewart	b Caddick	0	2	1	0	0
JN Gillespie	lbw	b Caddick	4	13	8	1	0
SK Warne	c Malcolm	b Caddick	47	62	46	8	0
MS Kasprowicz	c Butcher	b Caddick	17	42	28	3	0
GD McGrath	not out		1	9	3	0	0
Extras	(w 2, nb 2)		4				
Total	(all out, 31.5 overs)		118				

FoW: 1-11 (Elliott), 2-15 (Taylor), 3-26 (ME Waugh), 4-28 (Blewett), 5-48 (SR Waugh), 6-48 (Healy), 7-48 (Bevan), 8-54 (Gillespie), 9-110 (Kasprowicz), 10-118 (Warne).

Bowling	O	M	R	W	
Gough	10	1	43	3	(3nb, 2w)
Malcolm	10	2	25	2	
Caddick	11.5	1	50	5	(2nb)

England 1st innings			R	M	B	4	6
MA Butcher	c Healy	b Kasprowicz	8	16	13	2	0
*MA Atherton	c Healy	b McGrath	2	10	4	0	0
+AJ Stewart	c Elliott	b Gillespie	18	52	33	3	0
N Hussain	c Healy	b Warne	207	437	337	38	0
GP Thorpe	c Bevan	b McGrath	138	290	245	19	0
JP Crawley	c Healy	b Kasprowicz	1	19	14	0	0
MA Ealham	not out		53	171	131	7	0
RDB Croft	c Healy	b Kasprowicz	24	70	56	4	0
D Gough	c Healy	b Kasprowicz	0	8	9	0	0
AR Caddick	lbw	b Bevan	0	11	7	0	0
Extras	(b 4, lb 7, w 1, nb 15)		27				
Total	(9 wickets declared, 138.4 overs)		478				

DNB: DE Malcolm.

FoW: 1-8 (Atherton), 2-16 (Butcher), 3-50 (Stewart), 4-338 (Thorpe), 5-345 (Crawley), 6-416 (Hussain), 7-460 (Croft), 8-463 (Gough), 9-478 (Caddick).

Bowling	O	M	R	W	
McGrath	32	8	107	2	(7nb)
Kasprowicz	39	8	113	4	(6nb, 1w)
Gillespie	10	1	48	1	(1nb)
Warne	35	8	110	1	(1nb)
Bevan	10.4	0	44	1	
SR Waugh	12	2	45	0	(2nb)

Australia 2nd innings			R	M	B	4	6
MTG Elliott		b Croft	66	145	113	12	0
*MA Taylor		c & b Croft	129	396	296	11	1
GS Blewett	c Butcher	b Croft	125	300	228	19	1
SR Waugh	lbw	b Gough	33	135	100	3	0
MG Bevan	c Hussain	b Gough	24	45	41	4	0
ME Waugh	c Stewart	b Gough	1	8	7	0	0
+IA Healy	c Atherton	b Ealham	30	66	48	5	0
SK Warne		c & b Ealham	32	51	34	5	0
MS Kasprowicz	c Butcher	b Ealham	0	1	2	0	0
JN Gillespie	run out (Crawley/Gough)		0	11	6	0	0
GD McGrath	not out		0	1	0	0	0
Extras	(b 18, lb 12, w 2, nb 5)		37				
Total	(all out, 144.4 overs)		477				

FoW: 1-133 (Elliott), 2-327 (Taylor), 3-354 (Blewett), 4-393 (Bevan), 5-399 (ME Waugh), 6-431 (SR Waugh), 7-465 (Healy), 8-465 (Kasprowicz), 9-477 (Gillespie), 10-477 (Warne).

Bowling	O	M	R	W	
Gough	35	7	123	3	(4nb)
Malcolm	21	6	52	0	
Croft	43	10	125	3	(2w)
Caddick	30	6	87	0	(3nb)
Ealham	15.4	3	60	3	

England 2nd innings (target: 118 runs)			R	M	B	4	6
MA Butcher	lbw	b Kasprowicz	14	15	10	2	0
*MA Atherton	not out		57	87	65	9	0
+AJ Stewart	not out		40	71	54	7	0
Extras	(b 4, lb 4)		8				
Total	(1 wicket, 21.3 overs)		119				

DNB: N Hussain, GP Thorpe, JP Crawley, MA Ealham, RDB Croft, D Gough, AR Caddick, DE Malcolm.
FoW: 1-29 (Butcher).

Bowling	O	M	R	W	
McGrath	7	1	42	0	
Kasprowicz	7	0	42	1	
Warne	7.3	0	27	0	

South Africa in England, 1998, 1st Test England v South Africa

Edgbaston, Birmingham
Result: Match drawn
Toss: South Africa
TV Umpire: JH Hampshire
Man of the Match: MA Atherton

4,5,6,7,8 June 1998 (5-day match)
Series: 5-Test series level 0-0
Umpires: DR Shepherd and RB Tiffin (Zim)
Match Referee: Javed Burki (Pak)

Close of Play:
Day 1: England 249/1 (Atherton 103, Stewart 28*, 92 overs)
*Day 2: England 462
Day 3: South Africa 192/5 (Rhodes 36, Pollock 0*, 75.2 overs)
Day 4: South Africa 343, England 170/8 (Croft 1, 45.1 overs)

England 1st innings			R	M	B	4	6
MA Butcher	c Kallis	b Adams	77	278	214	7	0
MA Atherton	c Boucher	b Donald	103	366	279	12	0
*+AJ Stewart	c Cullinan	b Klusener	49	188	128	5	0
N Hussain	lbw	b Adams	35	99	82	5	0
GP Thorpe		b Pollock	10	37	30	1	0
MR Ramprakash		b Donald	49	192	151	4	0
MA Ealham		b Adams	5	57	39	0	0
DG Cork	c Pollock	b Donald	36	127	109	5	0
RDB Croft	c Boucher	b Donald	19	32	21	2	0
D Gough	not out		16	35	15	2	0
ARC Fraser	c Cronje	b Pollock	9	29	21	1	0
Extras	(b 18, lb 26, w 8, nb 2)		54				
Total	(all out, 181.0 overs)		462				

FoW: 1-179 (Butcher, 69.6 ov), 2-249 (Atherton, 93.4 ov), 3-309 (Stewart, 116.3 ov), 4-309 (Hussain, 117.1 ov), 5-329 (Thorpe, 126.5 ov), 6-356 (Ealham, 141.5 ov), 7-411 (Ramprakash, 169.1 ov), 8-430 (Cork, 173.6 ov), 9-437 (Croft, 175.1 ov), 10-462 (Fraser, 180.6 ov).

Bowling	O	M	R	W	
Donald	35	9	95	4	(2w)
Pollock	42	12	92	2	(2nb, 1w)
Klusener	31	7	74	1	(1nb)
Cronje	11	3	28	0	(1w)
Adams	42	10	83	3	
Kallis	20	7	46	0	(1w)

South Africa 1st innings			R	M	B	4	6
G Kirsten	c Butcher	b Cork	12	81	55	1	0
GFJ Liebenberg	c sub (BL Spendlove)	b Cork	3	23	15	0	0
JH Kallis	c Stewart	b Cork	61	192	131	3	0
DJ Cullinan		b Fraser	78	220	193	8	0
*WJ Cronje	c sub (BL Spendlove)	b Fraser	1	8	6	0	0
JN Rhodes	c Stewart	b Fraser	95	228	156	8	1
SM Pollock	c Croft	b Fraser	16	16	18	3	0
+MV Boucher	c Stewart	b Fraser	0	18	9	0	0
L Klusener	c Stewart	b Ealham	57	119	90	11	0
AA Donald		c & b Cork	7	28	17	0	0
PR Adams	not out		6	24	17	1	0
Extras	(lb 5, nb 2)		7				
Total	(all out, 117.3 overs)		343				

FoW: 1-6 (Liebenberg, 5.4 ov), 2-38 (Kirsten, 18.5 ov), 3-119 (Kallis, 54.5 ov), 4-125 (Cronje, 56.5 ov), 5-191 (Cullinan, 74.4 ov), 6-211 (Pollock, 78.4 ov), 7-224 (Boucher, 82.3 ov), 8-328 (Rhodes, 110.6 ov), 9-328 (Klusener, 111.5 ov), 10-343 (Donald, 117.3 ov).

Bowling	O	M	R	W	
Fraser	34	6	103	4	(1nb)
Cork	32.3	7	93	5	
Ealham	23	8	55	1	
Croft	27	3	85	0	
Butcher	1	0	2	0	(1nb)

England 2nd innings			R	M	B	4	6
MA Butcher	lbw	b Pollock	11	23	21	1	0
MA Atherton		b Klusener	43	170	115	7	0
N Hussain	lbw	b Donald	0	14	5	0	0
*+AJ Stewart		b Donald	28	67	34	3	0
GP Thorpe		b Klusener	43	55	59	5	0
MR Ramprakash	c Kallis	b Adams	11	15	10	1	1
MA Ealham	c Pollock	b Klusener	7	12	12	1	0
DG Cork	st Boucher	b Adams	2	16	7	0	0
RDB Croft	not out		1	11	8	0	0
Extras	(b 10, lb 6, w 8)		24				
Total	(8 wickets declared, 45.1 overs)		170				

DNB: ARC Fraser, D Gough.

FoW: 1-24 (Butcher, 5.4 ov), 2-31 (Hussain, 8.3 ov), 3-80 (Stewart, 22.1 ov), 4-148 (Thorpe, 38.1 ov), 5-153 (Atherton, 40.1 ov), 6-167 (Ramprakash, 41.5 ov), 7-167 (Ealham, 42.5 ov), 8-170 (Cork, 45.1 ov).

Bowling	O	M	R	W	
Donald	10	1	48	2	(1w)
Pollock	12	2	43	1	(4w)
Klusener	11	4	27	3	
Adams	2.1	3	36	2	

New Zealand in England, 1999, 1st Test England v New Zealand

Edgbaston, Birmingham   1,2,3 July 1999 (5-day match)
Result: England won by 7 wickets   Series: England leads the 4-Test series 1-0
Toss: New Zealand   Umpires: SA Bucknor (WI) and P Willey
TV Umpire: R Julian   Match Referee: PL van der Merwe (SA)
Test Debuts: CMW Read, A Habib (Eng). Man of the Match: AJ Tudor

Close of Play:
*Day 1: New Zealand 226
Day 2: England 126, New Zealand 107, England 3/1 (Butcher 3, Tudor 0*; 1.1 overs)

New Zealand 1st innings

			R	M	B	4	6
RG Twose	c Thorpe	b Mullally	0	3	3	0	0
MJ Horne	lbw	b Caddick	12	38	29	1	0
*SP Fleming	c Thorpe	b Tudor	27	72	59	6	0
NJ Astle	c Read	b Butcher	26	75	53	4	0
CD McMillan	c Thorpe	b Caddick	18	76	53	2	0
CL Cairns		c & b Caddick	17	36	33	2	0
+AC Parore	c Read	b Mullally	73	205	140	9	0
DJ Nash	c Hussain	b Tufnell	21	120	100	1	0
DL Vettori	c Hussain	b Tufnell	1	13	15	0	0
SB Doull	c Butcher	b Tufnell	11	16	15	1	0
GI Allott	not out		7	43	38	0	0
Extras	(b 1, lb 5, w 1, nb 6)		13				
Total	(all out, 88.4 overs)		226				

FoW: 1-0 (Twose, 0.3 ov), 2-19 (Horne, 9.4 ov), 3-55 (Fleming, 20.1 ov), 4-73 (Astle, 27.5 ov), 5-103 (Cairns, 37.3 ov), 6-104 (McMillan, 39.1 ov), 7-189 (Nash, 69.3 ov), 8-191 (Vettori, 73.2 ov), 9-211 (Doull, 77.3 ov), 10-226 (Parore, 88.4 ov).

Bowling

	O	M	R	W	
Mullally	26.4	5	72	2	(2nb, 1w)
Caddick	27	12	57	3	
Tudor	11	2	44	1	(3nb)
Butcher	7	2	25	1	
Tufnell	17	9	22	3	(1nb)

England 1st innings

			R	M	B	4	6
MA Butcher	run out (Horne/Doull)		11	36	25	2	0
AJ Stewart	lbw	b Allott	1	9	3	0	0
*N Hussain	b Doull	10	32	21	2	0	
GP Thorpe	c Astle	b Allott	6	13	9	0	0
MR Ramprakash	c Parore	b Cairns	0	41	27	0	0
A Habib		b Cairns	1	45	27	0	0
+CMW Read	c sub (CZ Harris)	b Nash	1	25	25	0	0
AR Caddick	c Parore	b Nash	33	101	73	5	0
AJ Tudor	not out		32	99	62	8	0
AD Mullally	c Parore	b Nash	0	1	1	0	0
PCR Tufnell	c Fleming	b Cairns	6	12	13	1	0
Extras	(b 8, lb 11, nb 6)		25				
Total	(all out, 46.4 overs)		126				

FoW: 1-5 (Stewart, 2.1 ov), 2-26 (Butcher, 7.5 ov), 3-28 (Hussain, 9.1 ov), 4-33 (Thorpe, 10.2 ov), 5-38 (Ramprakash, 18.1 ov), 6-40 (Habib, 20.2 ov), 7-45 (Read, 23.6 ov), 8-115 (Caddick, 43.4 ov), 9-115 (Mullally, 43.5 ov), 10-126 (Tufnell, 46.4 ov).

Bowling

	O	M	R	W	
Allott	14	3	38	2	(2nb)
Doull	12	6	17	1	
Cairns	9.4	3	35	3	(4nb)
Nash	11	7	17	3	

New Zealand 2nd innings

			R	M	B	4	6
RG Twose	lbw	b Caddick	0	1	1	0	0
MJ Horne	c Read	b Mullally	1	16	13	0	0
*SP Fleming	c Read	b Tufnell	25	169	86	4	0
NJ Astle	c Read	b Mullally	9	18	14	2	0
CD McMillan	c Butcher	b Mullally	15	51	32	1	0
CL Cairns	c Read	b Caddick	3	7	7	0	0
+AC Parore	c Stewart	b Caddick	0	1	2	0	0
DJ Nash	c Read	b Caddick	0	16	13	0	0
DL Vettori		b Caddick	0	2	2	0	0
SB Doull	st Read	b Tufnell	46	63	50	8	0
GI Allott	not out		0	7	5	0	0
Extras	(b 1, lb 4, w 1, nb 2)		8				
Total	(all out, 37.1 overs)		107				

FoW: 1-0 (Twose, 0.1 ov), 2-5 (Horne, 2.2 ov), 3-17 (Astle, 7.2 ov), 4-39 (McMillan, 16.2 ov), 5-46 (Cairns, 19.1 ov), 6-46 (Parore, 19.3 ov), 7-52 (Nash, 23.4 ov), 8-52 (Vettori, 23.6 ov), 9-106 (Fleming, 35.4 ov), 10-107 (Doull, 37.1 ov).

Bowling

	O	M	R	W	
Caddick	14	3	32	5	(2nb)
Mullally	16	3	48	3	(1w)
Tudor	5	2	15	0	
Tufnell	2.1	0	7	2	

England 2nd innings (target: 208 runs)

			R	M	B	4	6
MA Butcher	c Parore	b Nash	33	77	67	4	0
AJ Stewart		b Allott	0	3	3	0	0
AJ Tudor	not out		99	182	119	21	0
*N Hussain		b Allott	44	79	57	10	0
GP Thorpe	not out		21	27	21	3	0
Extras	(b 7, lb 2, nb 5)		14				
Total	(3 wickets, 43.4 overs)		211				

DNB: A Habib, +CMW Read, MR Ramprakash, AR Caddick, AD Mullally, PCR Tufnell.
FoW: 1-3 (Stewart, 0.5 ov), 2-76 (Butcher, 17.4 ov), 3-174 (Hussain, 36.5 ov).

Bowling

	O	M	R	W	
Allott	15	0	71	2	(4nb)
Doull	7	0	48	0	
Vettori	6	1	22	0	
Nash	7	0	29	1	
Cairns	4	0	18	0	(1nb)
Astle	1	1	0	0	
McMillan	3.4	0	14	0	

The Wisden Trophy, 2000, 1st Test England v West Indies

Edgbaston, Birmingham   15,16,17 June 2000 (5-day match)
Result: West Indies won by an innings and 93 runs   Series: West Indies leads the 5-Test series 1-0
Toss: West Indies   Umpires: DR Shepherd and S Venkataraghavan (Ind)
TV Umpire: B Dudleston   Match Referee: GT Dowling (NZ)
Man of the Match: CA Walsh

Close of Play:
Day 1: England 179, West Indies 50/2 (Campbell 28, Lara 6*; 19 overs)
Day 2: West Indies 336/7 (Adams 66, Rose 33*; 109 overs)

England 1st innings

			R	M	B	4	6
MA Atherton	c Jacobs	b Walsh	20	82	52	4	0
MR Ramprakash	c Hinds	b Walsh	18	61	48	4	0
*N Hussain	c Jacobs	b Rose	15	121	82	2	0
GA Hick	c Campbell	b Walsh	0	9	7	0	0
+AJ Stewart		b Ambrose	6	40	25	0	0
NV Knight	c Lara	b King	26	85	56	4	0
A Flintoff	c Lara	b Walsh	16	40	20	3	0
RDB Croft	c Jacobs	b Walsh	18	33	19	4	0
AR Caddick	not out		21	94	67	0	0
D Gough	run out (Jacobs)		23	51	36	4	0
ESH Giddins	c Jacobs	b King	0	14	11	0	0
Extras	(lb 6, w 1, nb 9)		16				
Total	(all out, 69 overs, 320 mins)		179				

FoW: 1-26 (Ramprakash, 13.5 ov), 2-44 (Atherton, 17.4 ov), 3-45 (Hick, 19.4 ov), 4-57 (Stewart, 28.5 ov), 5-82 (Hussain, 39.5 ov), 6-112 (Knight, 46.4 ov), 7-112 (Flintoff, 47.2 ov), 8-134 (Croft, 53.5 ov), 9-173 (Gough, 65.4 ov), 10-179 (Giddins, 68.6 ov).

Bowling

	O	M	R	W	
Ambrose	20.5	10	32	1	(2nb)
Walsh	21	9	36	5	(4nb)
King	14.1	2	60	2	(2nb, 1w)
Rose	13	3	45	1	(1nb)

West Indies 1st innings

			R	M	B	4	6
SL Campbell		b Gough	59	157	120	7	0
CH Gayle	lbw	b Gough	0	11	8	0	0
WW Hinds	c Hussain	b Caddick	12	22	11	2	0
BC Lara	c Stewart	b Gough	50	143	93	`9	0
S Chanderpaul	c Stewart	b Flintoff	73	161	119	11	0
*JC Adams	c Flintoff	b Gough	98	391	299	9	0
+RD Jacobs	c Stewart	b Caddick	5	20	21	1	0
CEL Ambrose	lbw	b Croft	22	83	50	3	0
FA Rose	lbw	b Gough	48	63	54	7	1
RD King	st Stewart	b Croft	1	60	40	0	0
CA Walsh	not out		3	21	12	0	0
Extras	(b 6, lb 14, nb 6)		26				
Total	(all out, 136.5 overs, 571 mins)		397				

FoW: 1-5 (Gayle, 2.5 ov), 2-24 (Hinds, 7.4 ov), 3-123 (Campbell, 36.1 ov), 4-136 (Lara, 40.5 ov), 5-230 (Chanderpaul, 76.5 ov), 6-237 (Jacobs, 81.6 ov), 7-292 (Ambrose, 99.5 ov), 8-354 (Rose, 116.1 ov), 9-385 (King, 131.2 ov), 10-397 (Adams, 136.5 ov).

Bowling

	O	M	R	W	
Gough	36.5	6	109	5	(3nb)
Caddick	30	6	94	2	
Giddins	18	4	73	0	(3nb)
Croft	29	9	53	2	
Flintoff	23	8	48	1	

England 2nd innings

			R	M	B	4	6
MA Atherton		b King	19	116	75	2	0
MR Ramprakash	lbw	b Walsh	0	6	3	0	0
*N Hussain	c Jacobs	b Walsh	8	33	26	2	0
GA Hick	c Jacobs	b Walsh	0	10	5	0	0
+AJ Stewart		b Rose	8	14	12	1	0
NV Knight	c Hinds	b Adams	34	180	103	1	0
A Flintoff		b King	12	24	22	3	0
RDB Croft	c Hinds	b King	1	17	14	0	0
AR Caddick	c Hinds	b Rose	4	40	27	1	0
D Gough	not out		23	63	52	2	0
ESH Giddins		b Adams	0	16	17	0	0
Extras	(lb 7, w 1, nb 8)		16				
Total	(all out, 58 overs, 263 mins)		125				

FoW: 1-0 (Ramprakash, 1.3 ov), 2-14 (Hussain, 9.4 ov), 3-14 (Hick, 11.4 ov), 4-24 (Stewart, 14.5 ov), 5-60 (Atherton, 25.2 ov), 6-78 (Flintoff, 29.4 ov), 7-83 (Croft, 33.2 ov), 8-94 (Caddick, 42.2 ov), 9-117 (Knight, 53.3 ov), 10-125 (Giddins, 57.6 ov).

Bowling

	O	M	R	W	
Ambrose	14	8	16	0	(2nb)
Walsh	19	10	22	3	
Rose	10	1	43	2	(5nb)
King	9	4	28	3	(1nb)
Gayle	3	0	4	0	
Adams	3	1	5	2	

The Ashes, 2001, 1st Test England v Australia

Edgbaston, Birmingham — 5,6,7,8 July 2001 (5-day match)
Result: Australia won by an innings and 118 runs — Series: Australia leads the 5-Test series 1-0
Toss: Australia — Umpires: SA Bucknor (WI) and G Sharp
TV Umpire: KE Palmer — Match Referee: Talat Ali (Pak)
Test Debut: U Afzaal (Eng). — Man of the Match: AC Gilchrist

Close of Play:
Day 1: England 294, Australia 133/2 (Slater 76, ME Waugh 0*; 22 overs)
Day 2: Australia 332/4 (SR Waugh 101, Martyn 34*; 81.2 overs)
Day 3: Australia 576, England 48/1 (Trescothick 21, Butcher 15*; 13 overs)

England 1st innings

		R	M	B	4	6
MA Atherton	c ME Waugh b Gillespie	57	146	107	10	0
ME Trescothick	c Warne b Gillespie	0	5	2	0	0
MA Butcher	c Ponting b Warne	38	111	71	4	0
*N Hussain	lbw b McGrath	13	54	35	1	0
IJ Ward	b McGrath	23	50	39	2	0
+AJ Stewart	lbw b McGrath	65	130	82	9	0
U Afzaal	b Warne	4	11	9	0	0
C White	lbw b Warne	4	9	8	0	0
AF Giles	c Gilchrist b Warne	7	16	13	1	0
D Gough	c Gillespie b Warne	0	2	3	0	0
AR Caddick	not out	49	59	40	7	1
Extras	(b 10, lb 8, nb 16)	34				
Total	(all out, 65.3 overs, 289 mins)	294				

FoW: 1-2 (Trescothick, 1.1 ov), 2-106 (Butcher, 24.2 ov), 3-123 (Atherton, 31.3 ov), 4-136 (Hussain, 37.4 ov), 5-159 (Ward, 43.2 ov), 6-170 (Afzaal, 46.1 ov), 7-174 (White, 48.3 ov), 8-191 (Giles, 52.2 ov), 9-191 (Gough, 52.5 ov), 10-294 (Stewart, 65.3 ov).

Bowling

	O	M	R	W	
McGrath	17.3	2	67	3	(3nb)
Gillespie	17	3	67	2	(4nb)
Lee	12	2	71	0	(7nb)
Warne	19	4	71	5	(2nb)

Australia 1st innings

		R	M	B	4	6
MJ Slater	b Gough	77	111	82	13	0
ML Hayden	c White b Giles	35	71	41	6	1
RT Ponting	lbw b Gough	11	23	13	2	0
ME Waugh	c Stewart b Caddick	49	153	143	7	0
*SR Waugh	lbw b Gough	105	245	181	13	0
DR Martyn	c Trescothick b Butcher	105	222	165	15	0
+AC Gilchrist	c Caddick b White	152	205	143	20	5
SK Warne	c Atherton b Butcher	8	11	10	2	0
B Lee	c Atherton b Butcher	0	6	1	0	0
JN Gillespie	lbw b Butcher	0	2	3	0	0
GD McGrath	not out	1	36	19	0	0
Extras	(b 3, lb 7, nb 23)	33				
Total	(all out, 129.4 overs, 545 mins)	576				

FoW: 1-98 (Hayden, 14.6 ov), 2-130 (Ponting, 19.4 ov), 3-134 (Slater, 23.1 ov), 4-267 (ME Waugh, 63.6 ov), 5-336 (SR Waugh, 83.2 ov), 6-496 (Martyn, 117.3 ov), 7-511 (Warne, 119.6 ov), 8-513 (Lee, 121.1 ov), 9-513 (Gillespie, 121.4 ov), 10-576 (Gilchrist, 129.4 ov).

Bowling

	O	M	R	W	
Gough	33	6	152	3	(10nb)
Caddick	36	0	163	1	(12nb)
White	26.4	5	101	1	(1nb)
Giles	25	0	108	1	
Butcher	9	3	42	4	

England 2nd innings

		R	M	B	4	6
MA Atherton	c ME Waugh b McGrath	4	34	9	1	0
ME Trescothick	c ME Waugh b Warne	76	208	113	11	2
MA Butcher	c Gilchrist b Lee	41	95	73	5	0
*N Hussain	retired hurt	9	26	20	1	0
IJ Ward	b Lee	3	12	3	0	0
+AJ Stewart	c Warne b Gillespie	5	6	6	1	0
U Afzaal	lbw b Gillespie	2	10	6	0	0
C White	b Gillespie	0	8	6	0	0
AF Giles	c ME Waugh b Warne	0	22	12	0	0
D Gough	lbw b Warne	0	1	1	0	0
AR Caddick	not out	6	14	15	1	0
Extras	(b 1, lb 5, nb 12)	18				
Total	(all out, 42.1 overs, 218 mins)	164				

FoW: 1-4 (Atherton, 2.3 ov), 2-99 (Butcher, 24.2 ov), 3-142 (Ward, 32.1 ov), 4-148 (Stewart, 33.1 ov), 5-150 (Afzaal, 35.3 ov), 6-154 (White, 37.3 ov), 7-155 (Trescothick, 38.1 ov), 8-155 (Gough, 38.2 ov), 9-164 (Giles, 42.1 ov).

Bowling

	O	M	R	W	
McGrath	13	5	34	1	(5nb)
Gillespie	11	2	52	3	(4nb)
Warne	10.1	4	29	3	(1nb)
ME Waugh	1	0	6	0	
Lee	7	0	37	2	(2nb).

Sri Lanka in England, 2002, 2nd Test England v Sri Lanka

Edgbaston, Birmingham — 30,31 May, 1,2 June 2002 (5-day match)
Result: England won by an innings and 111 runs — Series: England leads the 3-Test series 1-0
Toss: England — Umpires: DJ Harper (Aus) and S Venkataraghavan (Ind)
TV Umpire: P Willey — Match Referee: GR Viswanath (Ind)
Man of the Match: MJ Hoggard

Close of Play:
Day 1: Sri Lanka 162, England 24/0 (Trescothick 9, Vaughan 14*; 7 overs)
Day 2: England 401/5 (Thorpe 30, Flintoff 14*; 112 overs)
Day 3: England 545, Sri Lanka 132/2 (Atapattu 56, Jayawardene 45*; 49 overs)

Sri Lanka 1st innings

		R	M	B	4	6
MS Atapattu	c Stewart b Hoggard	13	35	30	1	0
*ST Jayasuriya	c Stewart b Caddick	8	39	24	1	0
+KC Sangakkara	c Stewart b Flintoff	16	70	42	1	0
DPMD Jayawardene	c Flintoff b Caddick	47	91	60	7	0
PA de Silva	c Trescothick b Caddick	10	13	12	2	0
HP Tillakaratne	lbw b Tudor	20	76	53	3	0
RP Arnold	c Flintoff b Caddic	1	16	13	0	0
WPUJC Vaas	b Flintoff	23	84	52	4	0
DNT Zoysa	c Hoggard b Tudor	0	3	4	0	0
TCB Fernando	run out (Caddick/Tudor)	13	36	36	0	0
M Muralitharan	not out	0	5	1	0	0
Extras	(b 1, nb 10)	11				
Total	(all out, 52.5 overs, 239 mins)	162				

FoW: 1-23 (Atapattu, 7.6 ov), 2-23 (Jayasuriya, 8.4 ov), 3-76 (Sangakkara, 23.3 ov), 4-96 (de Silva, 25.6 ov), 5-100 (Jayawardene, 28.1 ov), 6-108 (Arnold, 32.1 ov), 7-141 (Tillakaratne, 44.1 ov), 8-141 (Zoysa, 44.5 ov), 9-159 (Vaas, 51.5 ov), 10-162 (Fernando, 52.5 ov).

Bowling

	O	M	R	W	
Caddick	17	4	47	3	(4nb)
Hoggard	17	4	55	2	(5nb)
Giles	4	1	7	0	
Tudor	9.5	3	25	2	(1nb)
Flintoff	5	0	27	2	

England 1st innings

		R	M	B	4	6
ME Trescothick	c Tillakaratne b Vaas	161	296	232	23	3
MP Vaughan	c Jayasuriya b Muralitharan	46	82	64	7	0
MA Butcher	b Muralitharan	94	260	209	13	0
*N Hussain	b Muralitharan	22	55	45	4	0
GP Thorpe	c Vaas b Fernando	123	316	229	12	0
+AJ Stewart	c Tillakaratne b Muralitharan	7	63	40	0	0
A Flintoff	c Tillakaratne b Muralitharan	29	69	51	6	0
AJ Tudor	c Tillakaratne b Zoysa	3	30	24	0	0
AF Giles	c Sangakkara b Zoysa	0	8	4	0	0
AR Caddick	c Sangakkara b Zoysa	3	9	6	0	0
MJ Hoggard	not out	17	126	94	1	0
Extras	(lb 19, w 6, nb 15)	40				
Total	(all out, 163.5 overs, 663 mins)	545				

FoW: 1-92 (Vaughan, 21.2 ov), 2-294 (Trescothick, 75.5 ov), 3-338 (Butcher, 88.6 ov), 4-341 (Hussain, 90.4 ov), 5-368 (Stewart, 104.2 ov), 6-426 (Flintoff, 122.1 ov), 7-436 (Tudor, 129.3 ov), 8-444 (Giles, 131.1 ov), 9-454 (Caddick, 133.2 ov), 10-545 (Thorpe, 163.5 ov).

Bowling

	O	M	R	W	
Vaas	41	3	141	1	(2w)
Zoysa	24	3	93	3	(9nb)
Muralitharan	64	12	143	5	(2nb)
Fernando	21.5	2	92		(4nb)
Jayasuriya	6	2	27	0	
de Silva	7	0	30	0	

Sri Lanka 2nd innings

		R	M	B	4	6
MS Atapattu	b Hoggard	56	207	152	5	0
*ST Jayasuriya	b Hoggard	12	34	28	3	0
+KC Sangakkara	lbw b Hoggard	1	6	7	0	0
DPMD Jayawardene	c Thorpe b Caddick	59	194	158	7	0
PA de Silva	c Thorpe b Caddick	47	130	103	6	0
HP Tillakaratne	b Caddick	39	92	59	6	0
RP Arnold	c Giles b Hoggard	4	14	5	1	0
WPUJC Vaas	st Stewart b Giles	28	34	28	3	1
TCB Fernando	b Hoggard	0	2	2	0	0
DNT Zoysa	not out	1	23	9	0	0
M Muralitharan	absent hurt	-				
Extras	(b 4, lb 4, nb 17)	25				
Total	(all out, 89.1 overs, 373 mins)	272				

FoW: 1-28 (Jayasuriya, 7.5 ov), 2-30 (Sangakkara, 9.2 ov), 3-135 (Atapattu, 51.3 ov), 4-156 (Jayawardene, 58.2 ov), 5-233 (Tillakaratne, 80.6 ov), 6-238 (de Silva, 82.1 ov), 7-247 (Arnold, 83.3 ov), 8-247 (Fernando, 83.5 ov), 9-272 (Vaas, 89.1 ov).

Bowling

	O	M	R	W	
Caddick	25	4	67	3	(2nb)
Hoggard	23	2	92	5	(11nb)
Flintoff	6	0	23	0	(3nb)
Giles	26.1	3	57	1	
Tudor	9	1	25	0	(1nb)

Bibliography

100 Years of Test Match Cricket at Edgbaston

A Who's Who of Warwickshire Cricket (Robert Brooke and David Goodyear)

Archie – a biography of AC MacLaren (Michael Down)

Birmingham Post

Birmingham Gazette

From the Sea End (Christopher Lee)

Hirst and Rhodes (AA Thomson)

Rothmans Football Yearbook

The History of Warwickshire County Cricket Club (Jack Bannister)

Wisden Cricketers Almanack

Wisden Book of Obituaries

Wisden Book of Test Cricket (Bill Frindall)

100 Greats of Warwickshire County Cricket Club (Robert Brooke)

http//www.ecb.co.uk

http//www.cricinfo.com

Roll of Honour

The following people have subscribed to 100 Years of Test Match Cricket at Edgbaston

Presentation Copies

Dennis Amiss MBE

MJK Smith

Sachin Tendulkar

Shaun Pollock

Allan Donald

Viv Richards

Ian Botham

Shane Warne

Sir Richard Hadlee

Imran Khan

Courtney Walsh

Richie Benaud

Subscribers

A. J. Collett, Nuneaton

C W Shilton

Chris Ivens

Chris Russell

Chris Sweet

Christopher Finch

Christopher Lockwood

Colin Summerton

D A Bessent

D J Osborne

Darren Cartwright

David Wilford

David Wilkinson

Iris Barford

Jamie P. F. Andrews

Jennifer McQueen

John A Gould

John Stubbings

Joshua Williams

Julie Apps

Leslie Fellows

Linda Perkins

Malcolm Handy

Martin J Cope

Maurice. F. White

Mr D Kent

Mr I M Dearman

Mr R T Slim

N. F. Taylor

Paul Burns

Paul Burton

Peter Woodroofe

Phillip Jordan

Rachel Burns

Revd. Michael C Dodd

Richard Long

Robert Brooke

Roger Marshall

Roger Williams

Roy Barker

Stephen Rand

Warwickshire C. C. C.

William A. Powell